WARRIORS OF THE TAO

Borgo Press Books by DAMIEN BRODERICK

WARRIORS OF THE TAO

THE BEST OF *SCIENCE FICTION: A REVIEW OF SPECULATIVE LITERATURE*

DAMIEN BRODERICK

& VAN IKIN

EDITORS

THE BORGO PRESS

MMXI

I.O. Evans Studies in the Philosophy
and Criticism of Literature
ISSN 0271-9061

Number Fifty-Six

WARRIORS OF THE TAO

FIRST EDITION

Published by Wildside Press LLC

www.wildsidebooks.com

DEDICATION

For Terry Dowling,

Singer of Images, Scryer of Dreams:
Science Fiction Co-Editor, Issues #1-38

CONTENTS

INTRODUCTION I
by DAMIEN BRODERICK

Pierre Marie François de Sales Baillot, who flourished at the turn of the nineteeth century and taught violin at the Paris Conservatoire, wrote in his *L'Art du violon*: "The quartet is a conversation among friends, communicating to one another their sensations, their sentiments, and their mutual affections." Literary genres—their texts, writers, readers—are time-lapsed conversations in somewhat the same way, each voice contributing, if only in the silence of one's head while reading, responding, deciding whether or not to read any more in this particular mode, or by this author, or to contribute some writing oneself to the great *fleuve* of story.

Think of the many-braided conversation (conveyed by speech, letter, email, blog) where interested people articulate their views of a given book or body of writing, sharing more penetrating and intimate reactions than just, "Hey, hated that," or "Oh, I *love* her stories, *so* romantic!"

Today, increasingly, that discussion is conducted by blog, listserv, and for all I know an endless nervy cascade of tweets. But the great historical record of conversations about imaginative literature is the magazines shared by a lively international community of readers and writers. This book is a selection from such a journal, one not easily available to US or British readers, since it was produced and funded by an Australian academic and science fiction fan, Van Ikin.

The leading characters in classic science fiction by, for

example, Asimov and H. Beam Piper had crisp but unfamiliar names: Hari Seldon, Salvor Hardin, Preem Palver, Tortha Karf or Verkan Vall. You could easily suppose from his name that Van Ikin, the editor and publisher of *Science Fiction: A Review of Speculative Literature,* came from the same futuristic lineage, and perhaps he does.

Van is a connoisseur of all the odd flavors of sf's menus. His first anthology, *Australian Science Fiction,* in 1982, was an early and exemplary sampling of the best sf from the island continent. John Baxter had released *The Pacific Book of Australian SF* and its sequel in 1968 and 1971, but these reached back only to 1955. Van's *Australian Science Fiction,* published by University of Queensland Press, delved back into the roots of fantastika in Australia in 1845, and forward to brilliant writers such as Peter Carey (later a multiple Booker Prize winner and US National Book Award finalist) who were opening out literary fiction in this formerly despised direction. In 1990 he edited the anthology *Glass Reptile Breakout,* published by the Centre for Studies in Australian Literature, and two years later he and Terry Dowling compiled the excellent anthology *Mortal Fire: Best Australian SF.*

This background of knowledgeable scholarship is the basis for the most important historical study to date of Aussie sf: *Strange Constellations: A History of Australian Science Fiction,* from Greenwood Press in 1999, co-written by Van with Dr. Russell Blackford and Dr. Sean McMullen, both contributors to *Warriors of the Tao.*

Van's chief contribution to the sf mode is his distinctive and long-running (if sometimes belated) critical magazine, familiarly known by the iconic initials *SF,* from which we have drawn the contents of this book. With its cleanly printed pages and a trademark yellow or ivory stiff cover and crimson title, always a cut above the traditional mimeograph-copied sf fanzines, *SF* was not quite an academic literary review nor a wildly anything-goes celebratory or controversy-fuming fanzine. The voices in

Van's magazine engaged in a long conversation, with no stuffily imposed tone beyond civility and a willingness to cite sources, usually good-humored, sometimes naive, sometimes hair-raisingly hieratic (like the splendid colloquium with famous sf theorist Darko Suvin—another of those names from Asimov or Piper!—included here).

Australia has been a serious source of science fiction and fantasy scholarship and reviews since at least 1966, with John Bangsund's witty *Australian Science-Fiction Review,* followed in 1969 by Bruce Gillespie's *SF Commentary.* The first *Encyclopedia of Science Fiction and Fantasy* was compiled and published by independent Tasmanian scholar Donald H. Tuck, published between 1974-83 before Tuck lapsed into long silence (he died in 2010). Two Hugo awards were shared by the greatest of all sf encyclopedists to date, Australian Peter Nicholls and Canadian John Clute, for their *Science Fiction Encyclopedia* (1979 and 1993). Van Ikin's small magazine fits into this trajectory as part of the long conversation, from its first issue in 1977 to its latest in 2010, a memorial number for the late brilliant independent sf scholar and fan John Foyster.

In *Warriors of the Tao,* from its cheeky, deliberately pulpish title (borrowed from Russell Blackford's opening essay) to the formidable cultural and political analyses of the closing interview with Professor Suvin, we have selected a mix of items that represent the many voices at play in *SF* during a third of a century (which of course extended, like science fiction itself, from the twentieth century into the twenty-first…). We hope to return to these accumulated treasures in a second volume. For now, enjoy the table talk—and watch the skies!

INTRODUCTION II

by VAN IKIN

The editorial in the first issue of *Science Fiction* began with a quotation from Australian poet Richard Tipping's "P(r)oem (1970)"

> First, to begin, let me say
> almost nothing

and went on to claim that "This journal will be formed more by its contributors and their interests than by its editor and his ideals." Looking back, we did live up to that claim, and the eccentrically eclectic content of various issues can now be seen as a snapshot of the Zeitgeist.

But perhaps it's more accurate to say it was a snapshot of *the shadow* of the Zeitgeist. From the perspective of thirty-four years later, two things seem crystal clear in that regard. First of all, *Science Fiction* was *always* running behind schedule, so our notion of what was "current" or "topical" was inevitably a peep backwards into time. (The first issue, published in June 1977, was originally planned for early 1976, and the June '77 launch was only achieved because I was due to get married in August '77....)

Secondly, our material was coming largely from people with university connections, and academe frequently identifies the Zeitgeist by its passing shadow rather than from full-on encounters. Initially that worried me a bit, back in the days, but over time I came to see it as an advantage: we didn't (couldn't) rush in on topical issues, and that provided the opportunity to provide a more contemplated, measured view. Whilst that might sound dull and cautious, the fact is that contributors were usually still passionate about new trends or ideas even after they'd run them through the mills of contemplation—so I tended to feel we were getting the best of both worlds.

If we did, it was because of the intellectual passion driving individual voices. A sane kind of cultural nationalism held sway in Australia in those first post-Whitlam years. It was an intelligent nationalism because it didn't try to claim ascendancy over other cultural products and nor did it try to exclude them (none of us would have for one moment abandoned our regular consumption of US and UK sf and television): it simply said, *Let's expand the possibilities so that they include what might be produced on our shores.*

There was also in those years a fascination with issues surrounding place and identity. In the wider cultural sphere this fed into the growing local film industry (because people wanted to hear Aussie voices and experience stories set in their own locales) and in the sf community it engendered an expectation that works of Australian sf would have their own "voice" and their own subtly distinctive range of concerns. The consensus view, when reached, was that it *didn't* and *couldn't* (because sf was itself a transnational concept with an international audience) but it was a debate that we had to have and it was one which motivated individuals to put fingers to the keyboard. Above all, it made us hunger for the "local product" and be eager to see what "local talent" might produce…even as we were satisfying ourselves that the local voices should more rightly be heard as part of a wider global utterance.

Damien's Introduction expresses this paradox with the tantalizing image of a "many-braided conversation." Whilst *Science Fiction* often missed out on one strand of the braiding (for letter-column debate was only intermittent), it did subscribe to the ideal and like any other "serious minded" journal of commentary, it tried to insist that the conversation had to go beyond the guttural of *loved it* or *loathed it*. That, to me, is part of the dignity and cultural significance of all such conversations: they are a civilizing attempt to link our pleasures and pastimes with the issues that shape our lives and emotions.

That first-ever *Science Fiction* editorial concluded with an optimistically rhetorical flourish:

> And when the Great Australian SF Novel does arrive, *Science Fiction* will be waiting to acclaim it.

To be honest, we felt there was a chance this might happen In Our Time but you wouldn't have bet too much money on it. As things turned out, the Australian sf field was to bloom beyond our imagining over the decades beyond 1977, rapidly reaching the (glorious but frustrating) point where it became impossible to keep up with the yearly output. It would be politic to say that from the perspective of 2011 the words of 1977 make me cringe—but that would be disavowing the moment, and I don't want to do that. It was a *good* moment, part of its time—and when seen in the context of what we subsequently discussed and reviewed, it turned out to be far less parochial and limiting that it might now appear.

This volume is going to take you from 1982 (when the voices were discussing Cordwainer Smith and Gerald Murnane) to 2008 (a discussion of the career of Norma Hemming, the iconoclastic Australian writer of the 1950s whose achievement is about to be honored through the Norma K. Hemming Award for excellence in the exploration of themes of race, gender, sexuality, class, and disability). I hope you'll be drawn in....

WARRIORS OF THE TAO
DAVID LAKE'S XUMA NOVELS

by Russell Blackford
[1984]

In *Human Society in Ethics and Politics*, Bertrand Russell indicated the world he would like to see:

> one where emotions are strong but not destructive, and where, because they are acknowledged, they lead to no deception.... Such a world would include love and friendship and the pursuit of art and knowledge. I cannot hope to satisfy those who want something more tigerish.

Whether or not David Lake would welcome the comparison, I find in his novels something of the same presence of a kind and wise intelligence as I find in Bertrand Russell's writings. And Lake is a creator of worlds, one who revels in depicting cultures different from our own. Except that he occasionally creates memorable characters, he would epitomize the old critical cliché about science fiction: that it is concerned with fictional societies at the expense of fictional individuals. Moreover, at least some of the societies Lake has shown us, on the different worlds he has created, purport to be something like ideal. Lake has made several attempts to construct the kind of society which he (or his authorial persona) would like to see.

Lake's novels commonly depict a contrast, often a violent clash, of cultures. The norm is that our own industrial culture, or a surrogate, is contrasted with a kinder and wiser one. Lake's "good" societies are not traditional utopias, but they do share some features which Bertrand Russell mentioned: love and friendship, and the pursuit of art and knowledge. Though they are not static and constraining (they are fulfilling for individuals and tolerant of experiments in lifestyle), they are based on sustainable organization and technology. Above all, they are concerned with balance: different temperaments and social elements relate dynamically but without violating the social order, while their technology utilizes the ecological system without changing, and thereby endangering it. Lake even allows for an element of something more tigerish, as implied by the title of his latest novel: *Warlords of Xuma*.

The recent publication of *Warlords of Xuma* provided me an excuse to go back to the book to which it is a sequel. *The Gods of Xuma* was published in 1978 and did not necessarily cry out for a sequel; the new book is set a generation later and shares no major character with its predecessor. The two can conveniently be read independently. However, *Warlords* looks like the beginning of an ongoing series set on Xuma, possibly with recurring major characters.

Both Xuma books are competently and coherently plotted heroic adventure stories. Neither is marred by the excesses and unevenness of *The Fourth Hemisphere*, the other Lake book they most resemble, and to which they are closely related. (On the other hand, *The Fourth Hemisphere* is more ambitious, in some ways more poignant, and more daring in its vision than either.) Lake's achievement is to have used a popular and palatable subgenre to get across some fundamental thinking about the ethics and politics of humankind and human society.

In one stroke, Lake turns a potentially boring sf standby— the discovery of a civilization millions of years old—into a philosophical enabling device. The starship *Riverhorse 1,* departing what remains of Terran civilization (Earth has been rendered uninhabitable, leaving only heavily armed Lunar colonies locked in cold war), lands on the Marslike planet Xuma. In the starship are 100 colonists, fifty of each sex, who have the task of starting poor nasty humankind over again. They have journeyed at near-lightspeed in suspended animation most of the way; their ship is a spectacular example of Terran technology, and bristles with sufficient weaponry to carve up the surface of a planet. The Xumans, by contrast, display no technology that rides roughshod over the natural forces of wind and water. They have perfected ballooning, but must travel with the prevailing east winds, even to the point of occasional east-west trips being undertaken by circumnavigating the globe. One of the questions asked by *The Gods of Xuma* (especially) and its sequel is: *Which species has the higher technology?*

Virtually the first act of the protagonist when he arrives on Xuma is to disintegrate 120 mounted warriors with his laser pistol. Human technology certainly performs spectacular feats—but the Xumans have deliberately renounced the path to such gadgets. The beauty of their technology and way of life is that it is sustainable, adapted to last without depleting their planet over millions of years. It might be added that their non-technological learning—linguistics, philosophy—is sublime.

The Gods of Xuma presents the inevitable clash between human and Xuman values and desires. The story is craftily handled, with some neat use of a nation on Xuma which was violating the old balance just at the time the *Riverhorse 1* conveniently turns up, as well as of a previous encounter between Xumans and space-travelling aliens—and what the Xumans learned from this. If anything, *Warlords of Xuma* is still more a well-made adventure novel. By this time, the tiny human minority has found its place within Xuman society, but there are still those who seek mastery and those who would use technology to override nature.

One of the intriguing elements in both books is the attitude taken to violence. Planetary adventure is, of course, traditionally violent, and the ample laser-shooting and sword-brandishing cater to the anticipation of the audience. But early in *The Gods of Xuma* the main character is told, "Evil too has its rights"—and this refrain echoes through both books. Nobody flinches at wars which have been going on for a million years, and it seems that Xuman civilization is presented sympathetically rather than otherwise when it is shown as incorporating highly regulated, indecisive warfare.

This element in Xuman civilization appears to be part of its balance, and has an almost biological function: Xuman individuals pass through various sexual changes from sexless child, to male adult, female adult, and sexless elder. The males do not rule—that function is left to the wiser females—but a place is accorded to their characteristic aggression. Violence is presented with repugnance only when it is not regularized by a larger context, or when it can be carried out with the effect of mass destruction at a distance. Any concept of total war seems to be rejected, and it is best to kill your enemy face to face, so that you at least appreciate what you are doing.

If I am reading correctly here, it seems that the books' concept of a balanced society incorporates some outlet for aggressive feelings, which are apparently seen as basic to both humans and Xumans (at least the males of both species). The author provides something a little tigerish because the need for it is part of his concept of at least male nature. Possibly, there is a further implication that violence and danger are even good, when controlled, in contributing to the overall shape of life: a concept of balance and wholeness at the level of total civilization, again, as well as the individual psyche.

I am less certain about my interpretation of this philosophy of violence than my overall interpretation of the Xuma novels' attitude to culture and technology. I am also unsure of what to make of such a philosophy of violence. The larger case for a sustainable culture, by contrast, is convincing both philosophically and aesthetically.

However, this does not mean that *The Gods of Xuma* and *Warlord: of Xuma* are totally successful novels when judged by the highest appropriate standards. The plotting is competent and the writing clear and even, yes. But *The Gods of Xuma* especially suffers because it seems divided between sound speculation, telling the story as it would really work, and old-fashioned Edgar Rice Burroughs-style planetary romance. As a result it is often engrossing as neither. The protagonist is puerile and irresponsible in obvious ways—which speeds on the action but seems incongruous with his position and training. The imperialist villains in both books possess neither glamour nor subtlety.

Finally, I draw breath to blast Lake's treatment of sexuality, a proper theme for a writer who is concerned with the success or failure of culture in meeting individual needs. Lake seldom depicts sexuality with imagination or daring, so much so that I often fail to see the point of his frequent depictions of nudity and quick assurances that much sexual activity is taking place. There is a tension between providing bounties of casual eroticism and safely planting the heroes and heroines of exotic worlds in good bourgeois marriages.

In the Xuma books too much is made of the poor fit between human and Xuman plumbing. *The Gods of Xuma* is largely devoted to this idea. Only in *Warlords* are there dark hints that a Xuman male can find ways to please a human female, so I infer that Lake read Masters and Johnson some time after 1978. Unfortunately, what is implied is some intolerably perverse practice. Lake, of course, is not the only author at fault here—many write as if they know nothing about the range of sexuality—but he is one who should be able to do better.

Works Discussed

The Fourth Hemisphere (Void Publications, Melbourne, 1980).
The Gods of Xuma (DAW, New York, 1978).
Warlords of Xuma (DAW, New York, 1983).

SEXUALITY IN SCIENCE FICTION

by Russell Blackford
[1984]

In Thomas Pynchon's *V.,* a text rich in parodic theories of history, we are told that if Benny Profane, a randy and sexist, aptly-named schlemiel, had amused himself with such theories he might have seen all political events as growing out of sexual desire: "...wars, governments and uprisings, have the desire to get laid as their roots; because history unfolds according to economic forces and the only reason anybody wants to get rich is so he can get laid steadily, with whomever he chooses."

The kind of intense and pervading sexual motivation that a Benny Profane could be expected to attribute to political actors is strong in a proportion of men and a somewhat smaller proportion of women, according to the research I've read, and irrespective of any unfalsifiable theory that sexuality is at the root of all behavior in all people.

To what extent the statistical difference between men and women is a cultural artifact and to what extent it is biologically coded is a subject of vigorous debate among feminists and others. It would be an ideal subject for science fiction writers, who are placed to create imaginary cultures in which different sexual expectations rule. Some interesting writing along these lines has been done in sf, mostly by women. Ursula Le Guin's *The Dispossessed* and *The Left Hand of Darkness* and Vonda

McIntyre's *Dreamsnake* come to mind as books that treat sexuality in other cultures with some intellectual rigor. Even more than Le Guin's novels, *Dreamsnake* makes a concerted attempt to remain within the conventions of revised sexual mores. On a future earth where most people can control their fertility by bio-feedback, sexuality has become a less traumatic aspect of life for both women and men. *Dreamsnake* is no Utopian novel: it depicts a hard world with its own problems that are merely *different* from those of our world, and there are still crises involving sexuality. But sexual relationships in general are freer and less tense. Unfortunately, much of what is good about *Dreamsnake* is thrown away in the last three contrived and sentimental chapters, which back off from any radical relativistic approach to the nature of sexuality and love.

In general, sf has not been able to depict with any conviction alternative sexual conventions. The old ideal in our own culture was of sexual experience exclusively within the ambit of lifetime monogamy, qualified by certain double standards. The emergent ideal seems to be serial romantic heterosexual pairbonding. Sf has had great difficulty in presenting more than half-heartedly any convention outside of these. Heinlein's original attempts to describe line marriage and coterie promiscuity were interesting at the time, and still strike me as genuine examples of what sf should attempt; however, in retrospect, they appear embarrassingly parasitic on sexist and merely sentimental cultural norms. George R. R. Martin's *Dying of the Light* was a courageous attempt to write a love story in anthropological perspective, and it succeeded to some extent on this level, though not notably on others.

I am dismayed that the simple depiction of nudity and sexual activity is *seldom* impressive in sf. Even in *Dreamsnake,* the reader is more told of sexual experiences than shown them, presumably in deference to cultural taboos. Le Guin has resorted to mystical pseudo-Lawrentian circumlocutions. Worse still is the sort of thing to be found prominently in Silverberg's *Shadrach in the Furnace.* Early in the novel, the hero's lover,

Nikki Crowfoot, is described. The emphasis is on portions of anatomy: "heavy dark-tipped breasts," "powerful thighs," "flat hard belly," "strong shoulders," "narrow waist," "sudden flaring hips," "sleek muscular buttocks." She seems "something primitive, barbaric, primordial," in keeping, we are told, with her Amerindian ancestry. She dons a see-through gown that displays "Chocolate nipples," "hints of the blue-black wire-stiff pubic triangle," and "flashes of haunch and thigh." The woman is virtually reduced to itemized cuts of meat and hair. The only extra layer of description is in the references to her savage and romantic Indian quality—in prose that could have been written for a magazine centerfold. The passage is partly redeemed only by an ironic reference to Nikki's ability to twit the black hero about his own "savage ancestry."

Some short chapters later, Nikki and the hero make love: she "lets him know" that he can "skip" the foreplay and "get down to the main event." In *Penthouse* language, he "enters the taut hidden harbor between her thighs with a sudden unsparing thrust that brings grunts of pleasure from them both." The depiction of the feelings involved is crude, externalized, and without wit or real eroticism.

These passages could have been genuinely erotic—perhaps with only subtle changes of wording, providing that sexuality were used to enhance character rather than reduce it to pornographic anonymity. What Silverberg objectively describes is not offensive on any rational critical view of morality; it is the language and specific selection of detail that offends. It would be pointless singling out Silverberg, but the kind of language I have described is all too typical of the objectifying, leveling treatment of characters adopted by sf writers when they depict nudity or sexual action. There is no anthropological perspective here, merely a pandering to inartistic and insensitive cultural expectations of what is erotic. Until we can do better than this, we are doomed in any attempt at more ambitious depictions of alternative expressions and cultural organizations of sexuality.

SEX AS A HARD PROBLEM IN SCIENCE FICTION

by David Lake
[1985]

I have a few comments about Russell Blackford's views of sexuality in sf—both in his review of my Xuman novels and his article on sexuality in SF.

Blackford's view of my work is generally favorable—sometimes perhaps too kind. But in his last two paragraphs he "blasts" my treatment of sexuality. He doesn't like either the "casual eroticism" or the "bourgeois marriages."

But the fact is that most humans enjoy both, and I don't think there will be any change in this situation over the next thousand years (the period of my novels). By "bourgeois marriage" I take it that Blackford means simply "marriage." There is no other kind really viable today; even the (non-bourgeois?) communist states of Russia and China are grimly devoted to permanent monogamy. And in fact, long-term pair-bonding (= marriage) is natural to the human species; it has been naturally-selected, and people who reject it tend to get eliminated from the population in the fairly short-run—i.e. they don't produce as many viable offspring as the marriers. Especially if things get tougher (and I think they will), deviants will be weeded out.

As a matter of fact, like the vast majority of humans, I like marriage. It is the best kind of adjustment for long-term happiness, as I have found in my own life; I am sure it is here to stay; and that's why I make it the ideal of my sf. As for non-marital sex, well, that's nice too, especially as experimentation leading up to marriage. (By the way, I have not read Masters and Johnson. I was simply referring to masturbation, which needs no sexologists to teach us.)

The only real change we can make in marriage in the near future is to make it non-sexist. I entirely approve of that change. Women in fact are the essential human sex, and males are needed more peripherally, as fertilizers and protectors. Protectors mainly from other males, as Joanna Russ has rightly remarked. The trouble with us humans is that we have an unfortunate biological heritage. We are mammals, and in most mammals the males are bigger and more aggressive than the females. This paid off for a while, when we were tribal hunter-gatherers, but it doesn't pay off now. I suspect that if we survive our present crisis, over the next few millennia a new species will replace *Homo sapiens*. The new species may well have a different pattern of sexuality.

I did not plan a Xuman series (Blackford is right about that); but when I had written *Gods* I found that that planet was still alive in my mind, and its culture was becoming clearer, so I had to write another novel. I would dearly love to write a third, but the only rational plot I can think of would be a racial clash between multiplying human migrants and native Xumans. That story would be, to me, rather a depressing one—too much like umpteen countries in our present world, including probably, over the next fifty years, Australia. Of course I could write of the emergence of a new human species, perhaps influenced by Xuman sexual patterns. But it's really very hard to do a new human species—I think all attempts so far are brilliant fakes. Even *The Left Hand of Darkness* (a lovely book) centers on a fake—the Gethenians are really all men, as some readers have noticed; and Le Guin flinches from the physicalities of Gethenian sex where they would be appropriate (I agree with Blackford on that).

Yes, sex is a hard problem in sf....

AGAPE, EROS, AND THE ZOOPHILOUS

AN APPRECIATION OF PETER GOLDSWORTHY'S *WISH*

by Bruce Shaw
[2000]

Sexuality between human and non-human is a relatively rare theme, but Peter Goldsworthy when he writes explicitly on it in his novel *Wish* (1995) is not the first to have done so, though he has done it very well. The theme of sexual and companionate relationships and needs between the human and non-human can be traced back through a number of science fiction and fantasy works to the great nineteenth century myth of Mary Shelley's *Frankenstein* and beyond.[1] Such tales have at their best a mix-

---

1. One of the themes that writers of science fiction and fantasy have addressed since the invention of those cognate genres is the relationship between animals and humans when the former realize intelligence on a human level. Indeed the comparatively large number of short stories and novels on this theme make it possible to speak of a "subgenre." The most obvious applications are in fables and allegories such as the moral tales attributed to Aesop (fifth century B.C.) or when human hypocrisies and cruelties are observed from the viewpoint of a household pet, as in Lucius Apuleius's The Golden Ass (second century). Where sexual relations between humans and animals are concerned we can go back further to Greek mythology and tales of sexual exploits between humans and gods; the story of Leda and the Swan comes to mind. Another application is to explore the nature of intelligence itself, of sentience, reasoning, and humanness.

ture of humor (especially satire) and tragedy. When writing about animal-human sexuality there is a fine line between establishing reader empathy towards the protagonists while at the same time using narrative techniques that distance the reader from the actions of the main characters, because bestiality is a strong social taboo. On the other hand, beneath the sexual explicitness (eros) of the novel there are suggestions of spiritual love (agape) which, it might be argued, can be (should be?) extendable to cross-species intelligences.

1.

Peter David Goldsworthy was born in 1951 in the South Australian town of Minlaton. Holding Bachelor of Science and Bachelor of Medicine degrees from the University of Adelaide, he is in that enviable position of being able to earn a living in medicine while pursuing his clear love of writing. Goldsworthy is a poet, playwright (screenplays), writer of short fiction, and novelist. He is described as a humorist and satirist and, in the blurb to his novel *Honk If You Are Jesus* (1992), as a mixer of "sci-fi, medical marvel, satire and romance." His writing has earned him several awards, for example the Commonwealth Poetry Prize in 1982 and the Bicentennial Literature Award in 1988. His major works include *Readings from Ecclesiastes* (1982), *Archipelagoes* (1982), *Zooing* (1986), *Bleak Rooms* (1988), *This Goes With This* (1988), *Maestro* (1989), *This Goes With That: Selected Poems 1970-1990* (1991), *Magpie* (co-authored with Brian Matthews, 1992), *After The Ball* (1992), and *Little Deaths* (1993). By this reckoning *Wish* (1995) is Goldsworthy's eleventh book, published when he was forty-four. [2]

Wish is the designated name of one of the work's two principal characters, a female gorilla descended from the western lowlands gorilla subspecies and originally named Eliza by the couple who first raised her. She is dubbed Wish by John James—

2. *Who's Who of Australian Writers* (Port Melbourne: D. W. Thorpe in assoc. with the National Centre for Australian Studies, 1995), 256-57.

the other chief protagonist—because of her repeated use of that sign: crossed fingers in Auslan, the Australian signing language used by the profoundly deaf and which Wish's minders and John use to communicate with her. This double meaning—*wish* as name and as substantive—is the dominant motif of the novel.

Language in the broader sense as more than speech is another important motif. One of the novel's themes is the difficulty of communication between different categories of person, between the deaf and non-deaf among humans and between humans and non-humans (animals), also between words and non-verbal communication. These pairings are set in constant juxtaposition.

There is frequent recourse to extra-verbal modes of communication, principally poetry and music but also forms of intertextuality such as television, film, and scientific treatises both real and fictionalized that allow for an element of parody. John James's growing understanding of Wish and eventual love for her is expressed in poetic terms: either through a direct appeal to poetry as "symbolic utterance" (109) or the creation of actual poems, as in those written by one of the other chief protagonists, the animal liberationist Stella Todd: "... I sniff the Sniff/ of Two Legs opening White Door:/ the Cold Kennel where Meat lives" (63).[3] These animal poems help to establish a sympathetic mood in the reader before the meeting with Wish. Stephen Muecke observes quite rightly that "[l]iterature often heightens its medium through poetic intensifications," but then puzzlingly claims that Goldsworthy does not need poetic intensifications "because he is doing something different... his is the double play of the language of words and the language of signs."[4] This

---

3. "Two Legs" recalls Gummidge the cat's naming of his human compatriots, "Old Horsemeat" and "Kitty-Come-Here," in Fritz Leiber's delightful short story "Space-time for Springers" (1958), in *The Best of Fritz Leiber* (London: Sphere, 1974), 208-21. The giving of nicknames to humans by sentient animals is a parody on the human predilection for applying unusual names to animals.

4. Stephen Muecke, "Goldsworthy's *Wish*," *Australian Book Review*, No.

suggestion that Goldsworthy has no need of poetic tropes I think misses the point. Goldsworthy throughout the novel consciously employs "poetic intensifications" that are part of the "language of words" in a stylistic policy that helps the novel move. The novel would lack some of its power without the poetic touches.

Wish/Eliza's first "spoken" communication—witnessed by John in a video recording and really a signed or mimed act—is described by John as a poem: "To the best of my knowledge Eliza had spoken the first symbolic utterance—the first poem—ever created by another species" (109). Similarly, John hails Wish's use of the "wish" sign as "a beautiful touch, an improvised variation, another poem which moved me..." (117). Poetry as "symbolic utterance" is important to the story because it demonstrates in Wish what is commonly taken to be a characteristic that defines humanness: the ability to communicate in abstracts, with symbols. Music is similarly associated with the rhythms of poetry: "As she closed her eyes and rocked her head in time, I realized that the main sense of those sweet songs was in the melodies; the words needed no translation" (203).

The narrative plot within which these stylistic modes operate is relatively simple. John James, a large overweight fellow, something of a misanthrope since his divorce from Jill, is asked by Stella Todd and her partner Clive Kinnear to teach Auslan to their young charge Eliza, who turns out to be a genetically altered gorilla. John renames her "Wish" and as their lessons in communication proceed a bond of affection grows between the two which culminates with them sleeping together. This occurs in Book Three and, appropriately enough, is the episode that marks the climax of the novel. Book Four is the denouement where they are discovered by Clive, who begins court proceedings against John; not from moral outrage, but with the motive of making Wish's case a cause célèbre for animal rights, especially those of an intelligent self-aware animal.

It is this duplicity that brings tragedy upon them, rather than

---

178 (February/March 1996), 47.

John's moral lapse. Wish is removed to the Adelaide zoo where in despair she suicides by hanging. Stella leaves Clive, and John becomes further estranged from his ex-wife and daughter Rosie. But a reconciliation of sorts is hinted at, firstly between Stella and John when the former visits John in his minimum security prison, and also between John and the now-dead Wish in a final touch of the numinous:

> A breeze stirred somewhere; I heard the shiver of the treetops, the sweepings of approaching debris across the carpark, then saw the wind catch and embroider and then divide the rising column of smoke, two fingers which briefly tangled, as if crossing index and middle, before joining again in a single smooth column rising upwards into the blue. (299)

Stephen Muecke observes, unnecessarily, "[o]nce he had the idea for this new work, Goldsworthy had to establish fictional plausibilities..."[5] The novel's "science" is important insofar as it helps attain suspension-of-disbelief. Human glands and the hormones they produce are a common factor in stories of this kind. Wish has been "biologically engineered" by the removal of the embryonic adrenal glands, an operation facilitating growth of the brain because the inhibitor of such growth, cortisone, is no longer present. There is a negative payoff, for without doses of corticosteroids daily such an animal would soon die (226-8). This is another tragic element, that the genetically changed animal is usually incomplete. Victor Frankenstein's Creature— the debt that Goldsworthy and many others owe to Mary Shelley—is fashioned from a patchwork of human parts culled from graveyards. Similarly, Wish is hampered by possessing an ape-like body with a gracile, almost human visage.

Wish raises Frankensteinian questions about social and ethical justifications for animal experimentation, dramatized in

---

5. Muecke, 47.

its climactic section by a debate between John and Terry, the scientist who originally took Eliza/Wish from the Melbourne laboratories. Partly disaffected with the project after becoming emotionally attached to Wish, Terry however largely retains the scientific point of view. One goal of the project is "to produce primates that could perform a range of intelligent tasks" (228) or, as John James instantly rejoins, produce "[s]laves for the assembly line!"—a common theme that has one thinking immediately of Aldous Huxley's *Brave New World* (1932). But there is a broader motive. "Think of the implications for human intelligence," says Terry (230) in an echo of Clive's thoughts sixty-five pages earlier: "We can learn much by looking at ourselves through her [Wish's] eyes" (165). The search for an understanding of ourselves underpins western science, a view that suggests a general truth, that we must always know ourselves in relationship to some other phenomenon. But is this motive any more redeeming that that of creating a labor pool? What can make this quest go awry is to forget the importance of the emotional life.

2.

Characteristics that make us human include self-awareness, an apprehension of consequences, a tendency to speculate about the meanings of death and life, and the experiencing of "human" emotions such as anxiety, fear, and love in all their permutations. But these appreciations come indirectly in the novel and not from a thoroughgoing characterization of Wish herself. In *Wish* the theme of a consciously aware Other questioning the world is muted and presented through John James's thoughts, in his debates with Clive and Stella and some of the minor characters, in his conversations with Wish, and in his interpretations of those conversations and Wish's actions. Wish in this light is an innocent, a naif protected from most of the harsh realities of the world. One of the strengths of the novel lies in her reactions to the real world, revulsion upon learning that humans eat animals, or anxiety about death—both good examples of defamiliarization that help us look anew at such issues ourselves. Wish rebels, but at a restricted level, as when she signs her dislike of Stella's badgering (109). The tragedy for Wish lies in her increasingly conscious awareness of and exposure to human cruelties, to which she finally succumbs. As John James says, Wish "still had an important lesson to learn, perhaps the most important: that the stupidity and cruelty of her cousin species, Homo sapiens, was limitless" (290).

Together with Wish's innocence, another central ingredient for tragedy lies in her quest for self. Wish is very nearly human in physiology: "She was almost adult sized, but her face was surely not the face of an adult gorilla. Her forehead was less protruding, her head disproportionately larger and more rounded—a child's big head" (99). And Wish's chief desire is to become more human. One of the most harrowing episodes in the novel is her attempt to shave off body hair, motivated in part by her jealousy on seeing Stella and John in bed together. Goldsworthy uses this anthropomorphic touch to assist in plot development.

John James recognizes anthropomorphism in the photographs in Clive's book *Primate Suffrage*, noting that they appear to have been selected "for cuteness—to find some human essence in the apes, a kinship with which the reader might identify" (89). This invented book, a parody on scientific treatises, helps to introduce another theme important for the novel's development. Goldsworthy takes the arguments of animal liberation rhetoric to their logical conclusion when Clive in a television interview says pedantically: "the rights of a particular individual of that species are far more important—far more tangible.... The client ape should be fully acquainted with the pros and cons and allowed to make an informed decision" (79).

Wish is, in Clive's words, "outside human culture, looking in," and to him this has the valuable scientific implication—as we have seen—that we can learn a great deal about ourselves through her eyes because Wish is "free from the preconceptions, the acculturation" (165). This is fallacious because Wish has already learned much more about human culture than Clive and Stella realize, as John discovers. In an extension of Clive's earlier point, John's argument is that just as the deaf should participate in the outside world while retaining their unique (Sign) language (139), so too should Wish be allowed similar outlets. In this respect, congruent positions are held by the two protagonists, though they are opponents in other respects. There is only then a relatively short step to the next freedom: "if Wish deserved human rights, she deserved human pleasures" (214); "If she is entitled to human rights, those rights should, I would have thought, include the right to fuck" (251), says John.

This brings us to companionship (by which I mean spiritual love or agape) and sexuality (sensual love, eros), which go hand in hand with John James's growing insights into Wish's intellectual capacities and her inner emotional life. There is a further twist to the plot when Wish, the object of study, begins to ask John about himself (168)—akin to the experience common among anthropologists when interviewees ask questioners about themselves, joke with them, and may even take their photograph. It reflects the curiosity of an enquiring, and therefore intelligent, mind. Wish jokes with John, she takes him into a high tree, into her natural environment, and after showing him her room where her drawings are attached to the wall she inspects his own sketches. At this point John feels "an odd sensation: of tables turned, of my artwork being scrutinised, searched for psychological clues" (171). Wish's drawings of John reflect the reality of his large bulk, as would a photograph. Perhaps, too, the psychological phenomenon called transference is taking place. John certainly responds: "Wish's growing puppy-love, adoring even when she was teasing me, added immensely to the pleasure of those days" (181).

John falls in love with Wish because "[w]e shared more than language; we also shared the nearest thing to a natural relationship in her life" (238). But is this a rationalization? At the psychological level John realizes that "my deepest need was for tenderness, for intimacy" (244). This said after the fact when, standing in the shadows of Wish's room before going to her, John overturns a joke made at his expense by Terry: "I felt, for once in my life, beautiful: a giant of a man, a human silver-back, in full sexual rut" (239). Wish's love is a powerful boost to John's self-esteem. In fact, it could be argued that the novel depicts John's quest for self as much as, or even more than, that of Wish.

In literature, the search for self and for companionship and sexual happiness can generate challenging and uncomfortable insights. That is one reason why such stories are written. But the same argument explains why not many really good tales are extant. In the better works, to question what is human touches on very powerful and archetypal cultural images. A writer treads unstable ground when depicting characters engaged in what the law calls bestiality, one of society's great taboos. Part of Goldsworthy's success in circumventing this limitation is stylistic. As Michael McGirr says of Goldsworthy's writing in general, "The progression... is so logical... that it is difficult to count back and find the precise point at which moral chaos got in under the brick veneer."[6] But how successfully the theme of "moral chaos" is handled depends on more than literary skill; its effectiveness can be made or broken by the prevailing mood in society. Goldsworthy can write explicit sexual passages, and get them published, because present day sociosexual mores admit greater tolerance.

3.

Stephen Muecke observes that "Goldsworthy is working in a society where the heterogeneity of desire is celebrated, and rapacious Man is no longer considered the centre of his

---

6. Michael McGirr, "Strange Talk," *Eureka Street,* Vol. 6, No. 2 (March 1996), 51.

long-suffering world."[7] That statement is a bit sweeping and needs some modification—the ideologues for human dominance are still among us—but it is certainly true inasmuch as a writer can get away with more in the 1990s, up to a point, than one could fifty years ago. Would Goldsworthy's novel have met with resistance if it had dealt too sympathetically with its characters?

I think Goldsworthy succeeds because he employs several distancing techniques that make it possible to confront the idea of bestiality. Firstly, most of the characters are unsympathetic, though not wholly so. And while Wish herself is presented very sensitively, our knowledge about her is relatively little. A great deal of Goldsworthy's work is about different kinds of hypocrisy masked beneath scientific rationalism or obscured by ignorance and misunderstanding. Most commonly, a lack of sufficient feeling, a dearth of emotion, lies at the heart of these. It is a contretemps between two Jungian functions of the psyche, thinking and feeling—the first articulated by Clive and Terry, the second dramatized by John James and Wish. Stella comes somewhere in between, at first joining in the experiment with Clive but redeemed towards the end when she rejects Clive's scientific ideology. This thinking-versus-feeling model is reflected also in the two sub-plots: John's conflicts with his deaf parents—a hostile and authoritarian father, a mediating and more affectionate mother; also conflicts with his ex-wife Jill in her studied reasonableness.

These functions are played out on the novel's center stage in the relationships between John, Clive, Stella, and Wish. The relationship between Clive and Stella towards Wish is characterized by paternalism. To Clive, Wish is a scientific object of study, a project; to Stella, Wish may be a surrogate child. Paradoxically, these preoccupations cause them to lose sight of the quality of feeling in Wish's almost-human nature: "to both of them, Project Wish came first, even at the expense of Wish's

7. Muecke, 48.

happiness" (189). Clive is depicted as measured, over-controlled, prissy (29), qualities about which Stella often confronts him so that it becomes a marital game: "They were playing their favorite game again: spot an emotion" (190). And at one point Stella says, "'Clive tends not to see what she [Wish] feels—only what she says... Clive doesn't believe in emotions'" (128). John above all sees himself in opposition to these people, perhaps to the world. He is dominated not only by feeling but also by a degree of intuition derived from his unique childhood: using Auslan, watching for subtle physical clues in people, their body language. This is the yardstick by which he measures others.

There appears also to be some arrogance in his dealings with those around him. He constantly compares his skill at Sign and greater sensitiveness towards other's feelings with the hypocrisies and double-dealing that he believes are contained in the spoken word. My reaction was at first to be intrigued by the descriptions of Auslan, illustrated effectively throughout the book by line sketches, only to grow disaffected by John's chauvinism. This was perhaps intended by Goldsworthy. Privately John derides the efforts of all attempts by others to learn that direct, sublime but difficult mode of communication. He makes that commonest of insider's claims, that others will never really understand, an outlook that is essentially self-defeating.

At bottom, John James is a misanthrope. He is large and awkward, acutely aware of his bulk and operating predominantly at the level of feeling and the sensual. He is highly susceptible emotionally to the tactile and the olfactory—his earliest attraction towards Wish triggered by her not unpleasant musky smell—to such an extent that he is greatly dependent on those senses. He escapes from the cares of the world by donning a wet suit and floating in the still waters of the Glenelg beach front, and later in the dam at Stella and Clive's farm immediately prior to having sex with Wish. (The physical setting shifts back and forwards from the Adelaide suburb of Glenelg in South Australia to the Hills, between John James's home and that of Wish respectively). This imagery of the sea as a natural float tank with cleansing properties and overtones of returning to the womb is a recurring motif, altering the novel's pace between the conflicts of interpersonal debate and moments of quietude (for example, 209). The image spills over at one point when towards the end of his conversation with Terry—before Terry chides him with the joke about being a silverback—there is a return to the floating, swimming motif, with a suggestion too of post-coital tristesse, though John and Wish have not yet coupled: "The day had been long, a heavy surf of emotions and ideas; I was exhausted, but not unpleasantly, beached in a tranquil aftermath" (233).

Essentially, John and Wish are outsiders. John especially is beyond the pale after he commits the offence of bestiality. Being outsiders is in fact true of many other characters. John's parents are outsiders because of their hearing disabilities. Clive, Stella and Terry have gone against the scientific establishment by taking Wish from the laboratories, and in their espousal of the scientific method they are also "deaf" to the emotional life. Wish is denied the rights of a conscious, self-aware, thinking and questioning being because physiologically she is not human. Being outsiders helps somewhat to evoke the reader's sympathy. And John is not an entirely unsympathetic character either. For tragedy to work, there must be a degree of reader sympathy towards the recalcitrant character—even someone like Macbeth—sufficient to allow the reader to suspend judgment. Clive is well-meaning, Stella is warm and somewhat lost in her partnership with Clive, John's parents evoke sympathy, and is there not always some residual sympathy for an overweight person? What in the end makes the tragedy most poignant is society's attitude that dismisses John's offence as a bad joke. He can be dismissed as harmlessly eccentric (293) by comparison with the pedophiles sharing jail with him, precisely because he has transgressed with a nonhuman: "finally, I was a joke, and therefore Wish also was a joke, consigned, again, to the inhuman world, and perhaps even to the inanimate" (294).

The most striking distance-setting factor is that after

Goldsworthy has depicted explicitly sexual acts between a human and a nearly-human ape he introduces mythopoeic imagery—for example, when Wish thanks John in Sign using all her limbs, "Her four hands, waving like those of some dark Hindu goddess, seemed at that moment the most beautiful thing I had ever seen" (242). This has an archetypal power, but it is communicated with a light touch combining the animal, popularly regarded as "less-than-human" and the godlike "more-than-human." The dictionary definition of anthropomorphism includes the religious or numinous and it may not be too far-fetched to see in Wish an appeal to mythology, namely the identification of Woman with nature, with the evocation of goddesses from religions that existed many hundreds of years before Christianity.

Imagery of woman's mystery permeates the novel. Stella for example is introduced in vaguely Earth Mother terms: "she had a comfortable thirty-something face, plenty of laugh-lines, a broad lopsided smile" (27). As a large-breasted "comfortable" woman she is a muted human reflection of Wish. And, like Wish, she attempts to seduce John, though unsuccessfully. Wish is human in her sentience and mysterious in her animal nature. The recurring images of the sea (the Gulf) and the Hills, well known metaphors for the feminine and the masculine, are I think no accident. In Jungian phraseology, the sea is John's anima and to Wish the Hills (or trees) represent her animus. One of the novel's messages is that modern humans have lost the old pre-scientific union they once had with the intuitive, religious mysteries. The tragic love between John James and Wish represents allegorically the separation in our psyches of reason from feeling, nature from culture, the scientific from the religious mysteries.

4.

Concerning authorial voice, are tales of this kind best told from the standpoint of the sentient animal or from that of human protagonists? It is partly a question of style, what critics lately call "discourse." *Wish* would have been quite a different novel had it been told from the point of view of Wish herself, but that is a tall order. To attempt a sustained development through an alien mind would test the skill of any writer.[8] Goldsworthy tells the story of Wish in the first person from John James's viewpoint and most of the novel traces the development of character through the relationships between John and Wish, John and his parents, John and his ex-wife, John and his boss, John and Stella and Clive, John and the police. The central character is John James, not Wish. This allows some distancing from Wish herself though there are plenty of incidents to illustrate her mixed human-cum-alien character.

To try too hard to create an alien viewpoint might be to create a clever text but one that becomes indecipherable to many readers. I have no particular text in mind here, but I think that to understand the Other we need to apply a process of "translation" or "appropriation"—though not in the pejorative sense used by many critics influenced by postcolonial studies—by bringing concepts into our language that were once alien, or very nearly so. We do this all the time, and not always with fidelity to the meaning or spirit of the original. Take for example the recent appearance of the word "mantra" as one of the latest buzz-words in journalistic commentaries. Goldsworthy does this by using the unfamiliar language of Auslan which from Wish's signed utterances becomes stripped down into "broken English." In this manner, it is possible in our literary imaginations to comprehend an alien viewpoint.

---

8. There are some notable examples where elements of the animal fable of old have been reworked for speculative fiction/science fiction in the twentieth century. Olaf Stapledon in his novel *Sirius* (1944)—often described as one of the best of its kind—approaches this difficulty by having a relatively minor character act as narrator, Robert the human boyfriend of the dog's companion Plaxy. Robert undertakes to write Sirius's biography and the third person narrative form seems to work well in *Sirius* as a means of distancing, for example allowing at times for the young man's jealousy to surface.

Humor is an important factor, and having one-dimensional characters is another way of creating distance. On satire, Muecke for example identifies "'signs' of political correctness" in the characters of Stella and Clive.[9] McGirr points out that the use of nicknames (which appear often in joking relationships) tends "to reduce characters to a single dimension." And when Goldsworthy has John James reading (that is, parodying) press reports about bestiality he is alluding to well-recognized topics for humor, the shepherd and his sheep or the woman and her large dog. But there are poignant edges to the satirical touches aimed at present-day mores. We are never far from tragedy. John feels that the note of amusement in the press reports is unfair to animals because "[t]hey are as much victims as any human victim, a crime against them is as serious as any human crime" (240).

Making the stigmatized the butt of jokes is both a means of handling the jokers' unease in the face of difference (which means that we will always have joking of this nature), and a means of excluding the stigmatized whether they are human or animal. This is where the counterpointing of a fictional animal possessing human intelligence against the real world experiences of the profoundly deaf comes into play. A common stereotype about even the partially deaf is that such individuals are frequently regarded as having a below-average intelligence, though the real reason is that they often miss the auditory cues that a hearing person catches without difficulty. The 1990s appear to be a decade of greater knowledge of, and tolerance towards, difference, though compassion and political correctness are uneasy bedpersons with suspicions of veiled hypocrisy often held towards political correctness. This seems to be another of Goldsworthy's messages.

What places *Wish* in the ranks of science fiction and fantasy is that it re-addresses such questions as those raised by James Gunn almost twenty years ago: "in the first forty years of the

---

9. Muecke, 48.

twentieth century science fiction began to ask questions that had never before been asked: Will humanity progress or regress? Will its social forms change? Will humanity survive?"[10] Now, as Muecke says, "A main point of the book is that ideal humanity is no longer the most important thing to strive for, but rather one has to rethink humanity as just one among many forms of life, and as still in a process of change as it encounters its Others."[11] Maybe so, and perhaps the "rethinking of humanity" might be extended to non-physical (meta-physical) "human" qualities— combinations of spiritual and sexual love, of agape and eros— plus a union between scientific and spiritual views. These are not really new ideas however. They are quintessentially eastern, as symbolized by Goldsworthy in his description of Wish as Hindu goddess. (What would James Gunn say about the state of the sf art today?)

So Goldsworthy's *Wish* belongs identifiably to the science fiction and fantasy genre, and within that mode of literature to the sub-genre of the human-animal allegory. The narrative technique of defamiliarization, which is a mainstay of science fiction, is put to good use. The work is balanced between tragedy and satire, with touches of parody thrown in. Its chief theme, the "hook" by which the author attracts the reader, is a sexual relationship between a human male and a nearly-human female gorilla. The imagery evoked has great power because the sexual act itself is the most intimate, most trusting physical relation-ship that can be had between persons. Because such intimacy is between human and Other, strong archetypal fears are brought to the surface. If eros, sensual and sexual love, was the only factor at work, the novel might belong more properly to the genre of pornographic literature. But Goldsworthy overcomes this hazard by suggesting the principle of agape or spiritual love with its emphasis on mutual respect and companionship.

---

10. James Gunn (ed), *The Road to Science Fiction #2: From Wells to Heinlein* (New York, NAL, 1979), 6-7.

11. Muecke, 48.

His narrative techniques raise the relationship between Wish and John James to a mythopoeic level, appealing to the poetic and the numinous, plus the employment of distancing mechanisms such as presenting most characters in an often satiric, less than sympathetic light. This saves the novel from crassness or banality. Readers are challenged by the questioning at one level of accepted scientific truths and at another level by the flouting of moral taboos.

Work Discussed

Peter Goldsworthy, *Wish,* Sydney: Angus & Robertson, 1995.

THAWING THE FROST GARDEN
KOMARR, BY LOIS MCMASTER BUJOLD

by Sylvia Kelso
[1998]

Komarr is not only a regular compendium but an exceptionally good balance of Lois Bujold's diverse strengths as an sf writer. It would be so easy to use that patronizing line, "This is a very good novel that just happens to be science fiction." Except that this is a novel that could *only* be science fiction: fiction based on science, fictional science, science becoming fiction—but *Komarr* pushes almost every side of the traditional sf envelope; which is where Bujold's diversity comes in.

Let me start with the science, whose most orthodox sf element is mulched deep into *Komarr*, set on a planet halfway through terraforming, with a plot that threatens both project and society. But like most very good sf writers, rather than lecture the reader *ad nauseam* on her borrowings from "proper" scientific hypotheses, Bujold almost entirely subsumes this basis of solid research. Instead, center front goes to the plot focus: the orbiting artificial mirror, or soletta, whose reflected light is vital to the terraforming. And as the novel opens, the soletta has been crippled by an accident in space.

From the image of the soletta, "a grand Winterfair ornament, hung in the sky like a snowflake made of stars" (Bujold, *Komarr*, 1), stems the who-dunn-the-wrecking plot that impels the novel, culminating in a delicious slice of entirely pseudo-science, based on the physics of wormhole travel: "a five-space needle of infinitesimal diameter and unlimited length, to punch through that area of five-space weakness called a wormhole, and unfold again into three-space on the other side" (230). This excursion into what Bujold calls "total handwaving" (email, 1) sits atop the novel's scientific ramifications like an exotic, spectacular flower. At the same time, while doing fictional science and science-sustaining-fiction, Bujold has never sacrificed the fiction to the science. If fiction equals the novel, and novels tell a story, as E.M. Forster long ago pointed out (26), then Bujold has consistently produced novels whose fast impelling stories unfold from both science and characterization with equal inexorability. Because, of course, the other thing the novel does is characters—and Bujold's characters, from Miles to the regrettably defunct Sergeant Bothari, were notable from the start. *Komarr*, however, takes a long step further into the traditional domain of women sf writers; beyond masterful character-making it revives that old strand of what my friend Justine Larbalestier, among others, calls *domestic sf.*

Such sf has flitted through the genre from Gernsback's day: women's stories mostly, rarely long in print, their tone resolutely unheroic, their focus determinedly on the nuts and bolts of not-so-everyday life. Connie Willis does the update: housing problems on a space station, the double-joke of aliens who appear on earth as normally nerdy human scientists ("Spice Pogrom," "And Come from Miles Around"). But this approach naturally militates against the high-gravity, save-the-universe tone of most sf; to combine them, without leaving the seams rucked awkwardly between the two, is one of the genre's hardest challenges. *Komarr* does it beautifully. More remarkably, *Komarr* does it structurally; using the technique initiated in *Mirror Dance*, *Komarr* splits the viewpoint between Miles and another character. But this time it's a woman instead of a man.

This split domesticates sf at a level previously inaccessible to Bujold's fiction, where "home life" was either the elevated milieu of Vorkosigan House, or the space-Utopia of Beta Colony. In *Komarr*, the woman's view reveals the off-Earth equivalent of a posted US army family: school-age son, colonial bureaucrat husband, non-working wife. Except on Komarr, such life's middleclass mundanities, grocery shopping, putting up guests, taking the kids to school, are all inexorably warped by the novel's givens: on Komarr, you hire gravity beds, live in oxygen domes, buy vat-grown meat and visit the countryside in a breather mask. This exotic domesticity simultaneously defamiliarizes the setting, that fundamental of sf, and highlights the alternating scenes of scientific investigation and thriller violence.

But the divided viewpoint also lets Bujold combine two previously diverse aspects of her sf, the male and female stuff. "Malestuff" is traditional sf, the staple of the Vorkosigan series. "Femalestuff," less common and correspondingly more difficult (Lake, 9), appeared most brilliantly in *Barrayar*. Like traditional, biologically based women's sf, such as much of Marion Zimmer Bradley's work, *Barrayar* centered on having babies; but as Miles matured, it seemed Bujold had sidelined this "femalestuff" out of the series. *Komarr* returns it stage center, with a new female protagonist. And yes, Miles has Met His Fate, and yes, she will give him a run for his money, and no, I won't say how it turns out. I will say that Ekaterin Nile Vorvayne Vorsoisson is one tough lady, in the proper sense of the word. She enters the novel as an unhappily married wife. She leaves a woman who has achieved self-determination, with firm prospects for a career in landscaping—from gardens to planets—and the kudos of knowing, despite a wall of security silence, that she could probably call herself the Hero of Komarr.

The real meat of the fiction, however, takes "femalestuff" to a level few mainstream novels have reached. The scenes between Ekaterin and her husband illuminate a loveless marriage to its nadir: not merely the squabbles, the endemic disagreements, the bitter strains of mismanagement or failed ambition, the public putdowns and social embarrassments, but the ghastly apparatus of loveless sex. When Ekaterin has to "study Tien warily" and decide "she had better offer sex very soon" because "it was past time to defuse him" (*Komarr*, 55), Bujold replaces the potential glamour of all sex-in-space with the excruciating truth of many "mundane" relationships; worst of all is the reader's understanding that this *is* normal for them. As *Mirror Dance* and *Memory* offer powerful studies of male characters suffering and struggling from a chrysalis of stagnation, the "femalestuff" of *Komarr* traces a staple of feminist fiction, including sf like Sheri S. Tepper's *Grass*: a woman's equally arduous metamorphosis from one suffocating life into something else that, however painful the transit, at least promises to be free.

The extra beauty in *Komarr* is that Ekaterin's struggles integrate with Miles's, letting dedicated Bujold readers have and eat the cake of a Vorkosigan adventure where "femalestuff" doesn't sideline Miles, and Miles need not be "a female in disguise" (Lake, 8) adumbrating women's physical and social problems. Instead, for Miles, this is the next step after *Memory*: the unfolding of the new personality that *Memory* heralded, at once more subdued and more redoubtable than Miles has ever been. Here the double viewpoint is highly effective: when Miles entered *Komarr* through Ekaterin's eyes I had a startled sense of seeing him for the first time. For me, knowing the series, he carries the baggage of growth from the womb on. But since to Ekaterin he has never been anything but an Imperial Auditor, he acquires an instant new stature to match his expanded personality; not to mention, since she first gauges his height as "speaking to her cleavage" (7), another instant adult status. For the first time, Lord Vorkosigan rather than Admiral Naismith appears as a sexual being.

This quantum jump is ably supported by the developing relationship; not the *coup de foudre* of sexual passion, or the giddy gavotte of teenagers' mating, but a rapprochement between two equally scarred, equally wary people, with mutual attraction but reciprocal embarrassments and vulnerabilities. Ekaterin sees Miles undressed, after the vintage Bujold comedy of the lake scene, then suffering a convulsion, and at the power station, she has to rescue him. Meanwhile Miles uncovers her computer secrets and overhears her second marriage proposal, sees Tien put her down and witnesses the violation of privacy when ImpSec fast-penta her. The overall honors go perhaps slightly to Ekaterin, since she does the heroics for the mirror-plot; while the final scene, despite his hilarious confessional, is also hers. "Can I take a number?" (310) produces a first for a Vorkosigan book: finally, *somebody* has poleaxed Miles!

If *Komarr* has a flaw for me, it is a kneejerk response to some of the imperial ideology. As an Australian, at once colonizer and colonized, my hackles rise at the tone of some of Miles's comments about foolish Komarran rebels who ought to know a benevolent tyranny when they see one. Throughout the series, Komarr seems to have shifted from the construct of the nasty but equal conquered rival sketched in *Shards of Honor* into the more orthodox position of subtly inferior colony; and at my gut-level, Good Guys are not colonists, however benevolent.

Apart from this cavil, I have rarely read a Bujold with more pleasure than *Komarr*, and her sf has given me considerable pleasure over the last decade. In this case, it's not least for the wickedly witty finales to both thriller and romance strands, which, as Shakespeare's Mark Antony remarked, "pardon me, I do not mean to read" (*Julius Caesar* 3.2.132). But if I had to take one Bujold book from a burning library, then despite the ill-fitting title, it might well be *Komarr*.

Works Discussed

Bujold, Lois McMaster. *Barrayar*. New York: Baen, 1991.
— *Komarr*. New York: Baen, 1998.
— *Mirror Dance*. 1994. New York: Baen, 1995.
— *Shards of Honor*. 1986. New York: Baen, 1993.
— Email to the author. 15th May, 1997.

Forster, E. M. *Aspects of the Novel.* [1927] New York: Harcourt, Brace and World, 1955.

Lake, Ken. "Interview with Lois McMaster Bujold." *Vector* February/March 1993: 7-11.

Shakespeare, William. *Julius Caesar.* Ed Norman Sanders. Harmondsworth: Penguin, 1987.

Willis, Connie. "And Come From Miles Around." *Fire Watch.* New York: Bluejay, 1985.

— "Spice Pogrom." [1986] *Impossible Things.* New York: Bantam, 1994. 126-222.

ME, HYDRA
POSTCARDS FROM A SWAMP

by Tess Williams
[2000]

> Single vision produces worse illusions than double vision or many-headed monsters.
>
> Donna Haraway

Not much is known of the Hydra. A monster from Greek mythology, it is generally seen as a hybrid of familiar creatures such as snake and dog, or possibly a species of dragon in its own right. Always female and always menacing. Hercules killed a Hydra as one of his great labors and it was a hard job. The Lernean Hydra had nine heads and every time Hercules lopped one off, two more grew to replace it. He finally defeated it by having Iolaus, his nephew, cauterize the necks as he hacked them through with his sword. In other stories the Hydra is seen as a creature of the water or marshes, a sort of sea serpent, and in yet others she is one of the critters that hangs around the gates of the underworld, waving her heads of snakes around and scaring the pants off questing heroes. As with many other mythological monsters, the Hydra interests me and I believe it is possible to construct a sympathetic reading of her as symbolically representing and containing some of the dilemmas of modern women—particularly the woman writer. Let me explain:

To start with, bugger this notion of wearing many hats—

hats are far too civilized a metaphor to describe the multiple roles regularly played by women in our culture. A hat suggests a neat process of exchanging attractive or serviceable millinery confections when they are not specifically needed, storing them tidily somewhere and taking appropriate ones out for special occasions—say the little black felt job for Aunt Molly's funeral or that plastic coverall for an accurately predicted shower. Good metaphor? Not. It just doesn't work like that in my experience. Not only is the wardrobe connection faintly patronizing and gendered to start with, but I find that the process of playing various cultural and social roles is much more like having multiple heads—not hats—ergo, it tends to work (or not work) very much like the hydra.

The hydra is not neat. She has an (often unspecified) number of necks and atop each one is a fierce head, face fixed in a bared teeth grimace, crowned with a nest of hissing wriggling snakes. So, which one is in charge? Answer: none. This is a slithering, hissing mess of multiple priorities which very nearly pulls the infamous dog's body (did you ever wonder where that term came from?) apart. Consider the creature's dilemma: while head number one is scaring the bejasus out of a prototypical hero, head number four is investigating a flea on the forepaw and head number six is feeling hungry—but not necessarily for the well muscled bloke number one is intimidating. Heads number seven and eight are locked in argument about how many angels can fit on the head of a pin, and this produces a sense of uncertainty in head number three which knows it has some kind of mission or job to do as it sits guarding the gates of Hades against intruders (Innana? Psyche? Mary Smith?). Meanwhile, head number two thinks it's been a long time since the whole shooting match had a relaxing swim in the swamp. It could almost be funny, if it wasn't my life I was describing!

For me the simple act of sitting down in front of a computer brings on a nasty case of Hydra-itis. First I have to decide: am I there in the capacity of a teacher? A student? A writer? All occupations I am regularly locked into, and all simultaneously needing work to be done. Yesterday. And a few of those are the kind that spring double replacement heads if you try to lop them off. The teacher may have her attention absorbed by equity projects at one university, extension courses at another, part-time semester teaching (up to three subjects at two universities), and guest lecture spots in various specialized courses. If I'm in my writerly identity I could be doing an article, a story, a section of a novel, a letter to a magazine. Or, I could be sliding into my student identity and trying to compile a week's research into one insightful paragraph. Is it any wonder there is a constant sibilant hiss in my mind(s) which resembles a badly tuned radio station? Is it any wonder that I'm not the friendliest at times?

I know well organized people will say that what is needed in this situation is prioritizing—figure out which jobs are most urgent, make a list, start at the top of the list and knock off each job as it gets finished. My reflexive answer to that is that well organized people don't choose my kind of life style in the first place. My more considered answer is, while I do concede that a degree of organization is essential to run a rig like the Hydra, it's probably a brand of organization that few people would understand, let alone subscribe to. This is because in a writer/student/lecturer/single mother kind of life prioritizing has to be organized and reorganized on a daily basis—sometimes even on an hourly basis, depending on what's coming in over the transom. And it's certainly not done in any way that would be approved of by a late twentieth century time and motions expert.

This is probably because the Hydra just doesn't fit modern concepts of time and space. She's illogical, anomalous, ancient and monstrous. She is an archetypal creature existing outside documented historical periods—straddling centuries, potent as a junction between a number of realities, refusing to be categorized and making a helluva noise. And she is not just some ancient Olympian genetic experiment gone wrong, her physiology and her habitat are still powerfully symbolic for us today. She reminds us uncomfortably of things that Walt Disney thought he'd expelled from nursery nightmares.

For a start, she is a creature of liminal spaces, spending much of her time in swamp lands. Sometimes she plunges into deeper waters for a cleansing swim, but often she walks on muddy land that sucks at her feet and she dips her body into murky, fetid marshes that are stagnant and reek of toxic algal blooms. As someone who has never subscribed to a rigid Freudian boundary between the conscious and unconscious, I can see that a creature which symbolically moves in the permeable interface between two such mediums as water and land has some kinship with the woman writer whose pen constantly scratches up against invisible borders and dredges up culturally denied muck. I can see the Hydra could be a muse of sorts to that kind of a writer, feeding visions of marginality, and exemplifying crossed and violated boundaries in her own existence, in her plural identities, in her (sometimes) unacceptable difference.

The Hydra's inarticulate heads (does she growl? bellow? whine?) could even be interpreted as the underrepresented, feminized impulses of our culture, the drives that are unacknowledged or designated inexplicable and inferior. Perhaps one of her heads emotes, operating from an intense kaleidoscope of feelings? Perhaps one is driven by instinct, that animal sense that bristles at danger and smells fear? It's possible that one exhibits the often derided psychic factor of intuition, reading patterns in patterns. These are alternatively experienced realities that women writers often try to give voice to. That process of giving/finding voice often starts as the sad and unearthly ululations of poetry and then may progress to the sticky autobiographical stories that so often threaten, like quicksand—like Tillie Olsen's vast cultural silences—to pull them back under.

Should the writer get as far as speaking her personal truth in her tales, she may well become a "Cassandra" according to the theorists, categorized as an hysteric, trying to express her suppressed female subjectivity by using phallocratic language. Be that debate as it may, Cassandra's madness only becomes an issue when she has already penetrated the temples and castles of Troy and encountered resistance there. The Hydra, the creature

I am interested in at the moment, predates the prophetess's more refined encounter with patriarchy. She is driven—as it were— from sub-aquatic comfort to mournfully bellow out a primal consciousness on an, as yet, uncivilized shore.

The Hydra is the urge to make sense of a complex life that is not orderly, the desire to participate and progress beyond designated roles. She is the creature that moves what is repressed and denied towards the walls of the city. Only, of course, to find that the homes of princes and peasants alike are defended from the appearance of problematic monsters like her by crews of heroic blokes with names like Odysseus, Hercules, Theseus and Perseus. But she persists. And in her uncoordinated existence as a category crisis, in her attempt to recognize multiple identities (her own and others), in her very impulse to write, she offers the first barely integrated manifestation of a feeling, intelligent, sensate, intuitive woman trying to find her land legs.

I know a lot of people could be disturbed to read such a primal and gendered construction of the processes of a science fiction writer, but this is what writing is like to me. It has never been a purely intellectual exercise. I'm not sure I want to sketch out blueprints for a new and better world, as much feminist utopian writing does, and I'm definitely not interested in producing social critiques from some sort of high moral ground. It's not that I'm apolitical, far from it. It's just that it's sometimes too easy to be a critic. And I certainly do not want to contribute to the shelves of overheated fantasies of technological and electronic mastery. No, I need to be a critic and a player in my own life. So my science fiction writing is ultimately a search for a personal and cultural synthesis. Technology is part of the synthesis, science is part of it too, as is social criticism. However—ultimately arresting as technology, science and social criticism are in their extremities—they must signify meaning for me personally or I cannot use them. The head is no good (however many one has) if it is detached from the body, the body will not reflect reality accurately if it is only feeding on one aspect of culture. If one head of the Hydra insists on only eating junk food, the other heads will become sluggish. Variety is needed. Balance is needed.

To me the genre of sf was always attractive because it allowed me to be grounded in my complex and sometimes painful realities at the same time as it allowed my flights of fantasy and my poetic vision. I have always wanted to write a literature that incorporates my personal process as well as my observations, experiences and knowledge of the world. I want to write maps of how to get there from here, even when I'm totally unsure of where there is. And I want to drag all of my idiosyncratic interests with me—my feminist politics and my anxieties about feminist politics; my deep psychological attachment to myth; my interest in scientific knowledge and my simultaneous resistance to any absolute claims it might make; my understanding of culture as a subjectively experienced irresistible force; my belief in the necessity of spirit and beauty—even in a stainless steel age; my many, many skepticisms, questions and contradictions, and the challenge of my self-perceived monstrousness and differences.

It's a big ask, a genre/theory/creative expression that can accept and represent such an eclectic and personalized approach, but it exists. A school of thought underwrites my fiction, permits my grab-bag of knowledge, rewrites boundaries with me and offers the distorted intellectual mirrors I love to gaze into. I discovered I am a cyborg.

The Hydra is not only monster, it is also cyborg—it defies conventional biological taxonomy, blurring borders both within its body and its environment. Its many necks insinuate over each other in reptilian caresses while a loving, loyal mammalian heart beats within its canine body. It patrols the gates of Hades, the boundary between life and death, the membrane between consciousness and non-consciousness, and I share some of its issues. I am monster and cyborg too. These blurrings, pluralities and dangerous border skirmishes are also mine—in my fictional writing, in my studies and teaching, in my political existence and in my very body.

Cyborg politics are heavily feminist. The cyborg represents a (not so) repressed desire to express difference, the cyborg exists on the borders of confusion and the possible, the cyborg is a carnivalesque creature which eludes conventional definitions. And that is me, in more ways than I really care to be. Monstrous and cyborg. As a single mother, I have spent nearly two decades surviving in the fringes of an ailing patriarchy. As a novelist I am currently rewriting humans as children of the sea. As a student and a teacher my passion is for remapping evolution and then using evolutionary theory to redraw cultural maps. My politics comes out on every level as I explore the "alien" that is within and without, and I see my life as the intersection of multiple—often competing—discourses (as I also see myself excluded from many other discourses).

And—finally—as a body? Well, it would seem almost too ironic if, in my search for synthesis in genre, I were to bodily prove myself a science fictional creature, a cyborg/monster, wouldn't it? But I can. Failing organs ensure that within a certain space of time I will have to avail myself of one of two options or find myself tapping on the gates of Hades for admission. The first option is to live through a machine which will clean my blood when my own kidneys can no longer do it. I've already had my body adapted to do that and my left forearm snakes with thickened veins which emit a constant, Hydran buzz. The second is to accept a transplanted organ, to accept a foreign body into my own, to know part of me as alien. To know myself, my own flesh, as a cobbled together reality, dependent on the overwhelming generosity of a friend or the overwhelming generosity of unknown people who support human organ donation after death.

There are likely, of course, to be other options in the future. Embryonic stem cells could be fused with my own body cells to regrow a kidney that would not be rejected. My own kidney, which would not necessitate the harsh intrusion into my body of immunosuppressant drugs—a dream, a fantasy, a science fictional reality bonding my body to my reading, my writing, my study. The ultimate synthesis. Or, in a strange parody of the tangled species line of the Hydra, I could receive the kidney of a pig bred with human DNA in its cells. In undergoing what is known as xenotransplantation, my body could cross one of Donna Haraway's famous cyborg boundaries and combine animal and human with an already recombinant animal/human entity. Human. Animal. Monster. Alien. In joining body, emotion, instinct and intuition I have become a surprising creature with an ancient pedigree. In synthesizing creative work, intellectual investigation and cultural boundary crossings I have become a living cyborg. I am skin deep a woman, but my spirit is unexpected, difficult for me to sort out and sometimes difficult for others to encounter. Unless, of course, they happen to be Hercules and one of his good mates. Then that might become a different story...

CATHARSIS AMONG THE BYZANTINES

DELANY'S *DRIFTGLASS*

by Terry Dowling
[1984]

I owe Delany a few. He came along with *Babel-17* (1966), *Empire Star* (1966), and *Nova* (1968) at just the right time in my growing involvement with science fiction. He offered true exotic adventure, a flood of genuine poetry and glistening style amidst an ironically austere and vitiated genre of imaginative fiction, conventionalized (with notable exceptions) by respectable forms, sober traditions, and the safe precedents of the Old Masters. The man had style.

His very strengths made him vulnerable, too, and he got himself savaged by other lights in the genre. But Delany's work survives such maulings. His stories are balanced on the fine line between excellent and overwritten, and the fact that he manages to tip the scales in favor of excellent almost every time is an indication of his very real skills as wordsmith and story-teller. Delany is the man who pulls off such image-lines as:

> As the sun at the horizon slit sky from water, pale gold bled on the waves. The evening was bruised with copper sores. (80)

The silver crew itself scatters across the pine nee-
dles like polished bearings. (162)

The eye-rag was knotted across his left ear. A splat-
ter of acne wounds made their red galaxy on his jaw.
(271)

Driftglass contains the very best of Delany's shorter work—
ten stories written between October 1965 and October 1968.
There are such award-winners as "Aye, and Gomorrah" (Nebula, 1967) and "Time Considered as a Helix of Semi-Precious
Stones" (Hugo and Nebula, 1969), which, with "Driftglass" and
"We, in Some Strange Power's Employ, Move on a Rigorous
Line," is one of three pieces set in the same universe as the
1976 novel, *Triton.* Enough of these stories share similarities
of design, format, and thematic staples to reveal completely the
man's approach as writer.

Delany is a Byzantine. By that I am referring to a synthesizing approach to subject matter, imagery presentation, and
literary form (the use of language, style, etc.). As with the
cultural profiles of the Hellenistic Period, the Byzantine Empire,
or the European Renaissance themselves, it involves a bringing
together of forms and images, of the traditional and the new, of
the pure and the decadent and even the outlandish, of the high
and the low. It is a cosmopolitan technique, extremely stylized,
vulnerable, and derivative by its corruption and amalgamation
of existing elements, but dynamic and exciting in its creation
of unexpected alignments and new possibilities. Vitality is its
keynote.

Nor is it surprising that, in using this technique, Delany has
so often been compared with fellow writer Roger Zelazny. They
both play the same "mythic" ball game, presenting the reader
with self-possessed and personable archetypal narrators, characterized by exotic names, attitudes, and life-styles, their adventures recounted in what—to pursue the earlier metaphor—is a
"mosaic" method of story-telling: the use of economical, self-

contained images in a firmly controlled structure. We need only quote the closing paragraph to "We... Move on a Rigorous Line" to see it at work:

> And often, almost as often as I think about that winter in Tibet, I recall the October mountains near the Canadian border where the sun sings cantos of mutability and angels fear to tread now; where still, today, the wind unwinds, the trees releave themselves in spring, and the foaming gorge disgorges.... (190)

Gerard Manley Hopkins is owed a debt here. This is a style of writing that shouldn't work as often as it does. It is contrived, mannered, worked and reworked; every image, every allusion, is carefully crafted and laid out as in the tonal and imagistic whole of a mosaic. The placement and structuring becomes quickly noticeable, almost obtrusive. The result, in theory, should be excruciatingly bad; but in practice, infuriatingly, it works! The obtrusiveness of pattern and contrivance is almost always lost in the flow of image and character, achieving a natural and easy relevance which produces a "yes" of approval from the reader.

Delany is good at relocating clichés—"reviving the standards," as it were—arranging them and tapping them in new contexts, using them as "exotifying" agents. What by our associations would seem risky phrasings and strained allusions, by some literary equivalent of euphony are made pleasing. In this way he brings to mind those other Byzantines—"mosaic" writers like Zelazny, Dick, Harlan Ellison, Cordwainer Smith, Jack Vance, J.G. Ballard and even Alfred Bester in *Tiger! Tiger!* We could row on down the mainstream and find ourselves in the domains of poets like Eliot, Dylan Thomas, Donne, and Hopkins—all with a strong imagistic tradition and a structural approach to the use of language. Many sf writers have set off eagerly along this same path, but their results have ended up as florid, fragmentary in the negative sense, and downright pretentious. The Delany game actually takes a great deal of skill, a true talent for placement.

Delany's stories are sometimes deceptive. A high order of crafting and intricacy of presentation does not guarantee a good story, just as a goldsmith's intricate and exotic setting does not necessarily hold a truly precious stone every time. Sometimes the means to the end of composing an entertaining piece is enough to entrance the reader emotionally and remain memorable, but the story thus staged may be anecdotal and slight in contrast to the telling. "Dog in a Fisherman's Net" is an excellent anecdotal story, spiraling out from an immediate resolution of its title to a larger, related framework of involvement. Others, without this story's simplicity of narrative style, do not fare as well.

A story like "High Weir" (a personal favorite, incidentally), though evocative and simply cast, is a case of a memorable setting to a slight story that doesn't quite work. It has Zelazny/Bradbury tinges, but that is no cause for complaint. Though typical Delany, it is simply not that good a story. "Cage of Brass" perpetrates its ambiguity of title in a way that annoys by its glibness even as it pleases by its aptness and economy of reference—its tying in of every possible loose end. It tells the story of Jason Cage, a new prisoner in the escape-proof interstellar prison, Brass, who, while helping two other prisoners escape, does not do so himself because he feels he should be justly punished for the crime that has brought him there. Again, it is typical Delany, formalized in the extreme, abounding with exotic-archetypal place and character names (Hawk, Pig, Sapphire, Bruno—to go with other names, in other works, like Comet Jo, Jewel, Kid Death, the Dove, Knife, Brass, Mouse, Lorq Von Ray, Prince and Ruby Red, etc.—names in a rogue's pantheon, a pirate's mythology). It employs the usual litanical narrative style:

"What world do you come from, Hawk?"

"A place called Krags, from a city called Ruption, where the streets are cracks down to the hot core of the planet and lava boils up with sulfur and brim."

"Yeah, yeah, you told me all about Ruption, where the green and yellow smoke twists up between the balconies of the rich palaces in the charred evening—"

"Shut up, Pig. Go on, Cage."

"Don't shut up, Pig. What about you?"

"You wanna know where I'm from, Mister Cage?"

"He's from a world called Alba, Cage."

"Yeah, Alba, an' a city called Dusk. Dusk is in the mountains, where we got caves cut way down in the ice, and sunset and dawn flame in the fog and make the ice dance like diamonds."

"I've heard it, Pig. Let Cage talk."

"Well I come from a world called... Earth... From a city called Venice." (192-193)

So it goes. If you can accept a rogue like Pig shifting from low-style to high-style this way, you will probably love Delany's work. This is sword-and-sorcery high-rhetoric heroics with Bronx hard edges. Everyone is a poet—or a Delany—for this is how he likes to write, agglomerating images just so. In stories about quests and a whole updated heroic dimension treating of equivalents of old classic struggles, conversations are suitably ranged between conventionalized high forms and the low talk of the gutters. It is an economy of opposites; a language of romance and survival.

Now consider Delany's story titles. There is a power in the arrangement of words, an actual intrinsic poetry in placement and in the subsequent suggestion of images. And Delany exploits this; he is a confirmed user of the provocatively evocative "hook" title. "Time Considered as a Helix of Semi-Precious Stones" is an excellent example of the reader gaining a very real pleasure from having that entrancing title located within the story, gradually, cumulatively, via a patchwork of intensifying images. The reader, having already been predisposed to the work by his own pure instantaneous "experience" of the title, then enjoys the act of placement, the economical resolve, the fleshing out of the exotic promise. It is little wonder that many of Delany's critics, who have divined this technique for what it is, along with his clever pyrotechnics of language, fail to be impressed (or, as they would say, deceived) by it. It is, after all, so obvious, though very difficult to duplicate. Delany is exploiting a sensitivity to the inherent limitless capacities of language and image that is natural to us all. To use "Time Considered..." again as a clue to technique, Delany's Singers in that story are typical of his whole handling of character—that special high order of exotic hybrids: "...whatever their origins, these diverse and flamboyant living myths sang of love, death, the changing of seasons, social classes, governments..." Delany contrives such composites in his stories, and it is undeniably one of his great strengths. To apply his requisites for a Singer to himself: "The required talents are poetic, theatrical, as well as a certain charisma..." *Theatrical* is a good description of Delany's process viewed as a whole. His staging of conflicts, of chance confrontations between characters, his building of dramatic tension, are clearly reminiscent of the theater and even the opera. (Musical analogies are interesting to make with this writer's work—literary equivalents of the symphony, the fugue, the litany, the improvised ballad, and the doggerel: sometimes played together in not the symphony but the cacophony of life.)

Given stories like "Corona," "Driftglass," and "Dog in a Fisherman's Net," I am reminded too of a comment made by Peter Brook, that "Catharsis can never have been simply an emotional purge: it must have been an appeal to the whole man." Catharsis is what allows Delany's poetry to function as well as it does. Every story involves a suffering, thwarted, striving humanity, a humanity both tormented and uplifted. Here, where full of its own buccaneer grandeur, the image is all, the mind always seems to serve the heart; science will always kowtow to poetry, as in "The Star Pit":

Ratlit and I were sitting under a street lamp with our feet over the Edge where the fence had broken. His hair was like breathing flame in the wind, his single earring glittered. Star-flecked infinity dropped away below our boot soles, and the wind created by the stasis field that held our atmosphere down—we call it the "Worldwind" out here because it's never cold and never hot and like nothing on any world—whipped his black shirt back from his bony chest as we gazed on the galactic night between our knees. (23-24)

Out of such striking settings, even as he is resolving his title, we can see Delany already crafting the dramatic and emotional flourish of an ending line:

But tell me, Ratlit; tell me Alegra; what better way to launch my live ones who are golden into night? I don't know. I know I laughed. Then I put my fists into my overall pouch and crunched homeward along the Edge while on my left the worldwind roared. (71)

Between them, Delany and Zelazny have recently led the world in the construction of marketable "mytholithic" fiction (to coin a term for the building blocks of their stories). They have brought synthesis to a new all-time high—melding one legend with another, transplanting, re-telling, but with a crucially important common touch. Their work is accessible. Many others have chipped away at such structures, but rarely within this mundane sweat-and-tedium setting. A mosaic is a busy and demanding way to present a single picture, especially if that picture is to remain true to life and is not to be merely distracting.

I am one of those people who regard the gift of images as one of the greatest—equaling the gift of ideas with which it is connected. This simple and vital gift extends down the ages—from Gilgamesh to the medieval minstrel, from the first fireside raconteur who found that style was of as much value as substance, down to the lyrics of Bob Dylan, where method is often more precious than message. And understanding of this twofold approach—and a mastering of it—is Delany's forte.

Work Discussed

Samuel R. Delany, *Driftglass*. New York: Signet, 1971.

THE NON SCIENCE-FICTION NOVELS OF PHILIP K. DICK

by Bruce Gillespie
[1993]

I.

What *are* the non-sf novels of Philip Dick? As happens often when discussing Dick's life and career, it is not easy to give a simple answer.

The books that I want to concentrate on comprise a series of novels that Philip Dick wrote during the 1950s with the aim of launching a career into the mainstream of American literature. For this reason, they might truly be called "mainstream" novels, much as I dislike the term. None of these novels was published during the 1950s or 1960s, and only one, *Confessions of a Crap Artist,* appeared during the author's lifetime. In his biography of Philip Dick, *Divine Invasions*, Lawrence Sutin shows that this lack of success was a constant, inconsolable disappointment to Dick until he died. In 1960 he wrote that he was willing to "take twenty to thirty years to succeed as a literary writer" (Sutin, 103). This dream had virtually died by January 1963 when the Scott Meredith Literary Agency "returned all of Phil's unsold mainstream novels in one big package that was dumped on his doorstep.... These rejections coupled with the ray of hope of the Hugo [for *The Man in the High Castle*], made it official. After seven years, Phil's mainstream breakthrough effort was formally at an end" (Sutin, 118). These 1950s manuscripts were later stored at the library for the University of California at Fullerton, and remained largely unread, except by scholars like Kim Stanley Robinson, until after Dick's death in 1982.

But Phil Dick's dream of mainstream success never left him. He had fond hopes that *The Man in the High Castle* would be a general literary success as well as a Hugo winner. This has not happened. In his last years, he begged Dave Hartwell at Timescape Books to market *The Divine Invasion* and *The Transmigration of Timothy Archer* as general novels. This happened, but removing these books from the science fiction category seems merely to have deprived them of sales within the genre.

Other novels of the 1970s and 1980s are so much based on Phil Dick's day-to-day experience that they might also be counted as non-sf novels. *A Scanner Darkly* is the most obvious example. Set slightly in the future of the year in which Dick was writing it, and containing only one sf device, it tells in an almost documentary way the story of the young drug addicts who shared Phil's house during the late 1960s and early 1970s.

In my Bibliography I also mention four novels as being "closely related to the 1950s non-sf novels." These novels, which are *Time Out of Joint*, *The Man in the High Castle*, *Martian Time-Slip* and *We Can Build You*, begin with highly realistic settings and characters that might just as well have been lifted from any one of the 1950s non-sf novels.

II.

Philip Dick, born in 1928, died in 1982 of a massive stroke. He spent most of his life in California, especially around Berkeley and San Francisco. He appears to have held only two regular jobs in his life, and by 1950 was doing his best to become a full-time writer, especially as he was no good at anything else. He had an early success in marketing science fiction short stories, and began to succeed with sf novels during the 1950s and early 1960s. In 1963 he won the Hugo Award for *The Man in the High Castle*. This boosted his reputation, which had grown slowly during the 1960s, and slowly he gained fame, both within and without the sf field, during the 1970s. Helped immensely by several film options and the completion of *Blade Runner*, loosely based on his novel *Do Androids Dream of Electric Sheep*, he was just beginning to gain his first real financial rewards when he died in 1982.

Philip Dick didn't do as well from sf as Isaac Asimov or Arthur C. Clarke, but he did better than most of his contemporaries. Given that Dick enjoyed an sf career that produced about 40 novels and about 80 short stories, why was he not content with success within the science fiction genre? Why was he so absolutely determined to become a mainstream literary writer, and why was this the one ambition of his life that was denied him absolutely?

The answers to these questions lie partly in the Sutin biography and other recent memoirs of the man, but much more obviously in the texts themselves.

III.

Part of the answer is undoubtedly that it was very easy for Philip Dick to write successful science fiction. He turned to it a bit too naturally. Like many of us, he began to read science fiction when he was twelve years old. Unlike many young sf readers, he was at the same time reading his way through the rest of world literature. By the time he began glimpsing a career for himself as a writer, his ambition was to become an American Maupassant or Balzac. His technique of interleaving chapters, each chapter based on a different set of characters, was drawn more from the great nineteenth-century European novelists than the works of anyone in science fiction. But before he could have any success in literary fiction, he met Anthony Boucher, editor of *The Magazine of Fantasy & Science Fiction*, who published his first story—a science fiction story—in 1951. Phil Dick had just been married for the second time, had no job, was highly ambitious as a writer, and needed to find money fast. Between that sale and the end of 1954 he wrote and sold 63 science fiction short stories, and wrote two sf novels and sold one of them (*Solar Lottery*).

But, as I've mentioned, during all this activity Dick did not see himself as an sf writer, except under protest. For a long time he ignored the sf fans entirely, and met very few other sf writers. At parties he would find ways of avoiding telling people that he wrote science fiction for a living. As my Bibliography shows, he still put a lot of time into writing non-sf novels, even while continuing to churn out torrents of sf short stories.

One fellow Berkeley sf writer with whom Phil did form a close bond was Poul Anderson. Together, they could talk over the facts of sf life: editors chopping stories, lousy royalties, no recognition outside of fandom. Recalls Anderson:

> I bitched, and so did everyone else. You have to remember that in those days a science fiction writer—unless he was Robert Heinlein—was really at the bottom of the totem pole. If you wanted to work in the field you had to make the best of what there was. But we didn't feel put upon.... Okay, you get shafted this time but there was always more where that had come from. (Sutin, 82)

But when Dick's second marriage, to Kleo, broke up in 1958, he found himself living with Anne, a lady with expensive tastes. After they married, there was a child. During the mid-1950s Kleo had worked, helping to bolster Dick's ambition to become a mainstream novelist. Married to Anne, Phil had to work flat out to make a living. The only way to guarantee this income was to write science fiction novels, which sold—but never gained advances of more than $2000 each. Even *The Man in the High Castle*, which was a Hugo winner and Book of the Month choice, made only $7000 at the time. By the early 1960s, sf was the only work that Phil could sell, but writing it condemned him to a life just above poverty level. The later breakup of his third marriage didn't help, either. No wonder that Philip Dick clung to his lifelong illusion: that those non-sf novels of the 1950s would someday be discovered and published, or that one of his new novels would be recognized by critics for *The New York Review of Books.*

IV.

So much for why Phil wanted to write his non-sf books. Why should any of us read them? This is a difficult question, one I can't answer to my own satisfaction, let alone yours.

During the early 1980s, Kim Stanley Robinson read them in manuscript, well before Dick had died or anybody had shown an interest in publishing them. Robinson's verdict, in his otherwise excellent book *The Novels of Philip K. Dick*, is uncompromising. His charges (Robinson, 4-5) are that:

(1) "All of the realist novels are prolix in a way that is utterly unlike Dick's mature work. Every scene, no matter how important to the novel, is dramatized at equal length, in a profusion of unnecessary detail."

(2) They are humorless: "A uniform tone of deadly seriousness is only occasionally replaced by attempts at black comedy that go awry."

(3) There is "an uneasy mix of realism and the fantastic. Despite making a very serious commitment to writing realist works, Dick's interest in the arcane and the peculiar crops up everywhere in these works, without being fully integrated into them."

(4) "They are dull."

The result, as Robinson summarizes his own argument, is "an artistic personality split down the middle. On the one hand were long, serious, turgid realist novels, not one of which sold; on the other hand were short satirical stories, which were very successful—within the bounds of the science fiction community" (12).

These are strong words, guaranteed to raise the hackles of any true fan of all the works of Philip Dick. Also, they did not square with my impression of the few non-sf novels that I had read before this year. I volunteered to give this talk so that I could refute these foul accusations, and persuade you to read the recently published lost masterpieces. In doing the research, I destroyed my own thesis. Philip Dick's 1950s non-sf novels are certainly nowhere near as interesting as his best sf novels, but not for the reasons given by Kim Stanley Robinson.

V.

Robinson's needling comments were not the only reason for wanting to investigate the non-sf novels. My other stimulus derives from the mid-1960s, when I persuaded a friend of mine to read some of my favorite Phil Dick sf novels. He had obviously not read any sf before, and still had the rather sniffy attitude to sf which one usually finds among otherwise well-educated Australian readers. His reaction was of cautious admiration, but he also said: "If it were not for the sf gimmicks in these books, you would not be able to stand the view of reality that they show you." I'm paraphrasing, but that's the gist. Since then I've often asked myself: what would Phil Dick's books have been like without the science fiction superstructure? Could you bear to read them, regardless of their literary quality? Would you be so appalled that you would never be able to finish such a novel?

This remained a theoretical question until, many years later, I heard that Dick had actually written and failed to publish several non-sf novels. Now, thanks to publishers like Ziesing, Morrow, Gollancz and Paladin, you and I have gained the chance to read them. Here, surely, would be the answer to my question. The trouble is that the answer does not answer the question.

VI.

Back to Kim Stanley Robinson. It occurs to me that all works of fiction are much less interesting to read in manuscript form than they are on the printed page. That's the only reason I can see why he would think the non-sf novels are humorless or that they contain too much realistic detail. Perhaps, holed up in a university library reading manuscripts, Kim Stanley Robinson's eyes nodded over the odd page or three.

Let me refute Robinson by looking at the novel that least resembles the science fiction novels. According to both Robinson and Sutin, *Mary and the Giant* is one of the very first of Dick's non-sf novels. To me it is the best. Like all the non-sf novels and some of the best sf novels, it tells of ordinary people living in a small town that is big enough to feel like a city, but which is basically only a commuter suburb of San Francisco. The time is mid to late 1953. The main character is Mary Anne Reynolds, described here in what is perhaps Phil Dick's best paragraph:

> In the tired brilliance of late afternoon she walked along Empry Avenue, a small, rather thin girl with short-cropped brown hair, walking very straight-backed, head up, her brown coat slung carelessly over her arm. She walked because she hated to ride on buses, and because, on foot, she could stop when and wherever she wished. (*Mary and the Giant*, 13)

Here is a girl with no special talent or features except she is good-looking and has a spiky sense of humor. She has a certain independence and flair, a need to run her own life in a small town where everybody else just obeys the rules. Mary Anne is young, restless, clever but not very well educated. She is, in short, the first of the young dark-haired girls who became the main obsession, both of Dick's fiction and his life, during later years.

Mary Anne Reynolds is jaunty in everything. She insists on hanging around the local bar, although she is under age, because jazz music is played there. Two of the performers, a white pianist named Paul Nitz and a black singer named Carleton Tweany, become involved in her life. At the same time, the new man in town, a tall middle-aged urbane chap named Joseph Schilling, falls for her immediately when she applies for a job at his newly opened classical music store. Into this small town also arrives Schilling's ex-lover, Beth Coombs, and her husband Paul. In turn, they have in tow a vapid chap named Chad Lemming. Beth and Danny are trying to get Schilling's support to launch Lemming's recording career.

> The young man had now emerged. His hair was crew-cut; he wore horn-rimmed glasses; a bow tie dangled under his protruding Adam's apple. Beaming at the people, he picked up his guitar and began his monologue and song.
> "Well, folks," he said cheerily, "I guess you read in the papers a while back about the President going to balance the budget. Well, here's a little song about it I figured you might enjoy." And, with a few strums at his guitar, he was off.
> Listening absently, Mary Anne roamed about the room, examining prints and furnishings. The song, in a bright metallic way, glittered out over everything, spilling into everyone's ears. A few phrases reached her, but the main drift of the lyrics was lost. She did not particularly care; she was uninterested in Congress and taxes. (*Mary and the Giant*, 78)

The weird sense of the ludicrous is shown in an understated way. Chad Lemming is an entirely new phenomenon, the 1950s folk singer, but he comes over as a nice dill. Mary Anne is mainly concerned about leaving the Coombses' apartment to go over to Tweany's. The other people in the room are promoting themselves in one way or another. Even Flaubert could not give a more accurate portrait of small-time people trying to be big-time. From our point of view, the main interest is that Dick is writing about people he knew well. Our other accounts of the 1950s in fiction tend to be in long hindsight. Phil Dick committed himself to putting on paper the life of his own time—and nobody wanted to publish him.

In *Mary and the Giant*, Dick's humor works on a number of levels: the straightforward satire of people like the Coombses and Chad Lemming, but also the humor that you get by pitching the viewpoint of a naive original such as Mary Anne against the viewpoint of people who think they are in the intellectual swim.

When all these unbalanced people go over to Carleton Tweany's grotty apartment, at two o'clock in the morning, they find Carleton still awake:

> Tweany, still wearing his pink shirt and hand-painted tie, was sitting at the table eating a sardine sandwich and drinking a bottle of Rheingold beer. In front of him, spread out among the litter of food, was a smeared copy of *Esquire*, which he was reading. (*Mary and the Giant*, 84)

Carleton Tweany is a thorough original: cheeky, musical, sexy—he goes against every clichéd view of black people held by whites at the time. He and Jim Briskin (a black character in several later novels, including *The Broken Bubble* and *The Crack in Space*) were presumably based on some very impressive black person Dick must have met in Berkeley during the 1940s. Sutin does not identify this person, but the power of his personality is so impressive that some future biographer should find out who he was. Certainly, by the 1950s Phil Dick scoffs at his fellows' racial prejudices.

At Tweany's place, the group begins a party, which quickly

degenerates into one of the great party scenes in American fiction. It is entirely different from anything in Dick's other fiction because here the characters really interact. All of the characters in all of Dick's other books are so fundamentally isolated that they can only interact in anger, alarm or despair. In *Mary and the Giant*, and to a lesser extent in the next non-sf novel, *The Broken Bubble*, people actually enjoy being with each other:

> Suddenly Beth leaped from the piano. In ecstasy she seized Lemming by the hand and dragged him to his feet. "You too," she cried in his astonished ear. "All of us; join in!"
>
> Gratified to find himself noticed, Lemming began playing wildly. Beth hurried back to the piano and struck up the opening chords of a Chopin Polonaise. Lemming, over-powered, danced around the room; throwing his guitar onto the couch, he jumped high in the air, whacked the ceiling with the palms of his hands, descended, caught hold of Mary Anne, and spun her about....
>
> "They're nuts," Nitz said, "They're hopped in another dimension." (*Mary and the Giant*, 90-91)

Needless to say, this spontaneous ecstasy degenerates quickly, as happens at so many parties, into a dark experience. Nitz, flaked out in the bathroom, falls and hits his head. Everybody else is going crazy. "The bull rumble of Carleton Tweany never abated, rising and falling, but contained within the frenzy of the little old piano" (92). Dick spins his themes ever closer together. Beth Coombs sheds her clothes. Paul Coombs, who turns out to be the only one of them who is really nuts, is suddenly outraged that Tweany, a black, should see his wife naked. The police arrive; they've been called by the woman who lives downstairs. Mary Anne escapes before the police arrest the lot of them. The last sentence of the chapter is "Outside, in the darkness, a bird made a few dismal noises. In an hour or so it would be dawn." (97)

VII.

This episode contains in it much that makes Philip Dick's non-sf novels refreshingly different from his sf novels.

(1) All the action springs from the personalities of the characters, not from exterior menacing forces. Only in Dick's non-sf novels do we find *collections* of interesting characters. In the science fiction novels there are isolated memorable people such as Tagomi and Robert Childan in *The Man in the High Castle*, Arnie Kott in *Martian Time-Slip*, and Joe Chip in *Ubik*, but the non-sf novels are composed of nothing but people. There are, for instance, the two couples—the Lindahls and the Bonners— in *Puttering About in a Small Land;* the memorable black characters, such as Tweany in *Mary and the Giant*, Jim Briskin in *The Broken Bubble*, and Tootie Doolittle in *Humpty Dumpty in Oakland.* There is the wonderfully sad Milton Lumky, the salesman from *In Milton Lumky Territory.* There is the great Jim Fergesson going on his last pilgrimage in *Humpty Dumpty in Oakland.*

(2) Ordinary people, looked at with the steady and sardonic gaze of Philip Dick, are funny most of the time. In other words, the non-sf novels are continually funny, not humorless, as Robinson asserts. But the humor springs from the inconsistency between the way people see themselves and the way they seem to other people and, of course, the much-amused author and reader. These novels contain very few ha-ha jokes.

The humor of incongruity can be seen most clearly in the novels where Dick puts up versions of himself, then shoots them down. *Mary and the Giant* includes an older idealized version of himself in Joe Schilling: obsessive about music and young, dark-haired girls. He gets the girl, but only for a few minutes and in circumstances that are equally humiliating to both of them. In the end he achieves dignity by leaving her to work out her own life. In *Puttering About in a Small Land*, Roger Lindahl finds himself drawn into a love affair, almost without meaning to, with Liz Bonner, his sexy and over-demanding neighbor. Faced with his wife's wrath, he can do nothing more decisive than hide naked under the sheets of the bed. Since Phil Dick's private life was in a particularly chaotic state when he was writing this novel, I suspect that much in *Puttering About in a Small Land* is drawn from memory.

(3) This is the truth of life in the 1950s in California as one person saw it. Dick is determined to be as truthful as possible. The urban landscape of the 1950s is often a major subject of the non-sf novels. For instance, a quotation from the first page of *Humpty Dumpty in Oakland*:

> As he drove, Jim Fergesson rolled down the window of his Pontiac, and, poking his elbow out, leaned to inhale lungfuls of early-morning summer air. He took in the sight of sunlight on stores and pavement.... All fresh. All new, clean. The night machine, the whirring city brush, had come by, gathering up; the broom their taxes went to....
>
> Nice sky, he thought. But won't last. Haze later on. He looked at his watch. Eight-thirty.
>
> Stepping from his car he slammed the door and went down the sidewalk. On the left, merchants rolled down their awnings with elaborate arm-motions.... By the entrance of the Metropolitan Oakland Savings and Loan Company a group of secretaries clustered. Coffee-cups, high heels, perfume and earrings and pink sweaters, coats tossed over shoulders. (*Humpty Dumpty in Oakland*, 7)

This is not merely description, because the rhythm and chatter of the prose sweeps the reader along, convincing us that we are caught up in the busy deliciousness of a new day. Since we know Phil Dick, we also guess that he is setting up his character for a perfectly ghastly day.

But there is more. Notice that "nice sky." I wonder how long it is since there has been a clear sky in San Francisco at eight-thirty in the morning? Readers could well drink up these novels in the same way that one drinks up the details of an historical wide-angle photo of one's own town.

(4) This telling the truth extends far beyond the details of buildings and food and roads and hills. In *Mary and the Giant* we find a sub-political world, largely untouched by Senator Joe McCarthy and the forces he was unleashing at the time, but in which people are fighting many of the battles that would dominate American life during the 1960s. In trying to find the reasons why the non-sf novels of Philip Dick remained unpublished in the 1950s, Kim Stanley Robinson fails to mention the obvious: their undisguised frankness on matters sexual and racial. In the 1950s there are two American battlegrounds, Dick seems to be saying: the bedroom, between male and female; and the street, between black and white.

As Dick's own emotional affairs became more chaotic during the 1950s, the battles between men and women in his non-sf novels become more ferocious. In *Mary and the Giant*, Mary Anne Reynolds likes to be involved with large, powerful men, but she is frigid. Sex was, to her, "very like the time the doctor had stuck his metal probe into her nose to break off a polyp" (*Mary and the Giant*, 69). But Mary Anne herself, with her cheekiness and willingness to break the stuffy old rules, is the heroine of her novel. She achieves a kind of balance between sexual and emotional needs.

By *Puttering About in a Small Land*, written only four years later, the two characters who represent aspects of the author are in retreat before the demands of vivid, purposeful female characters. A battle is raging. In one brilliant scene, Dick describes what would now be called rape within marriage. In a scene of quicksilver emotional parries, he shows the mixture of confusion and joy as the man achieves sexual ecstasy for the first time in months as he has his way, the fury of the woman as she realizes she has failed to put in her diaphragm and is likely to become pregnant, and the see-sawing emotions as both parties try to justify their actions, then berate themselves. There is even a strange and temporary truce at the end of the scene. No other American novel could have said so much, so clearly, with so little moralizing, before the late 1960s or early 1970s.

(5) In *The Novels of Philip K. Dick,* Kim Stanley Robinson concentrates on only one major theme of the non-sf novels. Since he covers it well, I quote him:

> Another abiding concern of [Dick's is] the effect, in American postwar capitalism, of business relations on the personal relations between employer and employee, and indirectly on all personal relations. Dick believed this effect to be profoundly destructive.... In *The Man Whose Teeth Were All Exactly Alike*, Dombrosio assaults his boss when his boss hires his wife. He becomes estranged from his wife after he is fired, and eventually tries to hoax his neighbor, with whom he once was friendly. In *Mary and the Giant*, Mary works in a record store for a disturbed owner and she is forced to conduct a sordid affair with him to keep her job. And in *In Milton Lumky Territory* this theme is expressed most fully. The protagonist, Bruce Stevens, marries his fifth-grade teacher of years before and takes over her business, a typewriter sales and repair shop. Business difficulties make the marriage a perpetual battle, and, as the business nears bankruptcy, Stevens becomes obsessed, and one by one destroys all of his personal relationships. (Robinson, 3)

These business relations give much of the special character to the non-sf novels, since all are based on the only job that Dick took before agoraphobia made him unemployable. This job was working in a small radio repair shop. Over and over again, in both the sf and the non-sf novels, Dick introduces the employee who is highly dependent upon the whims of a fundamentally worthwhile but often capricious or even dictatorial employer. As Robinson shows in another part of his book, Dick's meager experience of paid work made him both admire the manual worker as the epitome of the American good guy, and pity him for being stuck in a lowly job.

VIII.

I think I've proved that Kim Stanley Robinson is wrong in the reasons he gives for dismissing Philip Dick's 1950s non-sf novels. These books are indeed funny, although you need a sense of the sardonic and ironic to get the best out of them. They are not over-detailed; their detail is of the kind that the current breed of American writer—the so-called "dirty realists"—have accustomed us to. Dick's non-sf novels are certainly less romantic than those of, say, Larry McMurtry or Richard Ford or any of those people, but he does not have the lyrical gifts of, say, Anne Tyler or Raymond Carver. Like other American realists, Dick assumes that so-called ordinary people are always extraordinary, even gothic, if looked at with any insight.

However, if I have persuaded you that these novels have none of the faults pinned to them by Robinson, have I persuaded you that they are worth reading? Probably not. Yes, if you are interested in novels written about the 1950s where the viewpoint is not clouded by nostalgia or faulty memory. Yes, if you like novels about people being people. Yes, if you like well-written realist novels. All of these books are better written, in any formal sense, than most of the science fiction novels—hence, perhaps, Robinson's impatience with them.

But would you—could you—ever prefer them to Dick's best science fiction novels? This, if you remember, is the premise of Michael Bishop's cheeky but unsuccessful recent novel *Philip K. Dick is Dead, Alas*, which appeared in America as *The Secret Ascension*. In an alternate world, Dick has just died. He is known for the kind of novels I've been talking about. He also wrote a small number of sf novels, known only to aficionados. Etcetera. I don't believe it, as I don't believe Bishop has grasped the fundamentals of Dick's style or approach.

In the late 1950s, Philip Dick wrote three ambitious sf novels as well as some potboilers. The first two sf novels that we still value are *Solar Lottery* and *Eye in the Sky*. With *Time Out of Joint*, the third of them, Dick became a master of the sf field— but he couldn't have written that novel without writing the non-sf novels we have just been discussing.

The beginning of *Time Out of Joint* seems to be set in exactly the same small town that we enter in most of the non-sf novels. It has a downtown, and lots of shops and houses, and a public transport system, and lots of people, but basically it is quiet. Everybody knows everybody else. Business chunters along.

The scene shifts to Ragle Gumm, who is a bachelor sharing an ordinary house with his sister Margo and brother-in-law Vic Nielsen. Their neighbors are the Blacks, Bill and Junie. You can predict already that Ragle will have an affair with Junie. Ragle Gumm is the only bloke in town who does not fit in: the only man who does not go out to work every morning. Every day he sits and solves the *Where Will the Little Green Man Be Next?* contest. It comes in the paper every morning, and Ragle Gumm has been the national champion for three years running. Solving the puzzle each day obsesses him: "Spread out everywhere in the living room the papers and notes for his work formed a circle of which he was the centre. He could not even get out; he was surrounded" (*Time Out of Joint*, 9).

At this point the book begins to diverge slightly from the pattern set in the non-sf novels Dick was writing at the same time. Why is this man filling in these puzzles every day, apart from the fact that his constant wins provide him with a modest income? More mysteries slip into the story. Why, when Vic Nielsen reaches for the light switch, does he suddenly feel as if he should be reaching for an overhead light cord? Why, when walking up the two steps up to the front door, does he step up the third step, which isn't there?

These puzzles aside, for several chapters *Time Out of Joint* stays very much in the pattern of the non-sf novels. Compare it with, say, *Humpty Dumpty in Oakland*, which features Al Miller, the most completely failed small-time character of all Dick's small-time failed characters. "I'm a bum," he says of himself. "He absolutely lacked the ability to see how things really stood" (*Humpty Dumpty in Oakland*, 95). In *The Man Whose Teeth Were All Exactly Alike*, much of the action takes place because one of the characters finds himself stuck at home while all worthwhile American males are out making a crust. This also happens to Roger Lindahl towards the end of *Puttering About in a Small Land*. And in *Time Out of Joint*, sure enough, here is Ragle Gumm: "Stunning desolation washed over him. What a waste his life had been. Here he was, forty-six, fiddling around in the living room with a newspaper contest. No gainful, legitimate employment. No kids. No wife. No home of his own. Fooling around with a neighbor's wife" (*Time Out of Joint*, 39).

As readers of the Sutin biography will realize, all you need to do is substitute the term "writing" for "newspaper contest" and you have the exact way in which Dick saw himself at the time. Not only was writing very badly paid, but it somehow made him less of a red-blooded American male than anybody else. The consequences of this perception—"I'm a bum" combined with an awareness of the quality of his writing—played havoc with his third and fourth marriages.

The point I am making is that *Time out of Joint* is more autobiographical than the obviously autobiographical non-sf novels. This is because Dick no longer feels the need to stick to the surface facts of ordinary life. Behind ordinary life in an ordinary American town lies something else altogether.

Gumm has several extraordinary visions of his little town. In one of them, he walks up to a soft-drink stand, which seems to dissolve before his eyes.

The soft-drink stand fell into bits. Molecules. He saw the molecules, colorless, without qualities, that made it up.... In its place was a slip of paper.... On it was printing, block letters.

SOFT-DRINK STAND

(*Time Out of Joint*, 40)

In the second incident, he is sitting in a bus:

The sides of the bus became transparent. He saw out into the street, the sidewalk and stores. Thin support struts, the skeleton of the bus. Metal girders, an empty hollow box. No other seats. Only a strip, a length of planking, on which upright featureless shapes like scarecrows had been propped. They were not alive.... Ahead of him he saw the driver; the driver had not changed. The red neck. Strong, wide back. Driving a hollow bus.... He was the only person on the bus, outside of the driver. (81)

The exact status of this vision is never made clear in the story. Is it purely hallucination, or some supernatural view of the town? But its status in Dick's mind is made clear when we read in Sutin's biography that Dick actually had several such visions early in his life, long before he wrote this book. His distrust of his own perception of the world made him a virtual prisoner in his own house at various times in his life.

What we find in *Time Out of Joint* is that the bits and pieces of a science fiction superstructure, which gradually invade Ragle Gumm's consciousness, are actually more autobiographical, more real to the author, than the accurately drawn worlds he presents in the non-sf novels. It is for this reason that the non-sf novels fail, not because of any intrinsic demerits.

In *Time Out of Joint*, Dick finds metaphors for the very real paranoia which afflicted him from time to time. The miracle is that he finds coherent metaphors that he can use to construct an exciting story. Ragle Gumm happens to hear a broadcast that makes him aware that the world outside this town is very different from what he had imagined, and that Ragle Gumm himself is totally important to that world. When he tries to leave town, in what is one of Dick's most brilliant pieces of action writing, he is captured and sent home. On his second attempt, he travels from the world of 1959 to a totally alien and very frightening world of the year 2000. A war is on, between the "lunatics," colonists on the moon and throughout the solar system, and the One World government. Ragle Gumm's job had been, through the contest, to predict each day's strike from weapons sent from outer space. The town he had lived in was entirely a fake, with only a few people around him also sharing the illusion.

So here at last is the truth that Dick could not allow himself to write in the non-sf novels. In the end, they failed to sell because in them Dick was constantly pulling back from what he really wanted to say. This constraint improved his formal style, and the non-sf novels have little of the melodramatic flourishes that threaten to destroy so many of the sf novels. But having learned his craft, of showing the underlying reality of things through surface appearances, Dick had trained himself to write the sf novels, in which he could tell his own truth. The penalty for that was feeling that he had failed as a writer and as a man; yet, paradoxically, he came to feel that he was the center of the universe, that what he was telling people was more important than truths they could find anywhere else.

IX.

When I first tried reading *The Man Whose Teeth Were All Exactly Alike*, I could not get past page 70. I was constantly reminded of that statement made by my friend more than twenty years before. Without the metaphors of science fiction, Dick's intensely detailed account of the battle between two families, the Runcibles and the Dombrosios, seemed too painful to read.

One feels that there should be a filter between such emotional reportage and the reader. It's not a matter of entertainment merely; it's the fact that no general truth can be derived from such painful separate truths. In the science fiction novels, Philip Dick would put into his words his feeling that there is something generally wrong with the world. The non-sf novels have to take the ordinary world as a given. In the end, Dick felt this was untrue, and he was untrue to himself by portraying the world thus. During the 1950s and early 1960s, the so-called ordinary world became increasingly ghastly to Dick. He felt that we are all lonely stick figures out there on a plain, and vast distances separate us. Our only hope is to find out our individual realities and perhaps achieve some fragile fellow-feeling with some other human being. This feeling pervades the non-sf novels, but Dick cannot find an adequate way to express it. Give him a loony sf plot, plus the small-town setting that he uses in some of his best sf books, and the Phil Dick mind suddenly bursts into life. Paradoxes, ironies, and brilliant visions burst upon us. This is the real Philip Dick; the writer of *Time Out of Joint* and *Martian Time-Slip* and *The Man in the High Castle.*

What a terrible pity that he could never quite accept his greatness in the sf field, and never realized why the non-sf novels failed to establish him as a literary figure. The non-sf novels are enjoyable enough to read, and often brilliant, but they are important only because they point us to the real talents of Philip Dick, who never quite saw his own strengths.

[1 October 1990]

BIBLIOGRAPHY

1—The non-science fiction novels written by Philip K. Dick during the 1950s.

This list gives details of editions sighted. I suspect the British editions were all preceded by Morrow or Ziesing editions, but have no way of checking at the moment.

1942: *Return to Lilliput.* Juvenilia, lost manuscript.

1948-50: *The Earthshaker.* Lost Manuscript, perhaps never completed.

1952-3: *Voices from the Street.* Manuscript in Fullerton Library. Recently published? Not sighted.

1953-4: *Mary and the Giant.* Victor Gollancz 0-575-04243-5; 1988; 230pp.

1955: *A Time for George Stavros.* Lost manuscript. Known to have been recast as *Humpty Dumpty in Oakland.*

1956: *Pilgrim on the Hill.* Lost manuscript.

1956: *The Broken Bubble of Thisbe Holt.* As *The Broken Bubble*: Morrow 1-55710-012-8; 1988; 246pp.

1957: *Puttering About in a Small Land.* Academy Chicago Publishers 0-89733-149-4; 1985; 291pp. I'm told this had a British Paladin release.

1958: *In Milton Lumky Territory.* Victor Gollancz 0-575-03625-7; 1985; 213pp. Also had a British paperback release in Paladin.

1959: *Confessions of a Crap Artist.* Entwhistle Books; 1975; 171pp. Had an American paperback release (1978, also from Entwhistle Books) and one British paperback release during the late 1970s or early 1980s.

1960: *The Man Whose Teeth Were All Exactly Alike.* Paladin 0-586-08563-7; 1986; 245pp. First Edition (USA): Mark V. Ziesing; 1984 (This edition not sighted).

1960: *Humpty Dumpty in Oakland.* Victor Gollancz 0-575-03875-6; 1986; 199pp. No other edition sighted.

2—Sf novels by Philip K. Dick closely related to the 1950s non-sf novels

1958:*Time Out of Joint.* Penguin 14-002847-1; 1969; 187 pp. Continually reprinted. Original edition from Lippincott in USA.

1961: *The Man in the High Castle.* G. P. Putnam; 1962; 239pp. British edition continually reprinted.

1962:*We Can Build You*. DAW No. 14; 1972; 206pp. Still in print anywhere?

1962:*Martian Time-Slip*. Ballantine; 1964; 220pp. Often reprinted in Britain.

3—Basically non-sf novels lightly disguised as sf

1973: *A Scanner Darkly*. Doubleday 0-385-01613-1; 1977; 220 pp.

1978: *VALIS*. Bantam 0-553-14156-2; 1981; 227pp.

1980:*The Divine Invasion*. Timescape 0-671-41776-2; 1981; 239pp.

1981:*The Transmigration of Timothy Archer*. Timescape 0-671-44066-7; 1982; 255pp.

References

1989: *Divine Invasions: A Life of Philip K. Dick*. by Lawrence Sutin. Harmony Books 0-517-57204-4; 1989; 352 pp. Also available in a Paladin edition.

1982/84: *The Novels of Philip K. Dick*. by Kim Stanley Robinson. UMI Research Press 0-8357-1589-2; 1984; 150pp.

1987: *The Secret Ascension (Philip K. Dick is Dead, Alas)*. by Michael Bishop. Tor 0-312-93031-3; 1987; 341 pp.

THE GOLDEN AGE OF AUSTRALIAN SCIENCE FICTION

by Sean McMullen
[1995]

Introduction

In two hundred years of European settlement, can we single out any one time when Australian sf and fantasy was particularly outstanding? Certainly some themes in Aboriginal oral traditions parallel the genre, and these probably extend back before Europeans had invented the bow, but my own specialty is works published on the printed page, so the choice is within this constraint.

How are we to define the Golden Age of a nation's sf writing? A time when the local product is selling widely both at home and overseas? When plenty of new writers are emerging, and with new styles? When the genre is widely read by the general reading public? Many periods fit these criteria, and there has not been a year since the last decades of the nineteenth century when a work of Australian sf or fantasy has not been published. There were many Australians or Australian-born people contributing when the early pulps were emerging in America. D.W. Hall was *Astounding*'s assistant editor and a contributor as well, Gernsback himself praised Alan Connell as one of a new and progressive group of writers, James Walsh was selling whole novels overseas, and dozens of others were selling books and stories. More recently, after the World Science Fiction Convention was first held in Australia in 1975, there was a massive upsurge of local creativity in which Australian writing was displayed to the world, and some six hundred works were bought and published over the next decade.

My chosen period may surprise you, however, as it runs from the early forties to the early sixties. What, you may ask, was published in these years apart from some fanzines, Barnard Eldershaw, and a few short stories by Chandler and Harding right at the end? The truth is that this period was one of massive expansion of the local market. Per head of population more Australian sf was published between 1950 and 1962 than in the years since Aussiecon 1, and in absolute terms the amount sold overseas is actually greater. (Before you ask, Bertram Chandler's Australian output accounts for less than a quarter of all this.)

1: Isolation

You gotta laugh, mate.
—old Australian saying

Oddly enough, the Golden Age started with many works so bad that they were funny. Still, I suppose Australians needed a laugh back then. The period began as the War restricted the inflow of American sf (and most other) magazines to Australia. Small, cheap and nastily written novels began to appear and flourish on the local presses, and people bought them readily enough—there was nothing else. Mercifully much of this material was pulped for re-use as part of the war effort, but some copies survive in specialist collections.

Secret Weapons by Phillip O'Donnell was the first and worst of these books, appearing some time in 1941. It is ghastly beyond your wildest dreams, and the science appears to have been cribbed at random from popular science magazines of the day without the author understanding very much at all. The story begins with remote-controlled zombies, Nazis digging a tunnel to a Sydney insane asylum, a floating jelly a mile in diameter off Sydney Harbour, and an airship that was so light that it could fly to Mars. A zombie rat features in the bank robbery scene, a possible world first for Australian sf. In the end the hero steals a Nazi rocket and flies to Hollywood. Copies of *Mein Kampf* translated into Maori find their way into the story too....

The cover blurb declares that "This book has even horrified a Hollywood literary agent"—and I'm not surprised. The poor sod obviously knew something about elementary physics and chemistry, and had read stories of at least the caliber of Peter Rabbit's—whose style and plot are quite advanced in comparison. *Secret Weapons* was, I fear, the shape of things to come in several ways. In a concrete sense it pioneered the mixed genre of sf/crime/mystery that flourished in Australia in the late '40s and early '50s; in an abstract sense it showed what sort of writing would result if the local market was largely cut off from the rest of the world.

Australian writers had been published in overseas magazines all through the '30s, and even into the early '40s. People such as Alan Connell, H.M. Crimp, and the Australian-born James Walsh had met with some success in the US, but for the next decade the short stories of local writers all but vanished from overseas markets. At home, however, many bottom drawers were emptied to satisfy the demand of a reading public starved of print by the War. Walsh's own *Secret Weapons* novel was published by Collins in 1946, but was probably written years before. Currawong Press published three short novels by Alan Connell, all set in the reptile-ruled world foreshadowed in one of his mid-'30s works in *Wonder Stories*. Vol (Voltaire) Molesworth (1924-1964) had three sf novels published by Radio Records and one by Currawong—as well as general adventures. John Winton Heming (1900-53) wrote six sf novels for Currawong, along with his westerns, crime stories, and general adventure books.

Protected environments can hardly be expected to be the grindstones that hone the keen and shiny cutting edge of literature. At best the novels were okay entertainment, at worst they were Grade A horrid. It was, however, a pulp sf market, the like of which Australia had never seen before, and it was introducing the local product to a wide—if captive—audience.

Molesworth is an interesting example to consider. He wrote both adult and juvenile works, and was a devotee of sf from before the war, unlike many others who were just following a popular trend. *Ape of God* (published in 1943 when he was 19) is adult, and deals with questions of creators and creations— although not to quite the same depth as Mary Shelley's *Frankenstein* does. *Spaceward Ho* (1942?), on the other hand, was pure space opera, and chronicles the adventures of Major Lon Wynter and Zelie, his news reporter lady friend. Merv Binns, one-time proprietor of Space Age Books in Melbourne, remembers this as his first ever sf book, and I can recall similar material (such as *Space Patrol*) still being popular on radio serials as late as 1960.

> Reclining on this ornamental chair was a fat, ugly dwarf clad in rich silk garments, with a green star embroidered on the right breast.
>
> Lanning raised his arm in a full-length salute, while the Legionnaires saluted Earth fashion, hands raised to their peaked caps.
>
> "So," hissed the dwarf on the throne, "these are the Earthlings who flew from their world in a spaceship called the *Voyager*!"
>
> "How did you know that?" asked Lon coolly.
>
> Zee-Ka looked down at him, smirking. "My dear Major," he said, "there is not much about your world that I do not know. There are many Venusian spies living on Earth. They do valuable work, gathering information and sending it back here by special radiophone."

He paused and laughed unpleasantly. "They will also serve as fifth-columnists when we invade the Earth," he added suavely.[12]

State-of-the-art material this was not, though it was popular enough in juvenile circles. Lanning's salute, the evil dwarf, and the threat of invasion certainly would have struck chords with the young readers of the time.

Alan Connell's reptile trilogy was not as bad as it sounds. "The Reign of the Reptiles" was published in *Wonder Stories* in 1935 and republished in 1951. He wrote several more reptile stories in the mid-'30s, but as his interest turned to mainstream fiction these were forgotten. Faced with a market that would publish the likes of O'Donnell, Connell brought out his old manuscripts. The stories were primarily adventures, in the tradition of Edgar Rice Burroughs or Robert E. Howard.

In spite of the ludicrous cover, *Warriors of Serpent Land* (Currawong, 1945) is quite readable. It is also Connell's last sf work to be published. It centers around lost cities and tribes in a remote part of South America: a dirigible expedition lands there, and various dinosaurs and slithery beasties are found, along with a race of reptile people. After the usual sorts of power struggles among the reptile royalty, the expeditioners return to New York, but are planning a second trip by the epilogue.

Do not laugh. The Erle Cox 1925 epic, *Out of the Silence*, had enjoyed immense popularity over the previous two decades or so, and had even been serialized on the radio just before the war. This was the same sort of contemporary escapism then as *Star Wars* is today, and Connell was one of the best Australians writing it.

Unlike Connell and Molesworth, John Winton Heming was not an sf specialist. He was a prolific hack, who was said to have sat down at his typewriter on Monday morning, tapped away for the working week, then handed in a complete small novel on

12. Voltaire Molesworth, *Spaceward Ho!*, 36.

Friday evening. For all this, he was a competent enough writer. He wrote six works of fantasy and sf, all during the war, of which *From Earth to Mars* (Currawong, 1943) was the last.

For a general writer, it is really not a bad book, apart from being a bit dated even in its own time. Richard Portess and Bill Thomas travel to Mars in the newly invented Sunship, whose technology is kept mercifully vague by the author. They discover a utopian society with no money, politics or evil. Most of the book consists of a type of royal tour of Mars, encompassing everything from "women's work" and Martian home life in general, through to education, economics, crime and punishment, and high technology. After their ship is given a complimentary tune-up, grease and oil-change, the travelers head back to Earth.

In spite of the fact that there is no storyline, the book makes interesting reading. Heming was, after all, a very experienced writer, with a good sense of what his readers wanted to see and a personal interest in socialism. After several years of savage warfare in which their own country had been bombed, Australians would have found the escapism pleasant... and the ideas interesting, perhaps.

Dominic Healey was another mainstream writer who jumped on the sf bandwagon in the early '40s. In *Voyage to Venus* (Currawong, 1943) we discover, however, that the trend first seen in O'Donnell's *Secret Weapons* is showing disturbing signs of vitality two years later. It is called a "scientific thriller" and tells of human refugee-colonists on Venus, and how gangster politics is alive and well in the distant future. Thus a murder mystery is found in a setting little different to that of *Warriors of Serpent Land*.

The writers of western and crime fiction were projecting their genres' stories into future and/or other world settings in order to satisfy the demand for sf in an isolated Australia. What results is no more than adventures in exotic locations, with little innovation to speak of. Let us now consider a very superior overseas account of the first rocket into space to illustrate both this and the next point:

> We stood on the low observation hill about 300 yards away from the small stone house and the dilapidated stable. The first rocket took off. The sun was behind us and its rays illuminated the rocket in its coat of dull green camouflage paint, with its long, gleaming gas jet, as it rose vertically above the black woods. A great rumbling filled the air.
>
> I watched through my binoculars, following the rocket's rapid acceleration.... It rose higher and higher. Scattered white shreds of cloud hovered far up in the clear sky.
>
> The rocket had hardly glided past the clouds when I saw something I had never noticed before showing up distinctly against the dark background. It was as though the missile had suddenly had sugar icing poured over it. It shone brilliantly white in the dazzling sunlight. Moisture in the form of hoar frost must have been deposited on it from a warm humid layer of air after it had passed through a cooler layer. The phenomenon vanished as suddenly as it had appeared.... Then it was repeated higher up.
>
> ... Zigzags forming in vapor trails in a matter of seconds... indicated differences in direction and velocity of the wind in successive air layers—something well worth further study. The rocket reached a peak altitude of about 100 miles, 30 miles higher than the earlier firings.
>
> To be borne upward like this into... space—what a wonderful experience it would be for mankind! What a wealth of knowledge it could offer! I could imagine the eagerness with which meteorologists, physicists and astronomers would look forward to their first voyage into the stratosphere and ionosphere. How slight, after all, is our knowledge of the outer covering of our

small planet, based as it still is purely on conjecture and inference![13]

What is so special about this passage? Clear, simple prose describes the great event with both accuracy and awe, but then Wells was doing that sort of thing back in the 1890s. What puts the foregoing passage in a class outside sf is that it is not fiction. Major General Walther Dornberger of the German Army was describing the launch of the first V2 rocket to reach space. Although the events of that day in the early spring of 1943 would remain secret for several years, the first human artifact had flown clear of the Earth's atmosphere for some minutes: The *real* Space Age was born.

Unknown to the Major General, his rocket had also penetrated the frontiers of sf, and would in time cause quite a few problems for hack authors dabbling in the field. Rockets that could take off from Earth and do a return trip to Venus with fuel to spare would become increasingly unacceptable to the public. The number of readers who knew about payload to fuel ratios, the specific impulses of real rocket motors, and what was needed to achieve escape velocity was about to take a quantum leap—just as Australia was beginning an sf boom based on the most absurdly naive, tenuous grasp of real science that one could imagine. Many overseas authors rose to the challenge, but Australia was isolated from such stimulus.

It is rather hard to imagine juvenile sf so bad that it makes your teeth hurt just thinking about it, but Winifred Law's *Through Space to the Planets* (New Century, July 1944) is just such a work. In *Science Fiction News* #93 Graham Stone writes: "The otherwise unknown author wrote (these books) without the least interest in space flight or the solar system, and with only a hazy general impression of how the prospects were represented in writings for the under-tens early in the century.

---

13. Walther Dornberger, V2, 213-214.

The result is absurd, and was absurd in its time."[14] There is an aircraft that flies high enough to reach a planet called Aureela which is populated by short, blond, telepathic Nordics.

> "Gosh! I hope they don't keep us here long!" exclaimed Allister.
>
> "Let us sing!" returned Tom. "It will keep us from moping."
>
> "All right," agreed Allister, whose clear sweet voice had been greatly admired at home. "What shall we begin with?"
>
> "Land of Hope and Glory?"
>
> "Right!"[15]

Winifred Law had *Rangers to the Universe* published in 1945, a year which also saw a reprint of her first book. At that point the war ended, along with Law's sf career.

What we have seen thus far is the birth of a local pulp sf industry, built up around a few local writers who knew the field, and a lot of others who thought that they could adapt to it anyway. What resulted was some passably entertaining writing for the time, along with a lot of devastatingly bad rubbish. The island was isolated, and the dodos were thriving.

Import restrictions were not lifted with the end of hostilities, however, and that dreaded Australian invention, the "scientific thriller," was about to undergo a massive expansion in popularity. Amid all this lowering of brows and standards came M. Barnard Eldershaw with *Tomorrow and Tomorrow* in 1947. Written mainly by Marjorie Faith Barnard between 1942 and 1944, it was published by Georgian House in Melbourne and Phoenix in London, and is the only book from the first half of the Golden Age that has been reprinted since. The authors were

---

14. Graham Stone, "Notes on Australian Science Fiction," *Science Fiction News* #93 (March 1985), 5.

15. Winifred Law, *Through Space to the Planets*, 51.

both teachers, and were active on the political left between the Wars.

The book is a view of Australia from both past and present, using a twenty-fourth-century writer, Knarf, as a medium. Even though the technocratic socialists of the future have conquered war and want with the help of both the social and physical sciences, we still have corruption in high places. While the book is basically quite an advanced political critique—it is the only Australian sf book known to have fallen foul of the government censor—the effects of technological advances are not forgotten. In particular there is a sort of psychic polling device for decision-making, in my opinion the first step along the road to living in a hive. I am not sure whether the authors are trying to warn us about this prospect, as the idea is not taken much further. A hive would be made up of truly alien beings, after all, and I presume that Barnard and Eldershaw wished to make a statement about contemporary people and society.

In my opinion this attempt to remain politically realistic at the expense of investigative technological projection detracts from the book, and kept it from gaining the stature of *Brave New World* or *Nineteen Eighty-Four*. This is a minor quibble, however, as the book towers above all other Australian sf of the time. It deserves reading even today—for what it says about contemporary political theory as much as its utopian/dystopian predictions. It is interesting to read it after *From Earth to Mars*, to see how the other end of the literary spectrum was designing utopias. (Heming's concept of socialism was influenced by Bellamy, and he had ideas of starting a movement.) The public response in 1947 was unenthusiastic but the novel's reputation has grown since then. Virago published an uncensored version in 1983.

2: Arcadia

The man who laughs has not yet been told the terrible news.
—Brecht

In November 1948, Transport Publishing Co. Ltd launched a new series of small novels under the banner of *Scientific Thriller*, and the second part of the Golden Age was launched. They were all self-contained stories by writers using pseudonyms. The covers were printed in batch lots with the author and title already fixed, so that the actual writer usually wrote a story to match. In the tradition pioneered by O'Donnell and Healey, conventional crime, western and adventure themes were projected into the future, or onto other worlds. The resulting lack of originality leaves one gasping, but the starved Australian readership of the time soaked up forty three of the ghastly things before increasing imports of higher quality killed the series in 1952.

Copies of *Scientific Thriller* are rare today, but we can learn a lot from what survives. In *Cosmic Calamity* by Belli Luigi, the printer forgot to remove G. Clive Bleeck's name from the title page, so that we know that this mainstream Australian author contributed to the series. Bleeck was fairly careful with his dabblings in the genre, and tried hard to keep his adventure stories plausible. In *Cosmic Calamity* a mad scientist finds a way to allow deadly rays from outer space to penetrate the protection of the atmosphere, and as he tests his weapon, mysterious charred circles appear in the countryside. A scientist investigating the circles is kidnapped by the felon's gang, but his intrepid assistant tracks them down, then escapes to bring help before the villains can char Sydney and Melbourne. All fast moving action in a local setting, and just the sort of thing that my much older brothers would have been reading if they could have afforded the eight pence.

Other titles included *Atomic Death*, *Blackmarket Brains*, *Death is a Habit*, *Curse of the Mummy*, and *The Freezing*

Peril Strikes. There was a new *Scientific Thriller* on the news-stands practically every month, so that it was only natural that Transport Publications would soon decide to try out its own sf magazine.

One day in March 1950 this new magazine was introduced to the reading public of Australia. *Thrills Incorporated* has the distinction of being the country's first pulp sf magazine, and it was most certainly run in the tradition of the great pulps over-seas. In his autobiography, Alan Yates gives us a rare view into the routines of this magazine, describing how the editor would hand him a piece of ghastly artwork for a cover that advertised an unwritten story by a non-existent writer, expecting him to produce 3,000 or so words on the theme by some deadline.[16] In *Loving Reminiscences of the Dying Gasp of the Pulp Era*, Harlan Ellison describes a very similar situation with *Amazing* in New York in 1955.[17] There was a market for that sort of adventure, and even good writers needed to eat, so they churned out these unashamed space westerns. Note the distinction: the stories were frontier/crime adventures with off-world setting and so very little science that the description space opera lends them a legitimacy they do not deserve.

Thrills was superficially similar to the US pulps of the '20s and '30s. In content most stories were all adventure and very little else. The science that was included was pretty rank as far as even a pretence to accuracy was concerned. There were occasional science fact features, and for a while cartoons with futuristic settings were introduced. These were almost as funny as the supposedly serious illustrations. Predictably, perhaps, *Thrills* carried the same sorts of advertisements for sex educa-tion books that *Amazing* and *Astounding* had once featured for the benefit of the spotty, male adolescents in their audience of the '30s. Two issues went on sale in Britain under the name

16. Alan Yates, *Ready When You Are, C.B.!*, 31-32.

17. Harlan Ellison, *Loving Reminiscences of the Last Dying Gasp of the Pulp Era* (tape).

Amazing Science Stories, and did very poorly. The genre overseas had evolved far away from this sort of fatuous and dated writing, and soon the new, advanced sf would be pursuing *Thrills* back to its home.

We cannot be sure of the authorship of all the *Thrills* stories, but we know that G. Clive Bleeck, Norma Hemming, Alan Yates, Durham Keith Garton, Russel Hausfeld and (possibly) Stanford Hennell contributed under various names—sometimes their own! Ace Carter, Belli Luigi, Roger Garradine, Paul Valdez, and Al Ryan existed only for editorial convenience. Today the magazine is best remembered for running pirated stories by overseas authors, notably Clifford Simak and Ray Bradbury. This was not editorial policy, and research shows that one author using three pseudonyms pirated five of the eight stories that he sold to *Thrills.* There were cries of outrage from the more widely read members of the Australian fan community and the culprit disappeared from the pages of *Thrills* by issue 10, January 1951.

This is not to say that the quality of either the stories or the production control improved at once. "Jet Bees of Planet J" was attributed to Paul Valdez on the cover and Roger Garradine in the index—all the while being written by Alan Yates. In issue 12, however, Graham Stone ran an article and book review, introducing the hope of some sanity in issues to come. With the next issue it shrank to digest size with fewer stories. Yates, Hemming, and Bleeck were featured under their own names, and the quality of the work began to improve marginally. Stanley Pitt began illustrating the covers and internal drawings, and even Ray Cavanagh began to produce a better class of artwork—most notably the flying horse for the cover around which Norma Hemming wrote "Amazons of the Asteroids."

After twenty-three issues *Thrills* folded, in June 1952. The last issue had a Stanley Pitt cover for a story by Hemming, and other stories by Yates, Bleeck, and the Herscholt and Carter pseudonyms. In a sense it had everything going for it, and it did not need much in the way of money for production. Graham Stone's general summary of Australian sf magazines of the period probably explains its demise: "At their worst, publishers neither knew nor cared what sf was all about or what readers expected, and yet somehow expected the suffering public to support their miserable apologies for magazines."[18] *Thrills* specifically took a number of crime/western story situations and projected them into the future to acquire a veneer of science. The trouble was that by now those ideas and themes were out of date, and such magazines as *Fantasy Fiction* and *American Science Fiction* were offering superior overseas works to the Australian public. Worse, British magazines (both original and American reprints) were becoming widely available in Australia and *Thrills* had no hope against such competition.

Did *Thrills* have any redeeming qualities? Did anything of worth appear in its pages—aside from what was pinched from Simak and Bradbury? I would love to say yes, but... Otherwise talented authors had to work to criteria which precluded the possibility of anything original being written. Clive Bleeck was a competent and experienced author, who had had mainstream books published in the 1940s, and whose short stories had appeared the *Bulletin*. As we have already seen, he made sure that there was a plot, some science, much action, and that the text read easily. He had been told to write space westerns, and he did a good job on that obsolescent form. Norma Hemming's "Loser Take All" was published in the British magazine *Science Fantasy* in 1951, giving the world a look at what she could really do before working for *Thrills*. She tried her best to maintain her own standards within the constraints of *Thrills*, but it was too much, even for such a gifted author. While her eight stories were the best original fiction in *Thrills*, they were not her own best work. She was the only *Thrills* author to appear in other sf magazines, both Australian and British.

In "Amazons of the Asteroids," for example, a spaceship's crew discovers a race of Amazons riding winged horses around

---

18. Graham Stone, *Australian Science Fiction Index 1925-1967*, 156.

in the Asteroid Belt. The chauvinistic Amazons attack and take them prisoner, but they manage to escape safely after the usual sorts of Transport Publishing adventures. Hemming takes some trouble to set up a plausible explanation for the presence of air and other prerequisites of life in that region, demonstrating both the difficulty of writing for unsuitable cover art as well as her own wish to preserve at least a shred of scientific integrity.

Alan Yates' work was quite a different matter. He wrote for a living, loved writing, and wrote anything that would sell—crimes, westerns, and sf. His stories for *Thrills* were among his first, and appeared in parallel with his Paul Valdez novelettes in the *Scientific Thriller* series for the same company. While his style was slick and brisk, his grasp of sf was so bad that one wonders just who the editors thought would read it. "The Girl from Galaxy X" appeared in *Action Monthly* #10 in 1952, with two good illustrations by Stanley Pitt. This was perhaps the low point of Yates' sf career. The plot involves a spaceship that crashes on a strange planet, where the survivors are attacked by tiny humans. They are caught and shrunk also, but end up living happily ever after. Ghastly beyond bearing! Around now, however, one of the Transport editors remarked to Yates that the scientific content of his stories was so small that he might like to drop the pretence of being an sf writer and concentrate on detective fiction instead. Thus Carter Brown was born, and went on to sell tens of millions of books in the decades that followed.

Careful research indicates that "Ghosts Don't Kill" by Paul Valdez was in fact by Alan Yates. It is the thirty-third in the *Scientific Thriller* series, but is a pure detective story set in Cornwall. An upper-class detective and his ex-crim butler investigate the appearance of a ghost in a family mansion, and a couple of deaths associated therewith. The ghost turns out to be a perfectly live member of the family who is trying to cover up a smuggling operation by frightening people away. At no point does a transparent ghostly monk peer down into the cleavage of a young blonde's nightie, as the cover suggests....

The seeds of Carter Brown are here, alive and well, in this sf series. There was a good market for this sort of racy crime stuff, and once the sham of calling it sf was dropped, it took off with a vengeance. "Over 70 million Carter Brown mysteries in print," declares the blurb on the 1980 edition of *The Swingers* (copyright 1959).

Thus if *Thrills* did not produce any memorable stories, it did give some local writers a good deal of market experience before they went on to greater things. It also provided Stanley Pitt with some work, although hardly his most memorable creations.

By 1952 more and more overseas fiction was finding its way into Australia by various means. *American Science Fiction*, with its covers by Stanley Pitt, brought C.L. Moore, Henry Kuttner, Robert Heinlein, John Campbell, Murray Leinster and many others before the Australian public. Other local magazines followed, and the British magazines were on the increase too, carrying reprints of recent American stories. Faced with this caliber of competition, our home-grown "scientific thrillers" did not stand a chance. In May 1952 *Scientific Thriller* died, to be followed by *Thrills Incorporated* a month later. When *Thrills* folded we passed the high water mark of sf pulp publishing in Australia, murky and poisonous water though it might have been. It is ironic that the standard of the local writing began to improve from about now, probably under the influence of those very magazines that drove *Thrills* to the wall.

3: Invasion

Three little mice sat down to spin, / Pussy passed by and she peeped in. / What are you at, my fine little men? / Making coats for gentlemen. / Shall I come in and cut off your threads? / Oh, no, Miss Pussy, you'd bite off our heads.
—Beatrix Potter

This section is about what happened after some fool let the cat in—which, on the positive side, did lead to a faster and brighter variety of mouse through natural selection.

Australian writers were not all writing according to the rules of Transport Publishing in the early '50s. Norma Hemming, Wynne Whiteford, and Frank Bryning were all aware of both modern science and modern sf, and were writing accordingly. If there were no suitable sf magazines locally, there were general interest magazines that would buy their stories—and the overseas markets, of course.

The list of Australians who were published in overseas magazines in the '50s is very impressive, and contains some surprises. Bryning, Whiteford, Hemming, and Chandler are well enough known, but who knows that Dal Stivens had sixteen stories published in *Fantastic Universe* and *Satellite Science Fiction*, that Sydney fan Ron Nicholson had one published in *Galaxy* in 1953, or that Veronica Welwood had two stories in *Authentic Science Fiction* in 1954 and 1956? It all adds up.

Dal Stivens held a place in the sf of the '50s that is analogous to that of Peter Carey today. What he wrote was more in the line of fables or tall stories, but it was close enough to the genre to be adopted, even though the author was without question a mainstream writer. Frank Belknap Long calls him "our inimitable fabulist" and "a *Fantastic Universe* institution" in his introduction to "The Gay-Hearted Jay" in the June 1956 issue.

A jay falls in love with a nightingale, but is in the habit of chattering so much that the songbird cannot stand him. He tries to cultivate silence, but finds that it is against his nature, so he must face the prospect of losing his lover. At that point they are both captured for sale in a pet shop. Here the jay's chattering becomes a source of comfort to the nightingale, and she falls in love with him. A kindly old birdlover later buys and frees the nightingale, but the jay is so hoarse by now that the pet shop owner sets him free as well, and the two birds fly off together.

The story revolves around the futility of trying to change one's nature, coupled with the fact that one has to be flexible to achieve some things. Frank Bryning experimented with a similar style in the '40s, but fables never became widespread in the genre.

In 1987 the Sydney bibliographer Graham Stone published the results of his research in Australian men's magazines, showing that hundreds of locally written sf stories appeared in their pages between the late 1930s and the late 1970s.[19] There are many surprises. Darcy Niland's "Dark Lookout" and "Out of the Night" appear in 1945 and 1946. Many of Bertram Chandler's stories appeared, long before he came to live in Australia, sometimes for the first time, and once for the only time. The majority were by unknown authors, as might be expected, many of whom were journalists.

Gene Janes was one such journalist, and he wrote some fifteen stories between 1952 and 1972. Like Clive Bleeck, he wrote quite readable, intelligent stories that were pleasantly entertaining if not state-of-the-art. "The Unseen" appeared in *Peep* in December 1955. The first interstellar expedition is wrecked on a planet where the lifeforms are invisible to human eyes. The spacecraft had hit an invisible forest, but the inhabitants are intelligent and friendly. Very friendly, it seems, and so close to humanity from a genetic point of view that they can interbreed with the survivors. The mulatto children are only partly visible.

This is not the sort of thing to make the average reader do handstands, but good enough for the average Aussie male caught in the bathroom without his racing form guide, and a definite improvement on the "scientific thriller" school of writing. Janes developed a very strong interest in sf and began to read it a great deal, but after a final burst of writing in the early 1970s his output ended. He was, perhaps, the best of his type, a forgotten group that gave Australians much sf during a time when there were no local big names in the field.

After a few mainstream stories in the 1940s, Frank Bryning had his "Operation in Free Flight" published in *The Australian*

19. Graham Stone, "Science Fiction in the Man Group of Magazines," *Science Fiction News* #104 (May 1987).

Magazine in March 1952. This and his next three stories were later bought and reprinted in the USA by *Fantastic Universe* in 1955 and 1956. Ten of his stories were a sort of "space doctor" series, most of which would have sat comfortably beside anything that Asimov, Chandler, or Clarke were writing then. At the time I suppose it might have been realistic to think that Australia might one day have a network of space stations, but with science policy being what it is these days, it might have been better for Bryning to have used settings much further in the future.

Bryning actually thought that the Australian Aborigines were an excellent and unique theme for sf writers. He wrote several stories that featured Aborigines, and these also involved realistic science—unlike the lost race epics that Erle Cox and Phil Collas were writing in the years between the wars.

Wynne Whiteford began writing in the mid-1930s and appears to be the only Australian author from those years who was still writing sf half a century later. His works from the '50s were short stories, once again in a realist style similar to that of the better American and British writers; he was widely published overseas; and several of these stories were reprinted in the 1970s and 1980s. Like Frank Bryning, Whiteford was encouraged to return to writing by Paul Collins' publishing ventures in the late 1970s, and he went on to write a number of novels.

In addition to the British magazines a number of local efforts tried to cash in on the thirst for new and scientifically interesting fiction. *Science Fiction Library, Selected Science Fiction Magazine, Orbit Science Fiction,* and *American Science Fiction* were all produced locally. *Fantasy and Science Fiction* and *Astounding* had Australian editions, even though direct imports were prohibited.

More importantly, *Future Science Fiction, Popular Science Fiction,* and *Science Fiction Monthly* included a few Australian stories among their overseas reprints. The opportunities were not great, but the stories that did make it showed that Australian writers were climbing back to the standards set in the 1930s. Some stories from US authors were published in these magazines that never saw print in any other country, and local authors Frank Bryning, A. Bertram Chandler, Norma Hemming and Wynne Whiteford sold stories to them. Graham Stone and Vol Molesworth contributed reviews and items of interest to fans.

In early 1957 *Science Fiction Monthly* folded. It had been making a profit for the parent company, but the editor moved on to another job and nobody else on the staff was interested in taking over his work. I may be wrong, but this may have been the last Australian sf magazine to run at a profit. More importantly, it was the last sf magazine based in Australia for over a decade that offered local writers a chance to get into print.

The men's magazines and general interest journals continued to offer occasional opportunities, but in general writers began to turn their attention overseas with increasing determination, and with Britain's John Carnell, editor of *New Worlds, Science Fantasy* and *Science Fiction Adventures,* they found a powerful and generous sponsor. Bryning, Chandler, Hemming, and Whiteford had already been published in Britain, and after 1957 the rate increased. In 1958 Chandler averaged one original story published in Britain and America per fortnight, and Whiteford had six published in the following year. Bryning's output had begun to taper off, however, and Hemming was to publish only two more stories before she died in 1960.

About this time Chandler began to concentrate on his best known character, Commander Grimes, and his adventures in the Rim area of the galaxy. Chandler had been polling around the middle of the field in the *New Worlds* reader surveys until now, but with Grimes he established a fan following. Sea travel was still the main way of crossing oceans, and Chandler's paralleling of sea and space lore struck chords of recognition with a lot of people. The first of the Rim stories did not feature Grimes, but introduced us to the sprawling frontier scenario, along with its outcasts, slightly tatty ships, and exotic ports of call. In a sense it was like an updated version of the *Pacific Trader* radio serial of the same period.

Chandler had been writing sf since the mid 1940s, and had sold sixty stories by the time he moved to Australia in 1956. The combination of an easy, simple, and well practiced style with his experience of interesting and exotic locations produced stories that were easy to read, true to life, and even vaguely familiar to anyone who had travelled on a ship. He was a ship's master by now, and wrote sf in his cabin while off duty. Chandler was not the first author to introduce shipboard protocols and routines to spacecraft (Walsh was doing it back in the '30s), but he did it with more authority than anyone else.

In 1952, Walsh's 1932 epic, *Vanguard to Neptune*, which had first appeared in *Wonder Quarterly*, was republished in book form by Kemsley of London. Dated though the writing was, it was still not a bad yarn and it did well enough to warrant a French edition. While Australian born, Walsh had moved to Britain a few years before writing this story.

Back in Australia, Ivan Southall's children's novel *Simon Black in Space* also reached the bookshops in this year. Eleven years later a teacher (who knew that I read sf and that I had won a class prize with an sf story) discovered the *Simon Black* series and insisted that I, too, should experience "this marvelous Australian work." I was sent home with *Simon Black in Space*, and the following morning's conversation went like this:

"How did you like it?" asks the teacher.

"I didn't," I reply, returning the book with a sneer. "It's just *Biggles* modernized, and I'm too old for that sort of adventure stuff now."

"But it's Australian, and it's full of spaceships and other planets," he insists.

"So what?" says I, full of the not yet fashionable spirit of youth rebellion. "If I want to read about space travel I'll read good authors like Robert Heinlein, Isaac Asimov, and Arthur C. Clarke."

"Who are they?"

Bernard Charles Cronin, alias Eric North, had two sf books published in the 1920s in Australia, which were reprinted several times in the US. In 1955 *The Ant Men* was published in the US, although the setting was Australian. This book has also seen various reprints, and I bought one new in 1969. In essence it is a bit like Alan Connell's reptile world, with big ants instead of big reptiles. Some explorers are thrown back in time and meet up with a civilization of intelligent ants. The ants want their bodies—for transfer, not sex—but the humans escape back to their own time by the final page. Sounds terrible, to be sure, but even in 1969 I thought of it as a good adventure, in much the same class as a Tarzan novel.

What Walsh, North, Chandler, and later Shute had in common is that they all established themselves overseas, without having to rely heavily on a protected local market.

Mary Pratchett was a children's writer who tried her hand at sf early in her career, cashing in on the genre's lack of "good" juvenile material in the early 1950s. Just try to imagine a primary school nun using *Thrills Incorporated* in class for English Comprehension and you will get the idea. The situation overseas was much the same. In 1953 Lutterworth Press published the first of Pratchett's half dozen sf novels for juveniles. *Lost on Venus* came out in the following year, and is an ordinary little adventure of two boys lost on Venus, no less. They might just as easily have been lost in darkest Africa, with a few of the names changed. The location is exotic, the science is minimal.

Herein lies the problem. By the time some misguided librarian recommended this book to me eight years later, I was building my own model rockets and had scars to prove it! I strongly objected to the idea of precocious brats being allowed aboard rockets when every schoolboy knew (or ought to have known) that all astronauts had to go through years of rigorous selection and training procedures, and that the whole idea of kids in space was absurd.

Put less emotionally, Pratchett's original juvenile audience was pre-Sputnik, pre-Gagarin, and pre-Lunik. Suddenly one could no longer say "rocket" and expect the audience to sit back in wonder. In 1961 we wanted specific details of the propulsion units, and if the author could not provide them her book was going straight back to the Brighton Municipal Children's Library with a complaint! Pratchett's sf work seems to have had its heyday in the 1950s, predictably enough, then to have given way to more realistic themes, such as her popular Brumby books.

If a list of the best Australian sf novels of this time was ever compiled, Nevil Shute's *On the Beach* would have to be at the top. Published in 1957, it was made into a major film with wide distribution, and its message gave the world a well-needed fright regarding the consequences of nuclear war. In January 1988, I saw that a paperback edition was still on sale at Victoria Station in London.

Like Chandler, Shute came to Australia with a well-established literary career, but he quickly adapted his writing to his new home and wrote several books that are still popular today—two with sf-related themes. In its own way *On the Beach* is a simple story: a nuclear exchange involving cobalt bombs has poisoned the northern hemisphere, and the radioactivity is slowly making its way down south. In Melbourne, people are getting on with their lives, yet they are prepared with suicide capsules for when radiation sickness becomes too much to bear. Slowly the characters, who are disturbingly familiar and well-crafted, begin to die, and the world itself is close to death by the end. No hope is offered.

Shute's style is similar to Chandler's. It is very readable and transparent, with not much literary artifice to stand in the way of the story that he is telling. Stanley Kramer's 1959 film version followed the story passably well—and incidentally starred Ava Gardner, Gregory Peck, and Anthony Perkins. The combination of media spread the impact of this excellent story to a huge, worldwide audience. The sheer horror of people in a neat, well-functioning outpost of Western Civilization (Melbourne) calmly preparing for inevitable mass death was compounded by experts telling them "Well, sorry ma'am, but he's right. That's what cobalt bombs are meant to do—kill everyone."

I read *On the Beach* late in 1959, aged ten, and was devastated to find that there was no happy ending! Until the very last page I was sure that some scientist would find an unexpected cure for radiation sickness using powdered kangaroo liver or some such. Shute gave us no hope. For weeks thereafter I had nightmares on the theme.

Much of Shute's success with *On the Beach* lay with the subject being so very timely, together with the fact that he wrote about people readers could identify with. He did not dwell on technical detail, but it was as accurate as the science of the time could predict. In the tradition of the best sf he said, "this is a fact and this is what its effect will be on real people." In its day it was as grim a warning as Orwell's *Nineteen Eighty-Four*, and perhaps its greatest achievement was to help prevent its own prediction. There had been countless other post-nuclear war stories before 1957, but it took Shute to give the predicted tragedy a human face.

I think that Chandler and Shute represented the summit of the Golden Age's achievements, even though both were mature-age recruits from Britain. Their highly successful writing was identifiably Australian, with just the right balance of adventure and ideas—as opposed to the vacuous and unoriginal adventures by cut-out characters that were on offer in *Thrills Incorporated* and *Scientific Thriller*. Whatever their faults, they can still provide intelligent entertainment today.

There was one more period of conspicuous Australian achievement before the interval defined for the purpose of this essay comes to an end. As noted above, the important British editor John Carnell continued to take an interest in Australian writers, and in the early 1960s he began to publish the works of five new antipodeans. Stephen Cook and D. D. Stewart are not familiar names today, but John Baxter, Lee Harding, and David Rome (David Boutland) began substantial writing careers in

Carnell's British magazines.

The total number of Australian stories being published in Britain at this time was substantial. Between 1957 and 1962 they accounted for nearly ten percent of stories in *New Worlds*, for example, outnumbering those from American writers. For the first time, we can see a distinct group of Australian writers in the overseas literature, rather than just occasional stories by people who happen to live in Australia. Did these stories and their styles have any impact or influence, and how did the overseas readers react to them? Many magazines ran a readers' poll with each issue, and the results provide some clues.

Chandler, Baxter, Bryning, and Whiteford tended to average out at the middle of the field, while Rome tended to be a bit lower down. Lee Harding and Norma Hemming scored towards the top when their stories were polled, and two of Harding's stories in *New Worlds* actually topped the poll for their issue.

Thus Australian stories were about as well received as any that the average British author could produce, and were clearly of a standard that could survive in the overall market. Style is another matter, however. If one reads a couple of dozen works from this period it becomes clear that while our authors were writing good sf, there is nothing that is identifiably Australian in their work. This is not a criticism, as Australian standards had risen a great deal over the previous decade, which is much more important. Far better to write good sf than hack out the dreaded "scientific thrillers."

To all appearances this was another high point. Some local authors were prospering in overseas sf markets, and sundry lesser-known locals were having a slowly increasing number of works published in the *Man* group of men's magazines. Nonetheless, the local specialist markets were dead, and even Carnell's magazines were being eroded by the effect of television on the short story market. Although no year passed between 1962 and 1975 without at least a dozen Australian works being published, local writers were confronted with shrinking overseas markets, along with an editorial taste for the emerging

New Wave style. Our writers had been raised in the tradition of the pulp magazine just in time to see its decline.

4: Revolution

Waiting for the barbarians.
—British literary pastime of the 1950s

Like a gold rush boom town, the Golden Age was colorful, exciting, and full of exotic adventure. At the same time it was also crass, gaudy, and shallow. By 1962, say, Australia had a visible body of sf literature, at least half a dozen well-known authors, and a growing fan community. Unfortunately the market was about to shift again, and—unlike what happened in the 1940s—this time it would do so before the horrified eyes of those who had just clawed their way in. Even though the barbarians were wielding degrees in literature and television cameras, they were still ravening destroyers let loose in the Australians' newly-found arcadia.

We should not blame television and the New Wave too harshly for the changes as the pulps had a lot to answer for, and produced tons of muck for every ounce of brilliance. It may seem hard to imagine in the jaded 1980s, but programs such as *The Twilight Zone*, *Out of the Unknown* and *The Outer Limits* seemed to be too good to be true when they first appeared. I can remember such episodes as "The Sixth Finger," "Demon with a Glass Hand," and "Time in Advance" leaving me too excited to sleep—or do much homework.

Television was well established in Australia by the early 1960s, and the half-hour TV episodes of sf series were beginning to displace the mass audience short story market that the Australian Golden Age of the genre was built on. In 1967 a company re-released several old issues of *Popular Science Fiction* and *Future Science Fiction*, but with little success. They were competing with *Out of the Unknown*, *The Avengers*, *Star Trek*, *The Twilight Zone*, and *The Outer Limits*—just to name a few of the more prominent and successful examples of what television had to offer in that year. Specialist sf magazines have not had great success in Australia since the late 1950s, and they survive elsewhere only by the sheer size of the market.

If television was injury to these writers, the New Wave must have seemed very much like insult. The overall genre was definitely in a rut by the early 1960s: too many writers were writing about too few themes, and real space exploration was eroding traditional themes at an alarming rate. The first man in space now existed, and had a Russian name; Venus was known to be blazing hot beneath the clouds, and the far side of the moon had been photographed. There was still a market for good writing, but the readers wanted something new. By 1965 there were increasingly extreme experiments in progress by both British and American authors—but in general Australians were slow to respond. They had just learned to write well by the rules, and suddenly the rules were being changed, or even ignored.

The New Wave is impossible to summarize in a few lines, but in a very general sense it meant a shift in emphasis from the physical to the social sciences. It also saw a greater emphasis on literary form—in a field notorious for the banal nature of its prose. In general terms I like to see some degree of experimentation, even if the failure rate of the resulting works is high, but only as long as the terms "new" and "good" are not assigned the same meaning. Most of the time the New Wave did no more than substitute pretentious waffle for unpretentious garbage, but it did succeed in breaking the moribund high-tech mould.

David Rome was one of the very few Australian writers to try anything in the style of the New Wave when it was really new. "There's a Starman in Ward 7" appeared in the January 1965 issue of *New Worlds*, which was by now edited by Michael Moorcock. It is a disturbing account of a supposed alien by an inmate of an asylum for the insane, and one is never really sure if the starman is a true alien or a dangerous, clever, but human psychopath. It is the finest of Rome's stories that I have read. Rome was living in Britain in the early 1960s, and was thus closer to the new influences.

Other Australian authors either resisted the trend or assimilated it more slowly. In 1964, Moorcock took over the editorship of *New Worlds* from Carnell, then began to look for a new direction for the genre in general, and the magazine in particular. The Australian presence tapered away to nothing over the next two years. Carnell's more traditional policies lived on in the *New Writings in SF* original fiction anthology series (at 19, Damien Broderick placed a novella in the first of these quarterlies), and many Australians continued to find a welcome with him in this new venue.

Eventually, New Wave influences made some impact on Australian writing, but the process was slow. The rearguard action is perhaps understandable: the old high-tech style was still new and exciting for Australia, which had been isolated for so long. More importantly, much of the New Wave writing was not only incomprehensible, it was boring—the ultimate crime in such a genre. Some elements of the New Wave permeated through, of course, and perhaps this slower pace spared Australian writers and readers the excesses that were marketed as New Wave writing overseas. Baxter and Harding were using bolder prose and more surreal settings by the late 1960s, and with some success.

The last writer to come out of the Golden Age pointed the way to the future influences on the genre by beginning his career in a student newspaper at Monash University. Damien Broderick's first stories appeared in the Monash University newspaper *Chaos* (later renamed *Lot's Wife*) in 1963, almost beating everyone to the exploration and colonization of the planet Academia. (His first collection, *A Man Returned*, appeared from Australian publisher Horwitz in 1965.) While "All My Yesterdays" is neither New Wave nor high-tech, it could sit as easily in a better class pulp magazine as in a student newspaper. It is not typical of Broderick's later work, but it is a prophetic work nonetheless. Not a lowbrow adventure, not New Wave nihilism, but a light, literate entertainment describing the psychoanalysis of Lazarus. Within its own ashes the phoenix was stirring anew as the Golden Age ended.

5.

Before concluding, I would like to consider how the Golden Age looked to an average Australian sf enthusiast—as opposed to fan. While I was a bit young to do my own writing then, I was an insatiable reader by the late 1950s. I would read *Brick Bradford* in the *Sun* newspaper Children's Supplement, *Flash Gordon* and *Mandrake* in the *Herald*, and Basil Blackaller's *Ace O'Hara* in the *Age*. Nobody in my family bought the *Age*, but I would borrow copies from neighbors' postboxes to follow the serials. On the radio I seldom missed *Space Patrol, Tarzan*, and *Superman*, resorting to a crystal set when my tasteless older brothers hogged the family radio to listen to rock music. When one brother, an electrician, brought television sets home to repair I could watch *Jet Jackson* (*Captain Midnight* updated), and later *Men in Space*. *Batman* serials and an occasional full-length sf film were on show at the cinema. I had also been buying comics out of my lunch money from about age 7, and first encountered Wells and Verne in the Classics Illustrated series. After I discovered the local library I quickly graduated from comics to such books as *Level 7* and *The Green Hills of Earth*.

You may have noticed a continuous thread running through the previous paragraph. Not a single one of those examples of the sf that was delighting me during the late 1950s and early 1960s was Australian. In fact I did read Shute's *On the Beach* in the 1959 Christmas holidays, and in 1962 I read *The Rim of Space* without knowing that Chandler lived here. On the other hand, I did not really care whether something was the local product or not. I wanted to be entertained and amazed, and there was plenty of sf around to oblige. Even though Australian authors were producing plenty, it was submerged in the overall scene, which was immense.

Last year, a little old lady sold me a box of magazines that her son had collected in the 1950s, then stored in a shed. It consisted of nearly one hundred sf magazines: Australian issues of *Astounding, New Worlds*, and *Science Fiction Adventures*, but even more amazing was the fact that about a third of the items were locally produced and edited magazines such as *Science Fiction Monthly, Future Science Fiction*, and *Selected Science Fiction Magazine*. It was a stunning cross-section of what was available to the average young enthusiast in that period who was—like myself—not consciously looking for local works. While many of the illustrations were either original local artwork or local plagiarisms, the Australian component of the stories themselves was just two percent of the total number, these being by Chandler, Bryning, and Hemming. To make matters worse, most of these had already been published in overseas magazines, and this was at the time of a high point in local output!

One question needs to be asked in conclusion. What did the Golden Age achieve, apart from a legacy of rare and gaudy pulps? When Robert Bloch made that famous remark in the mid-1960s, "Tell me now you folks Down Under, do you have a sense of wonder?" he had most likely read over a dozen products of the antipodean sense of wonder in the previous decade without knowing it. A recognizable national identity is hard to maintain in the vast scene overseas, especially if there is no distinct national style. Nevertheless, the sense of national identity did exist by 1965, and those familiar with the Australian scene could talk about Australian sf, rather than just individual writers. The local genre now had a romantic pulp era and (rather terrible, but still endemic) local style of writing in its literary history. Above all, it had an identity, and in my opinion this is the most important achievement of the Golden Age. Beginners now knew that it was possible to be both Australian and an sf author. It should have also taught us that one cannot foster good writing in protected isolation, but I am not sure that it really did manage to convince us of that.

The author wishes to thank all those who provided unpublished background material for the talk upon which this article is based, especially those who were born in time to experience more of this period than himself. Graham Stone's assistance was particularly helpful, and his magazine *Science Fiction News* is recommended to anyone interested in the finer details of the history of Australian sf.

Selected Bibliography of Golden Age Authors and Sources

Bleeck, G. Clive. "Cosmic Calamity" *Scientific Thriller* (Sydney, Transport Publishing, September 1949)

Barnard Eldershaw, M. *Tomorrow and Tomorrow* (Melbourne, Georgian House, 1947) (rep.: *Tomorrow and Tomorrow and Tomorrow* [London, Virago, 1983])

Baxter, John. < 7 stories published overseas, 1962-1964 >

Broderick, Damien. "All My Yesterdays," *Chaos* (1963) (rep.: *A Man Returned* [Sydney, Horwitz, 1965])

Bryning, Frank. "Operation in Free Flight," *The Australian Magazine* (March 1952)

— < 20 stories published in Australia and overseas, 1944-58 >

Chandler, A. Bertram. *The Rim of Space* (UK, Avalon, 1961).

— "To Run the Rim," *Astounding* (January, 1959).

— < 55 stories published while living in Britain, 1944-1956. 96 stories published after moving to Australia, 1956-1964. 9 novels published 1961-1964 >

Connell, Alan. "The Reign of the Reptiles," *Wonder Stories* (August, 1935). (rep.: *Fantastic Story Quarterly* [Winter, 1951])

— *Warriors of Serpent Land* (Sydney, Currawong, 1945)

Dornberger, Walter. *V2* (London, Hurst and Blackett, 1954). (copyright 1952: *V2 Der Schussins Weltall*)

Ellison, Harlan. "Loving Reminiscences of the Last Dying Gasp of the Pulp Era," *The Harlan Ellison Record Collection: An Hour with Harlan Ellison*, Vol.I. (Copyright 1980, 1983 The Kilimanjaro Corp. HE 106A)

Harding, Lee. < 14 stories published overseas, 1961-1964 >

Healey, Dominic. *Voyage to Venus* (Sydney, Currawong, 1943)

Heming, John Winton. *From Earth to Mars* (Sydney, Currawong, 1943).

— < 6 sf novels published by Currawong, 1942-1943 >

Hemming, Norma Kathleen. "Amazons of the Asteroids," *Thrills Incorporated* no.17 (November, 1951)

— "Loser Take All," *Science Fantasy* 1/3 (Winter, 1951). < 14 stories published 1951-1959, 4 overseas >

Janes, Gene. "The Unseen," *Peep: For Men Only* 4/12 (December, 1955)

Law, Winifred. *Through Space to the Planets* (Sydney, New Century, 1944)

— *Rangers of the Universe* (Sydney, New Century, 1945)

Molesworth, Voltaire. *The Ape of God* (Sydney, Currawong, 1943)

— *Spaceward Ho!* (Sydney, Radio Records, 1942?)

— < 8 novels published in Australia, 1942?-1950 >

Nicholson, Ron D. "Far From the Warming Sun," *Galaxy* 6/6 (September 1953)

Niland, Darcy. "Dark Lookout," *Man* (April, 1946)

— "Out of the Night," *Man* (April, 1945)

O'Donnell, Phillip James. *Secret Weapons* (Melbourne, Wilke, 1941; Ace Detective Novels)

North, Eric. *The Ant Men* (New York, Holt, Rinehart and Winston, 1955)

Patchett, Mary. *Lost on Venus* (London, Lutterworth, 1954)

— < 6 sf novels published, 1953-1963 >

Rome, David (Boutland, John). "There's a Starman in Ward 7," *New Worlds* (January, 1965)

— < 17 short stories published overseas, 1961-1965 >

Shute, Nevil. *On the Beach* (London, Heinemann, 1957)

Southall, Ivan. *Simon Black in Space* (Sydney, Angus and Robertson, 1952)

— < 3 sf novels in the series, 1952-1959 >

Stivens, Dal. "The Gay Hearted Jay," *Fantastic Universe* 5/5

(June, 1956)

— < 15 stories published in overseas sf magazines, 1953-59 >

Stone, Graham. *Australian Science Fiction Index 1925-1967* (Canberra, Australian Science Fiction Foundation, 1968)

— "Notes on Australian Science Fiction," *Science Fiction News* #93 (March 1985)

— "Science Fiction in the *Man* Group of Magazines," *Science Fiction News* #104 (May, 1987)

Walsh, J. H. *Secret Weapons* (Melbourne, Collins, 1946)

— "Vanguard to Neptune," *Wonder Quarterly* (Spring, 1932) (rep.: London, Kemsley, 1952)

Yates, Alan Geoffrey (1923-1985). "Ghosts Don't Kill: A Supernatural Murder," *Scientific Thriller (Sydney, Transport Publishing, August 1951)*

— "The Girl from Galaxy X," *Action Monthly* #10 (1952)

— "Jet Bees of Planet J" (as Roger Garradine, or as Paul Valdez), *Thrills Incorporated* no.10 (January 1951)

— *Ready When You Are, C.B.!: The Autobiography of Carter Brown* (Melbourne, Macmillan, 1983)

— *The Swingers* (as Carter Brown) (Sydney, Horwitz, 1980; copyright 1959)

— < 8 sf stories, 1951-1952 > < several sf novels, 1951-1952 >

"I WASN'T
EXPECTING THAT"
THE CAREER OF
NORMA HEMMING

by David Medlen
[2008]

Norma Kathleen Hemming was the first Australian woman to have a career entirely dedicated to science fiction. A few female writers had used science fiction on occasion, such as in the nineteenth-century dystopias and utopias of Catherine Helen Spence and Henrietta Dugdale and then, after a sizeable gap, M. Barnard Eldershaw's *Tomorrow and Tomorrow* (1947). By contrast, every short story, essay or play in Hemming's nine-year career was related to science fiction. However, Hemming's life and career should not be celebrated because she was the first Australian woman to do something but because the passion and intelligence of her work deserves attention.

Norma Hemming was born in Essex, England in 1927 and migrated with her family to Sydney in 1949. A check of a number of bibliographies shows no indication of her publishing in British fanzines. However, I believe that she did submit her first professional work before leaving for Australia, but it was not published until Winter 1951/52. "Loser Take All," published in *Science Fantasy* (Vol. 1, 3), a sister publication to *New Worlds*, demonstrated Hemming's familiarity with the genre and her ability to manipulate clichés into the unexpected. The story starts with astronaut Mike talking to prototype spaceship "Liza" as if it is his girlfriend until interrupted by Jane, scientist daughter of the ship's designer Professor Lawrence. News arrives that nuclear war has broken out, with East and West blaming each other. Then the sighting of an alien craft at the launch site reveals the real culprits.

The first five pages of this story filled me with dread, not of the aliens, but of the hoary old chestnuts of science fiction being trotted out, of which Mike's "love talk" to the spaceship is especially nauseating. Hemming then turns this on its head. Within a few pages, assumed main character Mike has killed himself whilst destroying an alien base. Jane is revealed to be not the neglected love interest but the real heroine as the scientists race to create a weapon that will drive the aliens mad. The aliens are the Kalerians whose own home world has been destroyed. At war's end the Kalerians are in control but in such small numbers that they cannot survive, and Earth is becoming a backward ruin. A peace deal is negotiated by the professor, who becomes quite creepy, arranging that Earth will accept Kalerian government in return for technology and that Earth women will have to mate with the (entirely male) Kalerian fleet as part of the deal. With skin-crawling rationality he addresses his daughter:

> "They are not unattractive," he said quietly. "And if there is unwillingness, there is also hypnosis." He looked at her searchingly. "You are young, physically a... a fine specimen..." with a glimmer of a smile "and have a brain above average. Do you think you will escape." (96).

The traditional triumphant ending to the Earth invasion story is discarded; there is no clear victory and the professor has prostituted his daughter for technology. Unfortunately, much of the drama is undercut for the modern reader by the naming of

Earth's secret weapon—"The Vibrator"—leading to a number of unintended double entendres.

While "Loser Take All" was being considered and published, Hemming had become active in the Sydney fan scene and her work had begun to appear in the much maligned Australian pulp *Thrills Incorporated*. In this part of her career Norma Hemming was always credited as "N. K. Hemming," although *Thrills Incorporated* managed to misspell her name all but twice in the two years she wrote for the title. I had thought that the use of initials was an attempt to disguise her gender from readers, but when Robert Silverberg stated in a panel on C. L. Moore at Swancon 2001 (Perth, Western Australia) that Moore had used her initials to hide her writing career from her day job employers rather than to hide her sex, I had to reconsider. Certainly, males formed the majority of readers: a minor survey of a Sydney science fiction club in 1952 showed women were outnumbered by men at a rate of six to one—but did that automatically mean women writers hid their gender from their mainly male audience?[20]

Hemming "outed" herself as a female writer at the first Australian Science Fiction Convention in March, 1952. The moment was recorded in the fanzine *Stopgap* by Graham Stone during a debate on *Thrills Incorporated*:

> Incidentally it came as a surprise to fandom that "N. K. Hemming" of *Thrills* is the "N. K. Hemming" of *New Worlds* and an actual person, Norma K. Hemming. Why doesn't someone tell us these things.[21]

Hemming was prominent in fan politics, social events and publishing, so there was no attempt to hide her gender from the Sydney fan community that made up approximately 10% of the

20. Anon. (May 12 1952) "Take a look at yourself," Notes and Comment, 2, 1-3 (Uncredited but probably Ken Martin and Vol Molesworth).

21. Stone, G. B. (March/April 1952) "First Australian Science Fiction Convention," Stopgap; a letter, circular or publication, 43.

Thrills Incorporated readership.[22] Also, someone who turns up to a con ball in the mid-1950s as a Venusian swamp girl in a costume consisting mainly of green vegetable dye is certainly conspicuous.[23]

In 1953 Hemming wrote a short satirical essay for the femme fanzine *Vertical Horizons* describing how she had to disguise her love of science fiction from her workmates to avoid ostracism.[24] I think that this is possible evidence that, like C. L. Moore, Hemming used her initials to disguise her second career from her employers rather than her gender. In the latter half of her career Hemming alternated between her full name and her initials. When her final story was published in Britain in *Science Fiction Adventures* she used her initials but with the following introduction by the editor:

> Australian writer N. K. Hemming makes a welcome contribution to this issue of *Science Fiction Adventures*—and is, to let the cat out of the bag, our first woman contributor (although she had stories in *New Worlds* some years ago). However, Miss Hemming is extremely well-known in Australian science fiction circles and wrote a special play for the 1958 Melbourne Convention.[25]

---

22. This very rough figure is based on the numbers attending a convention in Sydney in 1953 (84 people) as proportion of the New South Wales circulation of *Thrills Incorporated* (800 issues). Sources of figures: Australian National Science Fiction Conventions (http://home.vicnet.net.au/~sfoz/ntcon1st.htm) and correspondence with Graham B. Stone (14th Nov. 2001).

23. Crozier, I.J. (31st June 1955) "Fourth Australian Convention Report," *Etherline*, 47, 3.

24. Hemming, N. K. (Oct. 1953) "On the Trials and Tribulations of being a Science Fiction Fan," *Vertical Horizons*, 5, 5-6.

25. Carnell, E. J. (1959) [Introduction to "Call them Earthmen"], *Science Fiction Adventures,* Vol.2 (10), 91.

1951 to 1952 marked the most productive period in Hemming's career with eight of her seventeen professional stories published in *Thrills Incorporated* in that time. However the lack of editorial assistance and tight schedules at *Thrills Incorporated* meant that this was not her best work. Fortunately for researchers, one of the writers making a start at *Thrills Incorporated* was to become perhaps the most successful author Australia has ever produced, Alan G. Yates. By the time of his death in 1985 he had sold eighty million books worldwide with most of his 300+ novels published under the pseudonym Carter Brown. However he started with short story pulps including *Thrills Incorporated*, where he wrote as A. G. Yates, Roger Garradine, Tod Conway and Paul Valdez and possibly under some house pseudonyms.[26] Yates' autobiography, *Ready When You Are C. B!* (Macmillan, 1983), is a goldmine of information on the pulp writing industry in the 1950s. Yates writes how, once under contract to the publisher, you were regularly told the name of the story and the pseudonym to be used. You then went away to produce a work to match both. Yates specifically mentions the editing style at *Thrills Incorporated*: "The editor was running to a tight schedule; he would have the art work already done and hand you a picture saying 'Three thousand words and a title, old boy, and I do need them by Friday'." (32).

Usually, to have your work featured on the cover of a magazine was a good thing, but starting with Hemming's second story in *Thrills Incorporated* (Dec. 1951), "Amazons of the Asteroids," we will see how it could be a curse. The story had to refer to both the cover art and the internal illustration which the writer had no control over and which could be totally unrelated. In this case Hemming had to create a hard science

---

26. As well as the pseudonyms assigned exclusively to an author there were also "House Pseudonyms" under which a number of authors would write genre material. The best example of this were the "Scientific Thrillers" credited to the non-existent Belli Luigi. The idea was to create a kind of brand recognition within a genre. Belli Luigi deserves a place in Australia's literary history alongside Ern Malley.

fiction story using illustrations with a strong fantasy element. I approached this story with some trepidation but found Hemming worked around the restrictions quite well. In "Amazons of the Asteroids," three humans and a Venusian are in a spacecraft exploring the asteroid belt, theorizing that it was once a habitable planet. The Venusian is a ball of electrically charged gas who moves by telekinesis, which is a change from the humans-with-green-skin aliens in other *Thrills Incorporated* stories. Hemming often added interesting sf touches to make her stories distinctive. One of the crew has a crackpot theory that humanoids migrated from this destroyed planet to earth, an event we remember through myths like those of ancient Greece. The ship makes a forced landing on a large asteroid where the crew are surprised to find a thick but unbreathable atmosphere, gravity, and...beautiful blonde women riding winged horses.

Soon the humans are captured by the physically dominant Amazons, who are armed with arrows tipped with a ball of acid which the men are afraid will penetrate their spacesuits. The Venusian, who avoids capture in this Freudian field day, finds machines from the time of the planet's break-up, no longer understood by the inhabitants, which give the asteroid its gravity. It engineers the humans' escape, but dies of exhaustion in the process. As they leave, the scientists decide never to reveal their discovery. Hemming uses interesting imagery and ideas, such as the Venusian, but is let down by corny dialogue and poor sentence structuring. For example: "The radio broke into strident life. 'Trouble' came Lee's voice, rather breathless, 'These blondes play rough.'" Hemming was later to parody the Amazon story in her play *The Matriarchy of Renok*.

Thrills Incorporated 22 (May 1952) had the Hemming story "Peril of the Sea Planet," which has the ironic cover illustration of a prawn trying to eat some people as *entrée*. And well may the man look nervous, he doesn't appear to be wearing any pants and has a condom pulled over his head. The story could virtually write itself with those elements! The internal illustration for the story is of a spaceship crashing into a rocky planet.

It would be easy to create a parody but Hemming takes these illustrations and the title, which constituted her editorial guidance, and creates a rather bleak story. A military captain of a ship carrying civilian VIPs crashes on a barren planet. Attempts to organize rescue fail as an airborne infection causes illness. The captain attempts to quarantine the infection but while exploring the planet with a haughty female passenger, Kay, he realizes that the passengers are mutating into the sea creatures that populate the planet. The infection is a means of reproduction. They return to the ship to find the passengers have fully mutated, killed the crew and moved to the sea. The captain and Kay realize that they cannot escape the mutation and commit suicide.

Thrills Incorporated 19 (Feb. 1952) gave Hemming the freedom of having to contend with only one illustration to which to match her fiction. However the printers cared as little as the editors and mis-aligned the two halves of the illustration. "Lifeline on Luna" is set in the near future (the mid 1960s) when the space race is more overtly part of the Cold War. Both East and West need a rare element, Cerium, that may be available on the moon, for weapons production. The western powers send a rocket containing three men and a woman, Julie Carruthers, to the moon to collect Cerium. A traitor on board lifts off in the rocket, leaving crewmembers Julie and Lee stranded on the moon and Doc set adrift in space. Luckily Julie and Lee come across a powerful alien spaceship. Everyone is saved, but the handsome alien ambassador refuses to intervene in Earth's affairs to prevent a war as he thinks humans are innately hostile to strangers. The humans suggest that this fear of aliens will prevent a war but the ambassador still refuses. Finally it is implied that Julie, who has a reputation as an ice maiden, seduces the ambassador into agreement.[27] The story concludes with Julie visiting the crewmembers to tell them the good news:

27. McMullen, S. and Blackford, R. (Spring 1998) "Prophet and Pioneer: The Science Fiction of Norma Hemming," *Fantasy Annual*, 2, 65-75.

Lee called after her. "Hey, where are you going off to?" She came back, a mischievous and gamin grin was the only way to describe it, spread across her face. "To further Vegan-Earth alliances," she said and the door closed behind her. Lee stood rooted. "Well, I'll be damned!" he exploded, "Julie Carruthers!" (23)

As I mentioned earlier, the editors of *Thrills Incorporated* were not fans of science fiction. While the reading public were aware of nuclear energy and warfare, the United Nations, early computers, etc., and these changes were reflected in overseas science fiction, *Thrills Incorporated* remained firmly stuck in the 1930s. Stories more often than not were of the mad scientist, monster and rampaging robot ilk. The editors knew so little about contemporary science fiction that when Durham Keith Garton submitted Ray Bradbury and Clifford Simak stories under his own name to *Thrills Incorporated*, no one noticed until fans pointed this out.[28] Earlier I mentioned Alan Yates getting an illustration to which he was to provide a story. This is what happened next:

> One picture he (the editor) gave me didn't allow a lot of scope as far as the title was concerned, I thought, so I called it "Jet-Bees of Planet J". He took another look at the picture when I brought in the manuscript, then looked at the title again. "See what you mean, old boy." He nodded approval. "Sort of self propelled by their own farts."[29]

Hugo Gernsback, this guy was not.

Yates was an unstoppable writing machine, who by 1963 was producing at least two novels a month in addition to other mate-

---

28. McMullen, S. (1994) "The Golden Age of Australian Science Fiction," *Science Fiction: A Review of Speculative Literature*, Vol.12 (3), 12.

29. Yates, A.G. (1983) *Ready when you are C.B.!: The Autobiography of Alan Yates alias Carter Brown*. Macmillan: South Melbourne, 32.

rial such as comics, radio plays, etc.[30] However, other authors found the *Thrills Incorporated* schedules difficult and the lack of editorial input showed. Hemming recognized this problem herself and in at least one fanzine appealed for contact details for overseas agents.[31] We know from reports from the first Australian Science Fiction Convention that fans loathed the low grade and often dated stories in *Thrills Incorporated*.[32] So why was this title produced and purchased?

Australia, due to balance of payment problems, had trade restrictions on overseas magazines, including all US and most UK science fiction titles. One effect was to stimulate the Australian fan scene as people formed libraries to exchange imported magazines and novels; another effect was to provide that most important aspect of fandom—something to bitch about. Fanzines produced by clubs provided news and contents listings of overseas magazines. I think it was similar to the situation in Perth in the 1990s where a number of pirate science fiction video screening clubs existed to give access to television sf years ahead of the TV networks. The trade restrictions meant *Thrills Incorporated* could publish knowing it would be cheaper and more easily available than superior overseas magazines.

The unsophisticated content can also be partly explained by the target audience. Graham Stone pointed out to me that *Thrills Incorporated* was a mass market title with a distribution of about 800 copies in New South Wales alone. Sales relied not on science fiction fandom but on casual buyers at newsagencies and street vendors[33] who were as likely to pick up a lightweight western or detective pulp.

I have often been asked how much writers were paid for their work. Alan Yates states that at that time he was paid one pound per 1000 words published, including worldwide rights. To put

30. Coupe, S. (February 1996) "Pulp Friction," *Mean Streets*, 16,.34-39.

31. Molesworth, L. (April 1953) [Editorial],*Vertical Horizons*, 1, 1-2.

32. Stone, G. B. (March/April 1952) op. cit.

33. Stone, G. B. (2001) [Correspondence to author dated 14th Nov. 2001].

that into context, Yates in his day job as an editor for the Qantas in-flight magazine earned just under £16 per week (£825 p.a.). A pulp novella written in his spare time earned an extra £20.[34] Norma Hemming in an essay indicates that she was an office worker, so the £3 from each 3,000-word *Thrills Incorporated* story was probably a nice top-up to income but hardly enough to allow her to turn professional.[35]

Early 1952 saw the easing of restrictions on directly imported science fiction. Fans now had access to overseas magazines to compare to the local product—and the local product was found wanting. By June *Thrills Incorporated* died, unmourned, but— like so many of the monsters from within its pages—it rose from the dead in the form of a general adventure magazine, *Action Monthly Magazine,* and a misguided attempt to export bad Australian science fiction to Britain called *Amazing Science Stories.* I can only assume that it was called *Amazing Science Stories* because the title *Amazingly Dated Stories* was already taken. Having missed the mad scientist/rampaging monster period in science fiction by twenty years, it folded after two issues. Hemming had at least one story published in *Action Monthly Magazine* that we know of. The continuing decrease in trade restrictions until their abolition in 1958 eventually stifled local science fiction publication.

Hemming's first post-*Thrills Incorporated* story appeared in a semi-prozine called *Forerunner* (not to be confused with similarly titled later fanzines) which wanted to publish local fiction of better quality than *Thrills Incorporated.* It only ran for two issues in 1952-53, of which only the first was widely distributed. Hemming's contribution to the first issue was "Starchild," possibly her longest work. This story of a boy developing psychic powers in a repressive post-nuclear society reminded me a great deal of John Wyndham's *The Chrysalids*, published three years

34. Yates, A. G. (1980) op. cit., 27, 31.

35. Hemming, N. K. (Oct. 1953) *op. cit.*

later. It contains many original ideas, such as the boy being able to communicate with a mental imprint of his dead mother. It also contains a familiar flaw in Hemming's work—that of telling rather than showing the reader. For example, we are told that the society is dominated by an oppressive cult, but this is obvious already from events in the story. A narrative Greek chorus probably is a hangover from the *Thrills Incorporated* style where it was necessary in setting up a plot in less than 3000 words. However the plot of "Starchild," dealing with sexual abuse by the cult, torture, and alien breeding experiments, is aimed at a more mature readership than *Thrills Incorporated*. It does mark a progression in the quality of Hemming's work.

For a short period the competition from imports did seem to stimulate the quality of local writing. Sister publications *Future Science Fiction* and *Popular Science Fiction* mixed local and imported stories and included local science fiction news and reviews. The editor seems to have been more knowledgeable regarding the genre and the stories were not illustration-driven. In March 1953, Hemming's "Symbiosis" was published in *Popular Science Fiction* (1), in which a super-intelligent but microscopic crystalline alien from a destroyed planet searches for a host to form a symbiotic relationship with. After an initial aborted attempt with one man, the alien—Muron—bonds with a poor urban boy, Andy, aged ten. Muron begins to communicate with Andy and to increase his intelligence. Andy's fear as he becomes more intelligent is well presented, but the story lacks any suspense. Muron's motives are never questioned and the increasing gap between Andy and the rest of humanity is only hinted at. It is as if Hemming simply wanted to do something, anything, that was the opposite of a *Thrills Incorporated* tale. In this fairy tale in modern guise Muron might as well have been a genie.[36]

A much better story was the 1954 "As We Were" in *Future Science Fiction* (5). While less a character piece than

36. McMullen, S. and Blackford, R. (Spring 1998) *op. cit.* 65-75.

"Symbiosis," it has tension in spades, pacing, and some good twists. The story starts with a great hook: an intelligence, possibly a computer, lies deep under an island. When people migrate to the island by boat and start to build, the intelligence starts to affect them, although we are not shown how or even when this occurs. Upon seeing these undescribed changes, the entire population of the island commits suicide. And that's page one!

Jumping forward to the twentieth century, a group of explorers, husband and wife (Mike and Carolyn) and her sister Jan, come to explore the ruins. Hemming creates a great deal of foreboding as the ruins are explored, ending in finding a tunnel to a crypt. Their presence in the crypt activates the computer, then an alien in hibernation, Kralin of the Garan-Doy. Kralin ominously tells them that he is from a race that colonized earth in primordial times before a space storm killed everyone else. Humans are a degenerate mutation of a planned replacement species. He states: "From you I have learned that yours is an incomplete race. It must go back to that from which it came. The Garan-Doy will return to earth." Kralin affects the memory of the explorers so that they have no recollection of their encounter. However, soon after their return home Mike begins to become violent and to have physical changes. After a frightening attack on Carolyn he is placed in an asylum. It becomes apparent that he is devolving. While having no memory of Kralin, Jan and Carolyn are certain the island has something to do with this. Jan returns to investigate while Carolyn, too, starts to devolve. At the end of the story, everyone ends up back on the island and Neanderthal Mike and Carolyn start to re-evolve as Garan-Doy. Jan is the last human left on the island and she cannot stop Kralin and the other Garan-Doy from erasing humanity every-where. In a final paragraph reminiscent of *Invasion of the Body Snatchers*, she cannot stop herself from falling asleep, knowing she will wake up alien. While problems remain with dialogue and narrative style, Hemming had improved to a stage where she was ready to return to international publishing.

I think *Happy Days* and *American Graffiti* have forever poisoned many people's ideas of social changes in the 1950s. People did not turn on the radio one day, hear Bill Haley sing "Rock around the Clock," and think to themselves "I must cast aside my conservative values." Sydney science fiction fans, while enjoying a non-mainstream genre, had conservatives and liberals like the rest of society. As mentioned earlier, Hemming revealed her identity and gender at the first Australian Science Fiction convention in 1952. At that time women could not be members of some science fiction clubs, only guests. Shortly after the convention, Rosemary Simmons attempted to join the Futurian Society of Sydney, a science fiction club that still exists today. After very acrimonious debate she succeeded on the third attempt, with Hemming being the second woman to gain membership. Simmons and Hemming, along with other women in the Sydney science fiction scene, went on to form the Vertical Horizons Femme Fan group with a fanzine of the same name— which I think are the first women's group and newsletter of its type in Australia.[37] Anyone who reads this newsletter (1952-53) will be struck by the passion with which these women wrote about their favorite genre compared with the contents of other fanzines.

Hemming was also involved in the social side of fandom, costume designing for convention fancy dress, a topic that would be the basis for one of her stories, and helping form a science fiction theatrical group, the Acturian Players, for whom she wrote and performed. She wrote several plays for both fandom and the general public but the script for only one exists today, *The Matriarchy of Renok*. This is a parody of the Amazon planet and the "teach me about this earth thing called kissing" clichés of pulp science fiction. Written in 1956 and performed in 1958 at the Melbourne Science Fiction Convention, the plot

---

37. Molesworth, V. (Jan. 1985) "A History of Australian Fandom 1935-1963: Chapter Four," *The Mentor* 85, 17-23.

involves an egotistical, sexist astronaut named Carter (but think Kirk) who lands on Renok, a female chauvinistic matriarchal society. He is taken prisoner and is dismayed to find males and sex are redundant due to a new incubation process. Men are just going to be left to die out. He escapes, taking Queen Vanaris, played by Hemming, hostage. However the matriarchy scientists are smarter than Carter and when he lands he finds he is on what is now matriarchal Earth. The play ends with Carter being dragged off stage by female guards screaming "YOU CAN'T WIN!" Very tongue in cheek: it would probably get as big a laugh today at a convention.

While Hemming continued to write more plays for local production, her next three short stories were published overseas. The interesting aspect of this period is that polling by the magazines gives us some idea of what contemporary readers thought about Hemming's work. "Dwellers in Silence," published in *New Worlds* (51) in 1956, starts with an alien baby as sole survivor of a spacecraft crash. The child is raised as "human" by a bachelor farmer, who names her Carol. Carol's telepathic abilities are so strong she cannot help but overhear the thoughts of everyone around her. After the death of her adoptive father she is sent to an orphanage, then to work in an office which she finds a living hell mainly due to the sexual thoughts of men. Eventually she accidentally makes contact with her race, mutant telepaths who use the distance of space to shield themselves from the thoughts of others. While I think the perfunctory ending weakens the story, the use of telepathy and office sexual harassment as horror is original and effective. Also, I think most readers would suspect this was written by a woman even if they didn't know who N.K. Hemming was. The story rated third out of six stories in the readers poll.

There is then a gap of almost two years until "The Debt of Lassor" appeared in a 1958 issue of *Nebula* (33). Alien tyrants have ruled Earth for thousands of years after an apocalyptic war which has laid waste to the planet, but this story is not about a slave revolt, quite the opposite. Humans are mindless, nameless, numbered slaves with no concept of individuality and freedom, while the aliens have matured from their brutal past and wish to free humanity. The question being, how to free someone who has no concept of freedom? The alien in charge of liberating Earth, Thorval, starts a two-pronged plan of instilling individuality in humans by giving them names and treating them with physical and emotional abuse so that they will hate as well as fear their masters. Soon the humans break their conditioning and start to realize what freedom would mean. Thorval can now plan to hand back Earth. This unusual angle to the old Earth revolts story went down well, with readers rating it second out of the six stories.

"Call Them Earthmen," published in October 1959 in *Science Fiction Adventures* (Vol. 2, 10), is set in the distant future where Earth is losing a war with a vicious alien race known as the Hamadans. The only hope may be in an ancient citadel which may contain weapons from a long ago terrible war with another alien invader. Finally the long-lost citadel is located and opened, but only seems to contain an alien in suspended animation. He is woken and to everyone's amazement states that he, Grant Bendal, is human and that the entire population of earth is alien. The super weapon that had been used in the last war was a kind of memory eraser. When fired for the first time the backwash killed all humanity except Bendal, who was in the citadel. The aliens invading the planet were reduced to the intelligence of cavemen and had re-evolved in the ruins of Earth assuming they were the humans. Bendal still hates the aliens due to the actions of their ancestors. However, Bendal eventually gives the aliens the technology to defend Earth when he hears the Earth alien soldiers refer to the planet as home. Despite a few narrative flaws towards the end, it is a well written story.

A few months after that issue would have arrived in Australia, Norma Hemming died of lung cancer at the age of thirty-two. Her career lasted less than ten years and produced only seventeen professional works.

§

The article "Prophet and Pioneer: The SF of N.K. Hemming" (1998) by Sean McMullen and Russell Blackford suggests that Hemming's favorite motif is the contact between human and alien. While this contact motif is present, so is an underlying darkness to her stories. Repeatedly we find stories that are apocalyptic or near-apocalyptic, involving the annihilation of a race or the annihilation of self through suicide. The majority of Hemming's work was written in a ten year period that was in the shadow of Hiroshima. This was a time when the risk of the Cold War turning hot seemed very real in a country whose paranoia about a "yellow peril" was interchangeable with one about a "red menace." We can laugh now at the idea of "domino theory" and monolithic communism, but along with the risk of global annihilation they seemed very real at the time. The 1950s were not Happy Days but scary days. A large portion of speculative fiction is taken up with what can be termed "horror for the rational," where our fears are played out at a distance, in the future or on another planet, but close enough for us to have some kind of catharsis. Hemming's apocalyptic futures reflected a 1950s' fear. Sean McMullen reflected on Hemming:

> There are a couple of really big ifs raised by all this: if she had gone over to a couple of American cons and met some publishers and if she had a chest x-ray in the mid 1950s, Hemming could have gained the stature that Le Guin or McCaffrey have today. Even as it is, her four or five plays made history. Add the surviving play to her collected short stories and there would be enough for a book. Probably what has prevented Hemming from gaining wider recognition is the fact she never had a standalone book published and she never

had a story in an anthology. Being published only in magazines is a first class ticket to obscurity.[38]

Norma Hemming achieved a number of firsts—first Australian female career science fiction writer, first Australian science fiction playwright—but it was only at the end of her career that she reached her potential. Only with the return to overseas publication did she overcome problems in dialogue and narrative structure which a sympathetic editor would have ironed out years before. Norma Hemming's greatest talent as a science fiction writer was that she always surprised the reader. Whether it was a gas alien, a tragic suicide, or a reformed alien despot, the reader could always say "I didn't expect that!" and to me that is what makes her work interesting.

§

Credit where it is due. Sean McMullen and Russell Blackford's research in "Prophet and Pioneer: The SF of N. K. Hemming" in *Fantasy Annual* 2 (Spring 1998) remains the quintessential source on Norma Hemming and was a template for my own research. Sean McMullen was kind enough to take time from his busy schedule to provide invaluable photocopies, tapes and opinions. He also put me in touch with Graham Stone who gave me the benefit of his first-hand experience of the Sydney science fiction scene in the 1950s. My sincere thanks.

---

38. McMullen, S. (2001) [Correspondence to the author dated 22 Aug. 2001].

DIASPORA, BY GREG EGAN

by Russell Blackford
[1997]

In the late centuries of the third millennium, the Solar System is inhabited by three kinds of intelligences, reflecting decisions made and philosophies adopted by different humans long in the past. First are the remaining "fleshers," who are embodied, as the name suggests, in the flesh—although almost all have become transhuman, genetically-altered "exuberants," some of them avian or amphibian in form. Some have genetically engineered out their speech facilities, becoming "dream apes," though such removal of capacities, rather than development of new ones, is a rare exception. Others are familiarly human in appearance and gross behaviors, but have been engineered with extraordinary neural structures for handling new concepts, perceptions, communicative possibilities.

Secondly, there are gleisner robots, or just "gleisners," which are conscious software beings embodied in human-shaped robotic hardware. Then there are the "citizens" of the "polises." These are beings of pure software running within virtual-reality communities maintained by well-protected supercomputers; the word "polis" refers to both a community of citizens and the physically secure hardware that sustains the software infrastructure for its shared reality.

The original polis citizens were uploaded human beings who entered their virtual environments in the late 21st century; this mass exodus into virtual reality is recalled, appropriately, as "the Introdus," and the word gives a name to "Introdus nano-ware," still available for uploading fleshers, initially into the form of crystalline "snapshots" of neural properties. Egan uses a system of gender-neutral pronouns for those characters who are, themselves, ungendered, which includes all the citizens of Konishi polis. Within this system, "ve" is used for "he" or "she," "vis" for the possessive "his" or "her," "ver" for the accusative "him" or "her" (and hence the word "verself"). Not all polis citizens are ungendered, however, since some polises have different attitudes to ancestral forms and behaviors and to the physical world; their citizens take on the virtual equivalent of sexual characteristics, though not necessarily of human form. The gleisners have apparently chosen to maintain gendered forms, though it is not clear (at least to me) whether any of them appear as physically female.

This posthuman setting, described with some inaccuracy on the UK Millennium-Orion edition's back cover, is a thoroughly worked out version of how the various possibilities for altering the human species might collapse into a reasonably stable logical conclusion. In itself, that would have been a considerable achievement, but it is only a starting point for Egan, who asks what might happen after such a point is reached in future history, and tells a story that takes his main characters, over a period of additional millennia, beyond the local Solar System to the stars—and, beyond that, into higher geometries of reality. The story is framed by a dialogue between two software characters, Yatima and Paolo, discussing how they will explain themselves to the godlike Transmuters, beings whom they have pursued through reality level after reality level, while most of the book, seen from this frame, is a flashback, tracing Yatima's story step by step.

It begins with Yatima's creation within Konishi polis and vis subsequent individuation as a self-aware consciousness. The opening chapter has to be read slowly, which will put off many readers, but it is something of a tour de force, as it portrays the process by which a polis citizen is seeded from the digital genome (the "mind seed") used in the polis, brought into existence, then nurtured into self-awareness by the resources of the polis and through interaction with other citizens. The infrastructure of a polis and the modular construction of a software citizen are worked out in fascinating detail that calls upon Egan's extensive knowledge of cognitive science and philosophy of mind. This chapter provides the digital equivalent of a baby's-eye view of its initial interactions with adults and older children, leading to its discovery of itself as an "I".

At the same time, Egan's account of Yatima as a rare "orphan" in Konishi polis pays homage to a well-known equivalent in Arthur C. Clarke's early writing, perhaps also stating a claim of successorship to Clarke's mantle of authority. Yatima is an orphan in the sense that ve has been shaped from the infrastructure fields (one might roughly say "citizen nature") and trait fields (personal nature) of the mind seed, without the contribution of specific parents to vis characteristics. This is clearly analogous to the position of Alvin, the main character in Clarke's *The City and the Stars*. Alvin's trajectory in life is shaped by his being a rare Unique created within the city of Diaspar (compare "Diaspora"), his personal characteristics created for the first time, rather than recreated from a previous human template by the city's matter organizers, which use information on the billions of humans stored in Diaspar's memory units.

Yatima's life unfolds through a series of episodes and developments that gradually take on overall meaning and structure (or a succession of such meanings and structures), through the book's eight formal parts, which are largely self-contained as well as being framed and interlinked.

Part One consists of three chapters describing Yatima's early personal development—vis birth and individuation in chapter one (as discussed above), vis interest in the "truth mines" of mathematical study in chapter two, and vis first encounter with the physical world of the fleshers in chapter three, at the initiative of vis friend, a restless and childlike citizen called Inoshiro.

In these early chapters, we gain a sense of various important characters, citizen and flesher, refracted through Yatima's own relatively undeveloped consciousness. Egan succeeds in some quite subtle characterization of the disembodied software beings who make up the community of Konishi polis, and their more fateful decisions as the story unfolds are believable results of their personalities exposed to the experiences that they undergo. There is a limit to how far our interest can be kept in the experiences of beings greatly different from ourselves, without taking away the sense of them as truly alien, but Egan is able to sustain a focus on the non-human attributes of his characters, making us understand their often strange reactions, while keeping our interest in their problems.

The action becomes far more dramatic and suspenseful in Part Two. On the Moon, Karpal, a gleisner obsessed with the study of astrophysics in solitude, discovers the beginning of a sudden decay in the mutual orbits of two neutron stars one hundred light years distant from Earth. The twin stars of Lacerta G-1 are about to collide. More precisely, they were about to do so at the time they emitted the gravitational waves now reaching the Solar System, and which Karpal uses to make his observations. It comes to the same thing, for the point is that this collision one hundred years beforehand will have released a powerful gamma-ray burst, due to strike in only four days—so Karpal calculates—and with such intensity as to destroy immediately the ozone layer over half the Earth, creating devastating storms, and shattering the balance of the entire biosphere. Once the implications are spelt out, and it becomes starkly apparent that the vulnerable fleshers, in particular, are confronted by imminent global cataclysm, this part of the book moves swiftly, with spectacular effects and moments of poignancy.

In the aftermath of Lacerta, and stirred by a new sense of their vulnerability in an unpredictable cosmos, the gleisners and the citizens of Carter-Zimmerman polis commence separate programs of interstellar space exploration. At this stage, Yatima migrates from Konishi polis to Carter-Zimmerman polis, and a vast odyssey of discovery begins. Egan engages in the creation of a detailed and plausible-seeming unified theory of physics, "Kozuch Theory," which conceives of elementary particles as the mouths of wormholes with differing topologies, existing in a multi-dimensional space whose geometric properties underlie both general relativity and quantum uncertainty. It turns out that this theoretical description of the physical Universe requires further correction and elaboration, and the remainder of the book works with the implications of this.

As the focal characters move out from Earth, they encounter strange aliens on the planet Orpheus, then the distinctive signs of alien intelligence left behind on Swift, a planet in another star system, where spectral analysis shows that the main atmospheric elements have been deliberately transmuted. On Swift, hydrogen, carbon, nitrogen, oxygen, and sulfur appear only in the form of heavy, stable isotopes; common isotopes such as carbon-12 and oxygen-16 simply do not exist. Following clues left behind by the Transmuters, Yatima finds vis way beyond the familiar geometry of four-dimensional Einsteinian space-time, leading into an increasingly rich vision of the underlying geometry of physical nature. In the process, the book grapples with questions about extraterrestrial contact, the importance (or otherwise) of connection with physical reality if posthuman technologies are available, and the morality of exponential growth and cosmic engineering.

I have attempted to describe the direction of the narrative without giving away the details that resolve *Diaspora*'s various crises and its overall plot development. Clearly this is an extremely ambitious novel. It is also a difficult one. The book has an austerity which resides in the fact that its author is only too willing to write difficult technical accounts of such matters as the operations of polises and citizens, as well as of the physics and geometry of his universe. Much of Egan's work— and this is an excellent example—can be read easily only if the reader possesses considerable mastery of the hard sciences, mathematics, and several branches of contemporary philosophy, especially philosophy of mind. At times, *Diaspora*'s plot is enlivened by danger and suspense, or by emotional tension among the characters—and the reading pace increases considerably—but when difficult concepts are explained, relating to the posthuman nature of the late third-millennium world, real work is involved in understanding this book.

I suspect that Egan will not take pleasure in the comparison, but I was reminded of Samuel R. Delany's defense, in his written interview with Kenneth James, of the careful, considered pacing of Lévi-Strauss's prose—and that of many other structuralist and poststructuralist writers (see Delany's *Silent Interviews*: Wesleyan University Press, 1994). Delany describes the rewards obtainable from reading work that contains a kind of "phenomenal retardation," whereby a description can take longer to read than the equivalent real-time event to happen. There is a necessary element of phenomenal retardation in much of *Diaspora*, anyway, since the time-sense of the main characters is eight hundred times faster than ours, but techniques to convey this are not really a feature of the book. Rather than that, even with the pace of events quietly adjusted to match our own time sense, Egan is often forced to interweave his descriptions with technical explanations to make us understand what is really going on. This technique is handled deftly enough, without quite becoming outright exposition, and certainly without the various clumsy substitutes for it such as characters who preface dumb questions with "Tell me, Professor...." When characters explain difficult concepts to each other, this is justified in terms of the narrative and their respective levels of knowledge, rather than being a transparent sop to the reader; when the ideas are difficult, then, Egan's pacing is slow, but his technique is never clumsy.

In an initial draft of this review I accused Egan of being uncompromising in the demands he makes on his readers. On reflection, that is not true, for he always writes with great clarity, at pains to make the concepts understandable. As a result, I expect that an intelligent and patient reader with no particular specialist background could work out all but the most technical parts of *Diaspora*—though not easily. Nonetheless, there is a sense that the author is determined, come hell or high water, to force us to grapple with concepts and theories from the fields that inform his thinking, and the result is a somewhat odd reading experience.

For me, the greatest amount of work—and so the greatest problem with the pacing—occurred in passages that invited me to follow explanations of concepts in mathematical topology and similar fields. I suspect the author has underestimated the difficulty of much of his writing for readers who are not professionally educated in math. Egan is a mathematician, and one of the morals of the book is the rather Platonic or Pythagorean one that a being which has truly transcended reality will find eternal pleasure in unfolding the mathematical basis of nature. For most of us, such a proposition goes against the grain. I am reasonably numerate, with a moderate interest in mathematical concepts, but that is the most I'd assert, and I often found myself in real difficulty. Other readers may have less of a problem here, but greater problems with other aspects, and this may tempt them to skate over considerable tracts, treating them as technical mumbo-jumbo. Yet, to indulge in too much of this will be to miss many of the book's rewards.

And *Diaspora* really *is* rewarding. It will delight most of Egan's existing fans, many of whom I expect must have at least some of the technical background required to make a book like this easier to read. As I've said, Egan writes clearly, with his usual rigor in working out scenarios, a fine sense of narrative structure, and an adroit approach to problems of characterization. Once granted the right to deal with difficult concepts, he shows no self-indulgence. Comparisons will inevitably be made between *Diaspora* and the other very ambitious Australian sf novel of 1997, Damien Broderick's *The White Abacus*, which also depicts a transhuman/posthuman scenario with ungendered characters and a system of appropriate pronouns for them. Stylistically, Broderick's novel is more flamboyant, but

Diaspora is more coherent and convincing.

Where I am left with a problem is that Egan appears to embrace somewhat uncritically a posthuman concept of personal identity, whereby characters can be uploaded (and, it is suggested, downloaded), copied, modified, split, or merged—all with no sense of philosophical or moral controversy, though references are made to the problem of defining what is constant about identity. At times, superfluous copies of the software-based characters are simply erased, with little sense of compunction at the destruction of a separate intelligent being, as long as another being with (in a sense) the same identity lives on. It would be wrong to accuse Egan of not having thought the issues through, and they have been a mainstay of his fiction for years now, but I find a misplaced confidence in the answers he seems to have reached. Perhaps that is not a legitimate criticism of *Diaspora* as a literary work, but Egan's fiction invites us to take it seriously as a body of philosophical thought experiments, and perhaps it is legitimate to engage with his latest novel on such a level.

Be that as it may, *Diaspora* is exciting work which should enhance Greg Egan's reputation. For my money, it is the most important genre novel of its year to be published by an Australian, and evidence that Egan is determined to go on exceeding the scope of his previous efforts with each new publication.

Work Discussed

Greg Egan, *Diaspora*. London: Gollancz, 1997.

"THE DISQUIETING TERRAIN OF THE SPIRIT"

GERALD MURNANE'S *THE PLAINS*

by Yvonne Rousseau
[1983]

I

The epigraph to *The Plains* is Major Mitchell's response, in 1836, to the Western District plains of Victoria: "We had at length discovered a country ready for the immediate reception of civilized men..."

In Gerald Murnane's novel, the Major's fanciful notion has been fulfilled, subverting the commonplace image of an Australian population that huddles together in eastern coastal cities, demoralized by the giant specter of an almost uninhabited interior. Instead, the "interior" of *The Plains* has nurtured a civilization which is consciously distinct both from the Australian coastal-city culture and from Old World or American models. Australia's populous (and barbarous) cities are scorned by the plainsmen as "Outer Australia"—"the sterile margins of the continent" (25)—and a second Australian commonplace, the influence of landscape on human sensibility, is transformed by its application to a landscape considered not hostile or indifferent, but receptive, to civilization.

As one scholar expresses it:

Anyone surrounded from childhood by an abundance of level land must dream alternately of exploring two landscapes—one continually visible but never accessible and the other always invisible even though one crossed and recrossed it daily. (38)

The plainsmen are disposed to philosophical speculation—upon Time and mutability, and upon those invisible plains which are "the disquieting terrain of the spirit." A flourishing publishing house of the plains is devoted to "remembrances of the misremembered"—whose worth is "enhanced, rather than diminished, by being inexplicable to others." The "vindicators of the evanescent" or "philosophers of the lost" comprise a widely read school of moral philosophy; their subject matter, in the Other Australia, would be thought proper to novels (but to novels very unlikely to secure any readership).

The peculiar spirit of plains-philosophy can be appreciated, however, only if the external aspects of the culture are also appreciated. It is a culture in which women are to be seen and not heard (and not sun-tanned); where wine is disliked, but there is heavy indulgence in spirits and in beer (of which nine varieties are brewed on the plains). Polo is the traditional game, and the great landowners have polo fields and pavilions as well as tennis courts. Their huge mansions (all with several wings, extensive libraries, and shaded verandahs) may have "porticos and courtyards," "pillars and pavements and pools," in addition to their halls and galleries, their conservatories and aviaries. The landowners devote enormous attention to the refinement of their own heraldic emblems, which are incorporated into tapestries, leaded windows, the settings of jewels; liveries and racing colors are similar modes of display.

Social events include quail-shooting weekends and woolshed balls, but also more intellectual gatherings (going by different names, and held at different intervals, in different houses), where the "salaried clients" attached to the household may be expected to present, before visitors, their most recent variations upon "the endlessly variable theme" of the plains. These "salaried clients" may be either artists (of any kind) or founders of religions; they will live at the great house which employs them, receiving a more-or-less generous stipend in addition to the payment of all their expenses, and sometimes with lifetime tenure. Plainsmen compete vigorously for such employment; and the narrator of *The Plains* is an Outer Australian who poses as a plainsman in order to be admitted, as a film-maker, to one of the great houses, where he will capture and disclose, on film, a vision of the plains as he, alone, is capable of perceiving them.

Readers will be aware (although the novel nowhere mentions it) that in Outer Australia the film is popularly thought to be an excellent method of representing the most distinctive characteristics of the country. Plainsmen, however, are as contemptuous as D. H. Lawrence of the belief that film can supply a "visible equivalent" of reality (as if the plains "were mere surfaces reflecting sunlight"!) (61). Nevertheless, one of the land-owners employs the narrator, who then moves on, as the years pass, to a second and then a third person, each change taking him to a more remote section of the plains.

II

The observations of the nameless narrator convey to the reader the only information available for assessing the plains (in whose existence, on external evidence, readers are likely to disbelieve); and the narrator himself is an outsider who only poses as "belonging," and who also (at first) frequently poses for himself as a man who is being observed, and wondered about, by the audience of a film like the one that he is planning. His approach is the alienated one of a child or an anthropologist.

When *The Plains* is coupled with Murnane's first novel, *Tamarisk Row* (Heinemann Australia, Melbourne, 1974; and Angus and Robertson, Sydney, 1977), the effect is of an exercise in "remembrance of the misremembered"—the genre so esteemed upon the plains:

the comparative study of scenes recalled by one observer alone and accounts of these same scenes by
the same observer after he had acquired the skill to
attempt a fitting description of them. (81)

The observer here is Clement Killeaton, the boy who, in
Tamarisk Row, invests with glamour not only the unrewarding
"bookies" whom his father romanticizes, but also Con McCor-
mack, the Western District grazier, in whom (at their only meeting) he confides the secrets of the miniature world of roads and
farms that he has laid out in the Killeaton backyard (*Tamarisk
Row*, 110-111). The landowners of *The Plains* dress as Con Mc-
Cormack might do, wearing suits and ties in the hottest weather,
and, in at least one case, oxblood-red lace-up shoes (elaborately
patterned in punched dots) with "massive leather soles." To the
narrator's eye, these men possess "sureness and elegance" (47).

The boy Clement's vision is "misremembered" because it
does not correspond with the reality that people around him
would agree upon; in the manner of childhood (which *Tamarisk
Row* quite startlingly evokes), he wonders about other people,
without having the means to communicate his conjectures, or
rectify his conclusions; he attributes interests—he imagines
contexts—which are utterly foreign to them. The grownup
Clement would perceive a different mystery in the boy's "far
glittering landscapes" and "plains far ahead": the mystery of
men with the outward habits and dress of the landowners, who
nevertheless devote the cares of a lifetime to the emblematic
arrangement of colors and shapes, by which they hope to interpret their lives; thus sharing the boy Clement's obsession with
color and shape—whereby the subtle irregularities of his rosary
beads challenge him to imagine hidden "glories" and inward
"mysteries."

Tamarisk Row does not dwell upon philosophic graziers, but
upon the boy Clement's glamorization of other unlikely material, to produce other beguilingly unexpected conjunctions. The
plains he imagines are not detailed; the most explicit instance of

transmuted remembrance is the case of a small marsupial which early settlers called a hare, and which they exterminated with little trouble or thought. From this information, the boy Clement conjures up a legendary Hareboy, who "tries to live like a hare in the sparse grass on the hard dry hills" (*Tamarisk Row*, 29), and whom other boys wish they could read stories about. In *The Plains*, the same "hare" has inspired among adults an influential and seminal movement—the Haremen —whose founder wishes to "recover the promise, the mystery even, of the plains as they might have appeared to someone with no other refuge" (29).

The mystery of the strange conjunctions in the two books (like the polo-playing graziers who profoundly commit them-selves as either Haremen or Horizonites) is in fact the mystery of the boy Clement's nature, as he projects his imagination upon a world which supposedly presents itself in similar terms to himself and to those around him. It is a mystery likely to prove insoluble, even in adult "remembrance."

The boy's vision (like the narrator's in *The Plains*) is what "he and no other could have seen": his imagined world is lacking from the world of adult consensus, where there also lacks (in general) a value for any intellectual life which cannot be made to seem common—so that Clement's private view is "useless," even to himself, except as evidence of childish maladjustment to reality. Philosophers of the plains take the opposite view, and one of their painters expresses an extreme position:

> The only merit of so-called real lands, he said, was that people of dulled sensibility could find their way about in them by agreeing to perceive no more than did others of their kind. (66)

The plains, as I see them, are the kind of world that forms in the boy Clement's imagination before he is capable of obtaining enough data to verify its non-existence; and the inhabitants of *The Plains* (with an adult presentation) are preoccupied with the exploration and justification of the kind of imagination in which Clement has indulged for their creation.

III

Certain Australian writers, of Murnane's generation, reveal in their work the effect of having grown up amid what Upton Sinclair (writing of the American experience) defines as "the horde"—"a being with a personality of its own"—one of whose characteristics "is that it does not allow you to be different; it persecutes those who do not conform to its ideas and obey its taboos" (*World's End,* T. Werner Laurie Ltd., London, 1940, 351-2). The Australian version of the horde is (or was) particularly strident in its insistence that there is only one right way of "seeing" things; and particularly diligent in its attempts to scrape off, from its fellows, any nonsensical accretions appearing upon the horde-worldview (which is obviously there, somewhere underneath the nonsense, since it is the only worldview possible). Refugees from such childhoods sometimes retain the sense that their difference is illegitimate; their personalities—as reflected in their writings—may even seem (to a slightly gothic eye) fragmented by a phantom horde-standard which thrusts itself up at the very center of their being, where it can never be assimilated, since for them it is only its forbidding walls—it was never native to their sensibility. (As a result, they can appear most wretchedly self-conscious.)

For such a writer, *The Plains* would obviously be a splendid vehicle for satire and revenge. The landowner-thinkers of *The Plains*, who are largely silent but who muse profoundly, could certainly be used to mock inadequacies in their outwardly similar counterparts in the Other Australia; experience teaches us that strong and silent people (of either sex), when they finally do speak, are all too likely to make one wince with some extraordinarily simple diagnosis of what is wrong with the world (or even one's digestion), and some equally stark scheme for putting it right again. The philosophical graziers could thus represent the ludicrous-overestimate method of revenge-upon-pretension. A simpler method of attack would be the plainsmen's dismissal of Australian city-culture as self-evidently contemptible.

My own impression is that Murnane feels no compulsion to be savage in this manner; to plainsmen, the barbarisms of our cities are, after all, only "seeming barbarisms"; and no plains philosopher ("bizarre" though some of their speculations are) has ever

> seriously entertained the possibility that the state of a man at some moment in his life may be illuminated by a study of the same man at some moment said, for convenience, to have preceded the moment in question. (85)

Thus, for them there is no possibility of being the "victim" of a horde-mentality; no need for one's adult ironies to be vengeful.

The ironies which do pervade the book include one which is referable to the sense of an Australian horde: the way in which the non-existent plains highlight the Australian reader's disbelief in any civilized "interior" at the heart of the country's "spiritual geography." Ken Stewart (in *Australian Book Review,* 47, December 1982, 24) has written that this is a part of Australia's "false 'common wisdom'"—for example:

> the mistaken impression that the history of Australian literary culture is a journey from one intellectual oasis to another, each one sheltering a separate literary tribe... which disdainfully looks out upon a vast but specifically Australia-shaped cultural desert.

The narrator of *The Plains* seems subliminally influenced by this "false 'common wisdom'," for his viewpoint is abnormally imbued with the sense of absences: if he sees more distinctly than usual, the cause is probably "the lack of something in the sunlight" (73); to wear a barbarous red cravat is "to avoid... the proper gesture" (17).

Other lacks and absences of the plains are characteristic of plains of the imagination, and of the childhood-dreamer's emotional atmosphere. Thus there are no mothers in the landowners' great mansions, but only wives and daughters (as limitlessly ideal as the queens and princesses of fairytale); and, although the landowners remember their fathers and grandfathers, we never hear of their sons. (Many outrageous remarks about the Australian masculine psyche could be made to follow from these absences; let other pens dwell on them.) There are no Aboriginal inhabitants of the plains, and no World Wars or any other violent irruption of circumstances to agitate the emotions.

IV

The narrator, having arrived at the plains, will avoid the imaginative error of childhood, which is to build too ambitiously upon an absurdly limited basis of actual information; he is determined to understand exactly how the plainspeople perceive themselves, before he "explains himself" and reveals "an unheard-of vantage point." He also avoids the ridicule which a child can bring upon itself by its unselfconsciousness; no one could be more ridiculously aware than this adult is of the presence around him of potential observers. But he is as powerless as any child to verify his conjectures, because to do so would destroy the impression he hopes to create—of having always been "secure in his own view" (102). The libraries around him provide limitless information about the inner lives of the plainsmen; yet his failure in self-awareness (as opposed to his mere uninformative awareness that other people are aware of him) means that the more he reads, the further any certainty recedes from him. (This is only one, very limited, "meaning" of the philosophical problems that confront the narrator; in ignoring the fundamental bias of plains-thinkers towards "particularity" as opposed to shared certainties, it "falls short of a complete explanation" and, for that very reason, might be acclaimed by a secretive plainsman.)

At the outset, the narrator's ambition is to comprehend the plains by penetrating the mystery of the way they appear to a particular woman—by divining, at last, the most inner plains of her imagination, which will be the key to his film: "the landscape after her own heart" (71). This phase ends in a scene containing the germ of an awareness that the investigation of his own appearance in the young woman's imagination (his place upon her inner plains) could possibly become merged with his initial conception of his quest. He has arranged a dummy with a paper face to represent his own appearance in the library window, in order to decide whether the woman, standing and looking (a few moments earlier), has been seeing his actual face. Having decided that she really was watching him, he poises his pen over the smoothed-out papers which have represented not just his face but something deeply interior—his face as it might have appeared in that woman's perception. And then, as if common sense had taken over, he sweeps the papers to the floor and goes on, instead, with his "work."

In his second patron's house, the narrator's interest has insensibly shifted—to the decipherment of his own image in some woman's awareness. However, he draws back from an obscurely threatened "explanation" between himself and his patron's wife; and he comes to admit that the daughter, "whose image should have meant more than a thousand miles of plains," can contribute nothing, since she is dispiritingly "blind" to his reality (105).

The final section of *The Plains* finds him convinced that he will never produce his film (for which, to the admiration of plains-connoisseurs, he has not even written a script). Moreover, when he poses for photographs, aiming an empty camera, he is not merely acquiescing in his current patron's gnomish joke of photographing people in "some uncharacteristic gesture" or "as only rumor or raillery would have them" (118); his defeat is so final that he actually asks to be photographed as if about to expose the non-existent film in the camera, in order to falsely impress some young woman, inspecting the photograph in the future, with the idea that he "recognized the meaning of what he saw" (126)—so distorted now is his original dream either of comprehending some young woman, or of being accurately reflected back to himself by a woman's comprehension of him.

Different readers will find *The Plains* amusing in different degrees, according to their own proclivities and (hence) the degree of contrast that they perceive between the book's manner and its matter. For some, the whole subject matter will be rendered merely ridiculous by the spectacle of a narrator who enacts the bathetic fate of *Middlemarch*'s Mr. Casaubon—which is, perhaps, every scholar's or writer's most effective nightmare: the endless accumulation of notes and drafts, and an utter inability to produce the awaited Work. These readers will not sympathize with certain plains-philosophers who have awarded worth "to all lives that seemed to arrive at nothing" (96); or with the recluses (103) whose "aim is to say nothing and do nothing that can be described as an achievement" (resembling, perhaps, English Regency aristocrats).

There are parodies, on the plains, of ways of thought fashionable in Outer Australia; for example, earnest efforts at nonverbal communication (17, 73); or the project of arriving at a "formula" enabling one to exercise unerring good taste for the rest of time (24); or the conviction that the public mind would disintegrate if it were allowed to become aware of certain philosophical truths (37, 89).

As in Stephen Leacock's *Nonsense Novels*, the narrator's version of events will not always convey to the reader the impression that he intends—as when he is taking extraordinary liberties with some paintings done by his first patron's daughter (72-3), or when he recounts the details of the unspoken communication between himself and his second patron's wife. The narrator's apparently humorless disposition also betrays him into wit—for example, in his use of "boldly" when, speaking of the defenseless "plains-hare," he tells how "the early settlers had walked boldly up and clubbed hundreds of the creatures to death" (28). A similar effect is achieved by his excessive arrays of depreciation: "a few diehards hunched over acrid wines in back bars or haranguing casual acquaintances on opening nights in inferior art galleries" (31).

The narrative of *The Plains* may be viewed in many different contexts, producing different (and equally troubling) perspectives of the plains in relation to the narrator, to Outer Australia, and to the life of the mind. In providing a context for much that seems otherwise inexpressible (inexpressible, certainly, in this review), the book vindicates Murnane's earlier claim for fiction as "not the opposite of truth but a more complete expression of it"; and his belief in fiction's superiority over "straight facts" as a means of communicating genuine human experience" (*SF Commentary* 35/36/37, 1973, 51).

Work Discussed

Gerald Murnane, *The Plains*, Melbourne: Norstrilia Press, 1982; London, Penguin, 1984; New York, Braziller, 1985.

"SF WORLDS IN DARKNESS AND JOY"
AN INTERVIEW WITH TESS WILLIAMS

by Van Ikin and Helen Merrick
[2000]

Merrick: *How much writing had you done before* Map of Power *(published by Random/Arrow in 1996)? Was this your first attempt at sf?*

It wasn't exactly my first attempt and I took a rather winding road to *Map of Power*. I was always a literate person and I clearly had some facility with language. This led to me teaching writing skills at university and doing a variety of writing and editing jobs—from hack reviews in small literary mags that I didn't invest a great deal in to sensitive and socially useful information on children dying in hospitals which I'm still proud of. All terrific training, though at the time I didn't realize it—I just thought I was making a living of a very humble sort. Meanwhile there was this sort of psychological rumbling underneath these activities which was becoming louder—a discontent with writing that was done only to meet other people's needs and expectations. It finally became so loud that I knew I had to get serious and find out what it was that I needed to write for myself.

I was pretty shocked when the stuff that rolled off my pen was clearly embryonic sf. For some unknown reason I had assumed I would be a "literary" writer and my very experimental "other worldly" pieces took me completely by surprise. However, I was very open to what that rumbling demanded and I decided it was best to let it have its wicked way with me. I've never regretted that.

I think I did about eight short "practice pieces" before I plunged into the novel. Few of those early pieces survived intact. One became my first real short story, "The Padwan Affair," which was published in *She's Fantastical* about a year before *Map of Power* came out. It seems to be one of the profession's little ironies that often a writer has to write a novel before they can manage a good short story. Ray Bradbury said of this that he wrote a million words before he wrote a good story, then he wrote another million before he realized what had made it good.

Ikin: *To the public you've had a dream-run as author, with your first novel eagerly snatched up by a major publisher, Random House, and then marketed as their Arrow Books lead title for the month of release. But the glamour of success hides long, hard work, doesn't it?*

Oh yes. A committed writer needs to figure out why they write, who they wish to speak to, what it is they want to say and then, finally, they have to figure out how to say it effectively. This is the involved process of "finding voice." It can be both grueling and joyful, but it is always work. *Map of Power* took me a long time to write—three years of working blind. All in all, a huge commitment in emotion, time, money and energy—a commitment which necessarily had to be made from a position where I had no real idea of my own capacities as a writer or much hope that there would be any interest in my work when it was finished.

As far as publication is concerned, I consider myself extraordinarily lucky. I came along at a time when the larger presses were beginning to show an interest in genre markets in Australia. Pan Macmillan and Harper Collins had already taken the plunge and Random House were looking for an sf writer. I fitted their particular niche well, a sort of "highbrow" writer in a popular genre. And I have to say that *Map of Power* really did everything that a hopeful writer would want their first novel to do. It was marketed as a lead title, obtained some good reviews from people I respect, and sold quite well. Maybe that's what "dream runs" are made of—a combination of commitment, hard work and good luck.

Ikin: Map of Power *reflects your belief that a writer's decision to work in the field of "popular fiction" does not preclude that writer from dealing with serious issues. Can you outline these views, and how they were formed?*

As an sf reader I had not encountered the pulps until quite recently, and my reading had always led me to thinking of sf as an "ideas" genre. My teenage reading was largely the British school of sf—John Wyndham, H.G. Wells, George Orwell, Arthur C. Clarke and even C.S. Lewis. My genre experience then jumped to an odd combination of television *Star Trek* shows and feminist writings, both of which expressed positions on social and scientific issues of the day. They fascinated me, but I suspect I was not a typical adolescent sf fan in that, although I was reading anything I could get my hands on in the local library that struck my interest, sf formed only a part of my diet. Among other things I read at that time, and continue to read deeply, are psychology, myth, experimental literature, general science writing, space exploration, art and artists, drama, biographies and poetry. My tastes have always been eclectic, thus a wide range of interests nourish both my reading and my writing.

The key for me with the writing is that I don't write sf just from loving and reading sf. I write sf because I think it is an ideal genre through which to express all the interests and strange obsessions I have. To me my writing is always a synthesis of my art, politics, experience and passion, and while the genre is an ideal vehicle for cultural commentary (and I take full advantage of that!) it is also a very personal journey that I am taking which transfigures my life understandings and my questions into narratives that I can share with many other people. I know that there are those who would find this a curious way to approach genre writing, and something that runs contrary to its public perception as formulaic, but it works for me.

Ikin: *The critical reception for* Map of Power *was of the kind that other writers would die for. How did you find your first major experience of reviewers? Did they pick up on the themes and issues in the novel that were most important to you?*

Overall I have been satisfied with my reviews. Most of them were quite decent and fair in acknowledging that my writing was good and the characters were credible and strong. Intelligent reviewers also identified some of the political and psychological patterns of the book, such as feminism and the focus on the paradox of the powerful/powerless outsider. However, most of them failed to really come to grips with the book. I don't blame the reviewers for this at all, rather I would say that my writing is slippery and it presents some real difficulties when trying to situate it in the field.

This is a problem which is directly related to the bogie of labeling and I have to say that I've changed my position on this considerably since first being published. My first concern when I submitted *Map of Power* was that I would be ghettoized into science fiction and I really wanted some of the more literary qualities of the work to be appreciated. My rather naive idea was that the book should be read *as it is*. I've since discovered this doesn't really work. This is partly due to reader expectations, critical confusions and market pressures, but it is also to do with a responsibility I have to identify my own position when I present a text. This was much easier to do as an editor than as a writer and the anthology *Women of Other Worlds* taught me a lot about positioning a book in a niche market.

In that anthology, Helen and I were able to quickly get an overview of the work and pick up certain threads. When you are an editor you can and must also act as a critic with the work you are producing. This is a much more difficult process with your own work. Particularly if many of the themes and ideas of a complex work are themselves maturing through the writing process.

Now, after I have finished my second book, a novella and some more short stories, I have a clearer idea of what it is I am doing and how I can best be read and present myself. I know, for example, that not only do myths lie at the center of my literary world, but the power of children's narratives and narratives about women and children are central to my work. It is as if my sf worlds in all their darkness and joy grow from the tales that impress themselves upon a child's psyche. Other things I now know are that I am not only a feminist writer, I am an eco-feminist writer. I am someone who doesn't just fantasize new worlds, I insist on dealing with this one by recognizing the threats and promise it holds and acknowledging that it is shared territory. To try and examine this I construct situations where there are conflicts of interest and no one voice is dominant. These partial perspectives also make my writing "cyborg," as I try to write those often uncomfortable spaces between biology and machinery, between visible and invisible and between human and non-human.

Some of this clarification came from reviews. More of it came from sensitive readers who did not put pen to paper but were prepared to be generous with their time and chose to read and discuss my work with me.

Merrick: *You are currently writing your Ph.D. dissertation at The University of Western Australia. What can you tell us about the topic?*

I was originally going to write on cyborgs and science fiction, paying particular attention to how traditional mythical narratives contributed to stories of composite creatures but—as is the way of PhDs—I read myself into somewhere completely different. Now I am looking at radical evolutionary theories or reinterpretations of traditional evolutionary theory and applying them as a critical tool to science fiction. There is some very juicy stuff there as science fiction is fundamentally a genre of evolution and change.

And I have to add—though I do enjoy it!—that reading hard core scientific writing about subjects like protobiogenesis, panbiogeography and non-mendelian genetic mechanisms is hard work!

Merrick: *How does the academic work sit with your creative writing—do the two overlap or feed into each other in any way?*

They do overlap and I was fortunate enough to do a Masters degree in Creative Writing at the University of Western Australia a few years ago. This degree combined a creative component with an academic component, thus marrying what are often perceived as quite different processes. I believe doing this degree gave me confidence in my academic work and it also gave my creative work a sophistication it previously did not have. This is not to say that a knowledge of theory is necessary for good writing, but it can prove very useful in refining many of the different facets of a work such as *Map of Power*, or the recent manuscript I have finished titled *Sea As Mirror*, and it is certainly useful in knowing how to present the work and where it fits in the field.

However, there are a couple of points I'd like to make about the intersection of academic and creative work. The first one is that strong lines have to be drawn between the creative and the critical processes, as it is almost impossible to write if one's internal critic is attempting to theorize the writing as it appears. Both the critic and the editor must be silent when the creator is at work. Later they can be as vocal as they want, and indeed they may be extremely helpful, but they just get in the way when the primary objective is simply to get words down on the page.

I know this sounds dangerously like compartmentalized thinking, but it isn't really. I've found that similar processes are present in committed academic writing as well. To write a thesis or an exegesis, the same rules apply: the creative drive must be allowed to synthesize information and ideas without worrying about being correct in every detail. In a first draft of anything there are always sloppy joins, repetitions, contradictions and grammatical atrocities. That doesn't matter. A first draft is like the first rough shelter to keep the rain away. Holes in the wall can be patched later and the windows can be waterproofed in time for the downpour. What is important is that the walls are up and the roof is on.

The second point is the intersection of ideas in the academic and creative sphere. This is quite complex too. For instance, I have a passionate interest in alternative (non-Darwinian) theories of evolution, and evolution is a theme and sometimes an actual mechanism that figures strongly in my long creative pieces. However, even in *Sea As Mirror*—a book which is about evolution—I could use only a fraction of the information I have from my study. If I went into too much detail, I would risk boring my readers to death as well as losing them in some of the complex notions I am examining. So I do a lot of work and some of it is directly relevant and useful, other work will possibly be processed into fiction at a much later date or may even remain of academic interest only.

Merrick: *You juggle a number of identities, in addition to writer and academic—including teacher of sf and creative writing and also editor. Could you tell us about these other activities, and how you manage to juggle them all?*

Don't leave out "mother"! That's a bigger and more demanding part of my identity than all the rest put together, particularly as I am a long-term single parent.

What can I say about it all? First, I'll steal a line from *Alien Resurrection* and say I think it's a "chick thing." Fragmentation has been identified as lifestyle for many women, and I have firsthand experience of it in several ways. It can be bad when it simply becomes serial role-playing and someone slips in and out of personas with practiced ease, eventually forgetting to link their various realities. The result of that is a loss of any sense of self. However, it can also be very good when those multiple identities are linked and therefore create, rather than evict, your life. Having wobbled between those two extremes in the earlier days of my patchwork career, I know it's very important to remember why I do things. At this stage I do the juggling because it is one way in which I can get some time to write, but the price is high.

That's the personal angle. The creative line on this situation is interesting. I believe it has ultimately been positive. My novel narratives benefit greatly from my ability to think in multiple streams and to patiently knit disparate experiences towards set, common goals or resolutions. One of the features of my writing that is often remarked upon is the credibility of the separate worlds my characters inhabit. I can write that way because borderline multiple personality is a daily experience for me. Kind of, "If this is Tuesday I must be...!"

My political angle on this is not so cool. Although the various aspects of my life are starting to come together now (I write, study and teach in roughly the same area), I have spent a lot of time unsupported and torn between important commitments. This has led me to be very overworked and underpaid and I think I am only one representative of a growing underclass of well educated women who are systematically exploited through insecure, part-time, short-term contractual positions. It's not a situation this country should be proud of and it's not a situation that the people who are affected should be happy with.

How long can I go on juggling so many roles? I don't know. What will I do when I can no longer reconcile the benefits of this lifestyle with the disadvantages? Once again, I don't know.

Ikin: *Do you think sf is unique in providing an environment where a writer can juggle so many roles? Are you starting to feel like you are part of "the community"?*

Sf does seem to be unique in this way. That's one of the things that Helen and I point out in our introduction to *Women of Other Worlds*. Many of the contributors to that volume are high-profile women sf writers, but they can appear in quite different roles in that book. We have creative writers offering essays, ficto-critical writing and fan reports, academics as fans and interviewers, and—of course—a creative writer and academic as editors. It really does make the sf community special in that it has a large number of versatile, talented people who are prepared to participate in the many different dialogues generated within the community.

With regard to feeling as if I am part of that community, I am actually a really shy and quite reserved person so it has taken me a while to become comfortable in the community and sometimes I still become confused by undercurrents of emotion and politics that I don't understand. There is so much history in fandom. I am, however, learning the ropes and I have to say that I think I'm very lucky in this respect to be in Western Australia. Swancons are usually good fun and the fans are really warm people. I know I haven't been accepted with open arms by everyone, but I've never had problems with anyone I respect and the general attitude has been very supportive of writers.

Merrick: *Can you give us a summary of what your Murdoch University sf course covers?*

A little bit of this, and a little bit of that! It was a course originally designed to try to boost enrolments in English—and it worked. It has a basic historical framework with some nice detours around areas like sf art and comics, Russian sf, feminist sf, fifties sf films, slashzines and cyberpunk. We start with Verne and Wells and end with James Tiptree Jr. and Kate Wilhelm. It's a bit of a cook's tour and can be frustrating for people who are very well read in the area, and a bit confusing for those who have never come into contact with sf before (Yes, Virginia, people like that do exist!).

It's a great course to teach, though at times it's like riding an unbroken horse and I really don't know what to expect. I always have one or two students who actively dislike the genre and others who know more about some writers than I do, because they have read authors who have not attracted my attention. There is also an amazing range of students—they come from all disciplines and they bring with them a vast range of theoretical approaches. Ironically, literature students can sometimes be my worst students as they just don't get it that not all literature has to be psychological. It can be hard for them to understand that the idea is the emotional core of the work and they resent the focus given to history, politics and particularly science in the narrative.

Merrick: *You have also recently been asked to join the Editorial Board of* Eidolon. *Where do you see your career going in the future? Will writing still be your main focus?*

I'm at an interesting point in my life as a writer right now. *Sea As Mirror* is finished and I am very happy with it. I also feel confident with my short fiction. I'm having fun studying and I'm teaching work that I like. My role at *Eidolon* is not terribly demanding and I'm glad to contribute in some way. There are some other things on the drawing board, but the most immediate major project in my future now is my PhD.

I do swear off writing every now and then, particularly when I'm feeling under-funded and under-appreciated, but I don't know if I could actually stop. Besides, I owe my readers the conclusion of *Map of Power*, so I know that I have at least one more book to write!

Ikin: *Your new novel* Sea as Mirror *had its birth in a short story of the same name.* "Sea as Mirror" *the story is obviously very, very different from* Sea as Mirror *the novel, so I wonder if you could take us through some of the stages of the evolution of this project?*

The short story "Sea as Mirror" was one of those early experimental pieces of writing done before I started *Map of Power*. It had a couple of airings. The first was at a workshop with the West Australian poet Suzanne Covich. She told me it was a feminist creation myth and she just loved it. That was very heartening. However, I did nothing more with it until it came out of the bottom drawer again for consideration by the Creative Writing group at the University where I was doing my MA. It had a much more mixed reception there. Several people resisted the idea of sentience in another species so violently I was quite mystified by their response. Obviously I had hit some sort of nerve. I had written one of those stories that people either really love or really hate.

With some encouragement I decided to pursue the story further. I did a radio script of the story first (I thought such poetic language read to bird calls, whale noises and the sea would sound lovely—I still think that!), then I decided to amalgamate the whale story with another of my experimental pieces called "No Less than Trees and Stars" which was about a human-whale relationship. The novel grew from there and I think it grew so well and so strong because I loved it so much.

For a long time, *Sea as Mirror* was like a well fed secret. Even when I had doubts that it would work as long fiction, the story had a 'rightness' to it that meant I had to continue with it. I think it was very telling the day that I was criticized for writing this piece: that was probably the first time I had not been personally affected by a negative reading of my work. I just knew those people were *wrong*! And a certainty about this unusual story grew from that which led to me wanting to do justice to the power and ideas in the story. And I think I have now.

Merrick: *The amount of research involved in* Sea as Mirror *was absolutely staggering: you had to gain an in-depth understanding of various aspects of evolutionary process, whale physiology, American geography, the issue of biodiversity and other things. You even had to read up on magazines like* Newsweek *and* Time *until you could mimic their journalistic style!*

This relates in some respects to the whole genre issue again. I do read widely and eclectically and I read the world and its issues in a very political and mythic way. That's why I can't just write about my own personal experience; I'm too aware of cultural issues to keep them out of my work. They become actors on my stage. You see, I don't see myself as writing hero-centered fiction which is the traditional form in Western culture at this time (even in fantasy and sf!). I write fiction with multiple foci: human and non-human, personal and social, mythic and scientific. No one character or idea is center-stage all the time. Elizabeth is important, as is her unusual relationship with the whales, Tachotic and Chiten—but then so is the unpleasantness of colonial politics and the way it shapes science projects. So are media vendettas and the wild cards the natural world throws up. Even religion gets the treatment in this book!

As for the journalistic style...! That was the part of the novel that gave me the most trouble. I couldn't stay faithful to the story and be truly journalistic, so I compromised and made the article someone's private column. That allowed the writing to be broader and be issue based rather than strict news presentation or editorial address.

And my final point answering this question is probably the most important. I graze on knowledge much like cows graze on grass and it is no problem for me to deal with lots of different kinds of information in a novel. When I was researching *Map of Power* I had to figure out what the environmental problems in Australia and the Antarctic would be in two hundred years and how to build a space station. But the book is ultimately not a collection of information; it has to have a heart. For me, the heart of the book is the nub of the matter. It's the point of synthesis of all the information and history of the people in the world of the novel to that point. The heart of the book is the profound cultural story that shapes the characters' psychology and drives the society—usually without anybody really knowing it. Figuring that out and how to address it takes some work. It takes what I call deep thinking. And that's what makes my books effective, I believe. Their depth even more than their breadth.

Merrick: *By far the most compelling and fascinating task imposed by the novel was the need to be able to work out how a whale might understand life and the universe. We lucky people who have read* Sea as Mirror *ahead of publication date have been astounded by the way you take us into a whale's conscious- ness and unfold its language and its cosmology. How on earth did you even begin to go about grappling with this utterly alien perspective?*

I've been interested in whales for years. When my oldest son was a baby, I used to play humpback whale songs to him to get him to sleep. I read about whales and I really thought about them a lot. I found their world amazingly different and I in- vested quite a lot of mental energy in wondering what it would be like. For example, every breath a whale takes is voluntary. If a whale loses consciousness, there is no autonomic nervous system to simply keep handling that vital function. So, how do they sleep? And that's only one of dozens of questions that I asked. What do the observations that have been made of whole pods breathing in synchrony mean for whale society? Why are there so many documented cases of killer whales electing not to take humans as food when they have the opportunity? Why do killer whales seem to lose about half of their young?

I sifted these and many other problems for years. Unable to do the direct observational research I would have loved to do, I did the next best thing. I built a creative vision of how things might be for the whales. I tried to imagine a society that would fit all these strange facts, and then I went further. I tried to imagine how it would be to live in water all the time. Not just in the postcard snaps we tend to have of whales breaching on lovely days, but during the night and in the storms. Out in the very deep. How would their senses read the world? This is very important because sight is not their primary sense and so much of their experience would be darkness. Seeing would not be as important to them as echolocation or hearing is—that is why I have them "listening the world."

I tried to imagine how language in such a society would be influenced by the movements of the waves, how speech would be soft and sensuous, interspersed with choppy, repetitive, rhythmic sounds. And how their thinking would have to be a little like that too.

I had to imagine what would be important to them as possibly moral creatures, so I gave them a deity, but I made the deity conform to whale biology. Just as we anthropomorphize everything, so I felt they would do that to the world in their own way. Their deity has three parts, the Mother which is the sea, the Father, which is land, and god-in-air which is a more indifferent, less personal entity and is embodied in the sun and the moon. The whales—the *Curore*—see the sun and moon as the eyes of god-in-air. That the eyes move independently is not a problem for them as whales have completely different views of the world through each eye.

Most of what I say is backed by some sort of information, but I have taken some creative liberties with creating the *Curore*. For example, what I often shorthand as "songs" in the whale chapters of *Sea as Mirror* is more likely to be lots of grunts, creaky noises and squeals from Killer whales!

And I like the words you use in this question. To me the whales are more "utterly alien" than most of the aliens that are written about in endless examples of speculative fiction. Their biology is largely known, and contact has been made. But how much further have we got with all our scientific approach? We can say little definitive about them other than to give the weight of their brains and to identify which organs are used for which senses. Human arrogance sometimes astounds me. I remember years ago arguing with people when the first radio packages were being sent out into space in the hopes of contact. I'd say, "What if this intelligent species doesn't speak maths?" or "What if they have no tools?." I can't tell you how many times the people I spoke to just didn't understand when I said something could be an intelligent life form and *not* be like us. Oh well, perhaps if some of those people read *Sea as Mirror* they'll finally realize what I was on about!

Ikin: *Another striking feature of both your novels is the way you present your female characters. Like Kass in* Map of Power, *Elizabeth in* Sea as Mirror *is not a stereotypical modern-Amazon style of female, but rather a realistically vulnerable woman whose feminist principles are not always matched by her actions. It is as if you seem deeply uncomfortable with the way so many recent novels (both sf and mainstream) show contemporary women as feisty, free, and independent—almost as if the battles of feminism had been won, and won easily....*

Absolutely. I see two significant issues here that are addressed by *Sea as Mirror*. The first is that we are not going to find any permanent solutions to any of our problems simply by turning women into mark 2 versions of men. Although battles for equity mean we are fighting for equal treatment and opportunity for everyone—which is sound—there is an inbuilt problem there. We can't just thoughtlessly aim to shape all the citizens of our culture to achieve a standard of living where their rights compromise others. For example, I believe we have a social responsibility to make sure people do not go without basic food, shelter, medical care and education, but meeting these needs does not include the right to export the costs of an affluent life to less fortunate countries, or the right to destroy the environment and other plant and animal species to obtain products that are fashionable. This is simply giving everyone permission to behave badly. That's not real equity. It's great to see female characters who do not lie down and do as they're told, but giving them a knife, a gun, and a "don't-give-a-damn" attitude extends certain problems rather than resolves them.

The second issue is the "post-feminism" idea that tends to be fostered by images of strong women. That whole construct is positively dangerous, as is the notion of "post-colonialism." It's like we're saying *Oh, we're so cool and grownup we've left all that stuff behind.* Bollocks we have! The battles of feminism and colonialism have a long way to go yet and we've only really just started to negotiate the environmental and world justice war. I think it is good to have positive and strong women characters in books, but that is not enough in itself. Portraying characters who were traditionally submissive as more powerful tends to mask a whole series of dominations and exploitations that are built into (particularly Western) culture and experienced very differently by different groups at different points.

For example, as an adult, Elizabeth fights many battles on many fronts. Some she loses, some she wins, some don't resolve clearly at all. Just like in real life. But one of the serious questions the book raises is that people have to experience life as children first. Where I don't necessarily see children as victims or completely powerless—some of my short stories have very strong children in them—my understanding is that children are generally a very disenfranchised and vulnerable group.

Ikin: *To misquote Helen Reddy, your character Elizabeth seems to be a woman who sometimes doesn't "roar" at the moment when she should (and when she* wants *to). But both of your novels are about power, and the point of your fiction is to show that real power—and real change—is the result not so much of "roaring" as of* doing. *Is that a fair statement?*

I think my two most powerful characters are Kass from *Map of Power* and Elizabeth from *Sea as Mirror*. Simply put, they are not traditional warriors. Their power comes not so much from "roaring"—though they both do speak out against what they see as wrong—but from following their truths. Sometimes this involves speaking out, as when Elizabeth tackles Granger or Kass tackles Hovar, but more often it involves going their own way and pursuing what they see as the most important reality. This is because power is complex and they can't hope to fix what is wrong simply by identifying it. If that worked we'd live in a perfect world because most people know what is wrong already.

I suppose one of the features that tends to identify my fiction as anti-heroic is that the character's internal sense of justice or "rightness" doesn't just simply win out in the end and leave everyone feeling good. By the end of the story, there is usually a victory of some sort, but it can be a pyrrhic victory. These women who understood so much were right but that sometimes didn't fix things. What they did do, however, is at least to open a door to a different future. Not a perfect one. Power is an ongoing issue. But as Joseph Campbell says of the myths and stories that govern our culture, they can change when people and/or societies are ready to deal with the issues that have kept us imprisoned in those repeated cycles of pain and destruction. Characters like Kass and Elizabeth, and even Gretheling from my story "Out of Time Come Prophets," do that. They deal. They might not win in every sense but they win in some important way because they deal!

IMAGINATION, FANTASY, AND FICTION

by George Turner
[2002]

"To him [Turner], imagination on the loose must be like a wasp in the shower."
—John Baxter, disdainfully reviewing Turner's *In the Heart or in the Head* for the Australian Broadcasting Corporation's *Books and Writing* program.

It is my practice to advise distraught writers never to answer their critics unless they can catch them in misrepresentation of the text, and that even then their cries of righteous anguish are not likely to be heard with any sympathy. (The way to deal with incompetent reviewers is to let them stew in their juice; they will soon lose credibility. If, as a reviewer, you can find nothing good to say of a book, the best action is to ignore it; save your effort for what deserves it.)

My second piece of advice is: always, once you have recovered your temper, take adverse reviews seriously, no matter how wrongheaded you may think the reviewer. The so-and-so just might be right.

Now, the remark quoted above, about "imagination on the loose," seems to have been based at least partly on the premise that I have no appreciation of J.G. Ballard (wrong) or Frank Herbert (right) because they are highly imaginative writers. In fact I like most (not all) of Ballard's fiction because he uses imagination brilliantly to point his metaphors and statements, and am unimpressed by Herbert's (mostly, not always) because its imaginative content is decorative rather than integral, with little purpose beyond bizarrerie.

The sharp-eyed reader will perceive that Baxter and I seem to be discussing different things; the critic has posited a generalized "imagination on the loose" and I have at once shifted my ground to the *use* of imagination. Perhaps, then, he is right to say that I have no appreciation of a generalized imaginativeness (Herbert), but for my part I have a great respect and enthusiasm for imagination harnessed to a purpose (Ballard).

All of the foregoing simply introduces my reason for discussing some aspects of the use of imagination in fiction. They were discussed in partial fashion in the book which aroused such patrician contempt, but the public comment has caused me to consider the matter more closely.

§

"Imagination on the loose" seems to me to mean imagination uninhibited and unbounded. But this is no more than a description of the process at the moment of initiation; all imagination is, in the moment of its birth, uninhibited and unbounded. So is an explosion, and a useless thing that is until it is tamed—as in, if you like, a car engine. Imagination is equally useless until something is done with it; writing it down barebones for a reader to drool over does nothing at all for the conception or the reader.

Imagination is, after all, the common possession of us all and its mere display is no more admirable than the ability to move and breathe. It has no value until it is put to use, and its major use is in creative art, of which the most popular branch is fiction. (This popularity may mean only that the writing of fiction is the easiest art in which to achieve an acceptable competence and to understand without specialized study, but that is another argument, for another time.)

The publication of tens of thousands of novels and stories each year makes appreciation a highly elective process if we are to achieve a personal taste or a roughly agreed-upon canon of outstanding work. We base this selectiveness on a number of critical shibboleths—language, word-play, descriptive power, characterization, argument, realism, dialogue, sub-text... make your own list. All these center eventually on a single artistic process, the disciplining of that imagination which without discipline is mere contemplation of the ego, uninterested in communication.

Fiction is, basically, a work of imagination. The Concise Oxford adds little to that: *fic'tion, n. Feigning, invention: thing feigned or imagined, invented statement or narrative....* So, wasp in the shower or not, all fiction is basically imagination. But not, I protest, "on the loose." It is imagination given form and point, shaped for communication to others. This does not mean that it need be in any sense restricted, only that it be made intelligible—because minds do not meet as a matter of course. It is a commonplace of psychology, as well as the root cause of most literary criticism, that understanding is rarely immediate and that the extraction of meaning is a process continuing throughout the life of a statement or a text. Another's imagination "on the loose" would almost certainly be unintelligible to a recipient with quite different personal references and outlook, a foreign language needing the discipline of translation into commonly held terms.

§

Or have I misrepresented the critic? Did he perhaps have in mind that most highly colored of all the sub-genres subsumed under the sf label, fantasy? Can that be the field of "imagination on the loose"?

The Concise Oxford again: *fan'tasy, ph-, n. Image-making faculty, esp. when extravagant or visionary; mental image;*

fantastic design; = FANTASIA; whimsical speculation. These seem to be the requirements of *any* fiction, even of a simple con-man's lie. So what is special about fantasy fiction? "... extravagant or visionary" would appear to be the words we need to describe such works as the "Conan" stories, Fritz Leiber's "Gray Mouser" series, the novels of Stephen Donaldson, and the sub-literate trilogies clustering like flies on the shelves of paperback booksellers, but these could be equally well applied to the plotting of a detective story or a historical novel or a Harold Robbins extravaganza. There is also "mental image," the expressed form of a fantasy, and these two words are worth considering. A specific story suggests itself.

Could a "mental image" of so commonplace an object as a doorknob be a fantasy? Hardly. But what about Henry Kuttner's doorknob, which opens a blue eye and looks at you? (*The Fairy Chessmen*, opening line.) At once reality recedes and fantasy-as-mental-image takes over. Later in the story it appears that the doorknob fantasy is a delusion fostered by scientific means, but does the cause render it less of a fantasy? I think not, but the usefulness of this example is that it postulates a connection between fantasy and the real world. The doorknob, offered cold in the first words of the tale, is what pulp writers call the "hook," the grabber of reader interest, so here it is fantasy harnessed to a very practical purpose—and Kuttner's usage is possibly one of the most telling in the whole range of science fiction. It remains in memory after nearly forty years as a dramatic entity in its own right, but it is not imagination "on the loose"; it is harnessed, disciplined and impeccably placed.

It might be thought that imagination "on the loose" would have little place in *science* fiction, at least for those of us who still draw some personal line between it and fantasy. (For the moment let us ignore the great gray area of overlap; we will move into it soon enough.) Unfortunately, that style of undisciplined type of fabulation plays a large and confusing role.

Science fiction, whose beginnings I place with Thomas More's *Utopia*, was a truly speculative genre until the early days of the twentieth century; its ideas began with the contemporary "today" and built new ideas, as distinct from fantasies, upon them. With the twentieth century the leap of imagination took over, owing little to science, probability or even possibility; *Weird Tales* and *Amazing Stories* were born. Responsible writers like Taine, Huxley, Campbell, Wyndham, Aldiss (the best, that is) and some others tried to stay within the bounds of reasonable possibility as they saw it, but most took the leap of imagination without regard to credibility and then forced it into fictional form. These last were not always the incompetent or the thoughtless; they were often writers with a point to make, a statement or a question to put forward, looking for a science fictional metaphor to express it without didacticism. The results often demeaned the work.

Philip K. Dick, running time backward in *Counter-Clock World*, became hopelessly bushed in the cause/effect problem which forethought would have warned him is logically insoluble, so that action and plot lost credibility. Stanislaw Lem, using an alien intelligence (in *Solaris*) to make the point that truly different *kinds* of intelligence can never communicate, gave so much detail about his alien as to convince this reader that communication with this example *would* indeed be possible. (What Lem went some way towards proving is that the human mind cannot conceive of an alien *kind* of intelligence; what emerges from the attempt is always twistedly human.) James Blish trying, in *Cities In Flight*, to describe an inhabited *universe* with planets no longer necessary as bases, recognized the need for immortality in such travelers but was forced to ignore the problems inherent in millennial aging of the mind; so what should have been a vast vision of the future collapsed into a sequence of interesting but minor adventures.

These and many more could have been rescued from ultimate failure (they were grand attempts) by giving thought to the central imaginative core instead of trying to wrap a fairly conventional novel around it. In good fiction the imaginative core *dictates* the form and content of the work, else it registers only as decoration; it becomes a liability wherein the reader perceives the intention but finally concludes that the extended metaphor does not work. Enjoyable in the moment of reading, these novels fail in retrospect; one wonders about the novel that could have been, with the conception pursued to a logical outcome... surely a more challenging and enduring volume than that which actually appeared.

Imagination is not enough; it must be pinned, observed, trimmed, extrapolated. (Is "extrapolated" still a dirty word in science fiction circles?) "On the loose," it is mere gimmickry.

Those science fiction works which have stood the reader-test of time and laid the foundations of the genre (I avoid such terms as *great* and *classic*, both critically meaningless), eschew fantasy in favor of hardheaded speculation enlivened by fictional examples. From More's *Utopia* and Bacon's *New Atlantis,* which between them provided the spirit and seed of every major science fiction development, to the milestone works of Verne and Wells and on to *Brave New World*, *Tomorrow and Tomorrow and Tomorrow* (Australia's sole viable contribution) and *Nineteen Eighty-Four,* the line of descent has been characterized by realistic exploitation of a central conception, pursued to its end with little concession to fantasizing. Each arose from a stroke of the imagination, seized and disciplined to display its relevance to the real world.

(Since I believe that the ultimate critic is time, the unforgiving selector of what is and what is not worth preserving, I hesitate to guess what may survive from the science fiction of the last thirty years, but I like to think that Tom Disch's *334* will be rediscovered and pondered over, that Ballard's "disaster" novels will be more clearly seen as commentaries on our attitudes to the future, and that Le Guin's *Left Hand of Darkness* and *The Dispossessed* will be recognized as attempts to elucidate social problems of urgent importance, problems whose full impact will only be felt in some fairly near tomorrow.)

§

It would be futile to suggest that unfettered imagination has no place at all in science fiction which everywhere wanders into the nearer reaches of fantasy with the pretence that these too might turn out to be realities, if only.... One can only reiterate that the enduring works of the genre are monuments to *controlled* imagination.

But what of pure fantasy, the involuntary surge of imagery from the mind, pristine, surprising even to its originator, before the narrowing interference of the intellect begins? I suspect that it may be partially found in any three venues of significance: the spontaneous expression of a very young child, the confessional of the psychoanalyst's couch, and the first explosion of an idea in an artist's mind.

The child learns early that private fantasies must give way to reality and that one's dream-desires are expected to conform to social and racial patterns; the unforced expressions that startle and delight with sudden revelation of private worlds become rare and disappear. Explosions of fantasy persist in the mind, but unspoken; they survive as reactions to joy too private for communication, as protest too incoherent for explanation, as desires too much at odds with received behavior to be risked even in confidence. Attempts at communication are futile; the images can be transferred only in trimmed and dulled parody, muted to the cliché forms of common understanding.

When the enclosed mind has suffered enough, its fantasies may be spilled to an analyst or a psychiatrist in the confessional secrecy which tempts truth out of hiding, but the confession is encumbered by words and limited by vocabulary; in the long run only the fantasist knows the content of his mind. What's left when the analyst-confessor has completed his reduction and explication is a poor shadow of the original.

The depictive artist—painter, sculptor, musician—may attain some expression of an unfettered imagining in the first rapid splash of color, the first vision of form exploding from a mass of clay, the inspired cluster of notes in a moment when mind and music are one—and then art sets in. The color must make a pictorial statement, the clay an expressive mould, the sound an intelligible composition. So the artist creates (within the limits of his/her "school" and training) a version, however rebellious, of the prevailing modes of expression and composition. Somewhere in the finished work is the echo of the mental detonation which began it, shaped and tidied and given meaning, or gloss of meaning, and for the most part buried.

§

The term "fantasy" as a description has become as hopelessly debased and generalized as "science fiction." It belongs with Damon Knight's only partly ironical definition that science fiction is "What I point at when I say it." It is too often used to describe the lowest common denominator of non-realistic fiction, the basic stratum of curiously *un*imaginative tales wherein monstrous landscapes are infested by dwarfs and dragons, magic flourishes in a fashion mysteriously vulnerable to a smart sword slash, overmuscled nitwits double as heroes, heroines teeter precariously between sex and swordsmanship and convince at neither, prose is given a gloss of often shaky archaism and each book seems to duplicate the general tenor of the last. There are cosmetic changes—different titles, different names for the characters, different derivative periods for the same activities—but they belong finally with a group of a few composite works shared among the authors. Incest. Or, maybe, cannibalism—they eat and regurgitate each other.

There is little imagination in settings lifted from half-digested archaeology, themes from mythology and prose from a scrapheap of "fantasy" vocabulary. That they swell by the thousand and give pleasure to those who need such gimcrack is not my complaint; there is room for all kinds in the entertainment spectrum. It matters only that we do not pretend that they all have equal claim to attention; I am content to avert my eyes from a copy of *Murder Song of the Deathworm: Volume IV In The Heroic Saga of Hotcha of Hothel.*

§

With each year it seems more certain that the finest modern imaginative fiction belongs to neither fantasy nor science fiction but to that gray area of overlap between rococo splendor of vision and hard common sense of intention. Looking over my own shelves I see (aside from the predictable Ballard and Priest), Borges, Calvino, David Ireland, Rodney Hall, Peter Carey, Frank Moorhouse, Alasdair Gray and John Calvin Batchelor, at a quick glance—all fathering conceptions ranging from the gently subtle to the extravagantly vast. And in every case (except perhaps Christopher Priest, who seems to be still searching for his statement) the writer's eye is firmly on craft and common-sense and his conception is shaped, chiseled to an artistic whole. Nothing "on the loose" ever made an artistic whole.

Sometimes these imaginings are merely fun-loving; mostly they are metaphors, often surreal, for the mysteries underpinning reality, areas of existence suspected but undiscovered; they are never meaningless evocations of the weird and strange for its own tawdry sake.

The first notable characteristic of my short list (a selection only) is that the writers do not form an identifiable group sharing the relationships and limitations that form a genre. They are individuals. One might link Borges and Calvino as following modes with a superficial resemblance, but in fact their pursuits are very different; Borges moves inward to turn imagination back on its own wellsprings and ask new questions about meaning, whereas Calvino moves outward from his fantastic base to arrive at conclusions which insist that fantasy and reality are one. Set Borges's "Garden Of Forking Paths" against Calvino's "Tau Zero" stories and they move poles apart. In the same way Carey, Moorhouse and Hall might be seen as cruder Australian fantasists who demonstrate that our realities are themselves fantasies wherein the way of living life is itself unreal, but they are deeply divided in their attitudes to satire, responsibility and forgiveness.

So, too, might Gray and Batchelor be observed as two sides of the metaphysical coin, Gray producing grim and hideous portraits of humanity while Batchelor dances with gaiety over precisely the same egotisms and stupidities—until you notice that it is the dour Scot who promises hope and later laughter while the jesting American sees only the victims dancing on the crater's rim. To read *Lanark* (Gray) and then *The Further Adventures of Halley's Comet* (Batchelor) is to travel with two of the most evocative imaginations of our day; their two novels are a *Pilgrim's Progress* of our time, with intentions not far removed from Bunyan's. Their imaginative vigor makes "heroic fantasy" a juvenile scribble, science fiction a genre in decay and the creations of Tolkien adolescent. Yet there is nothing of the fantastic "trip" about these books, nothing of imagination "on the loose"; it is directed, in all this group of modern magicians, directed to a known and unfrivolous end.

Whether the end derives from the imaginative content or whether the imagination was set to work to illuminate the statement is irrelevant; what is relevant is the *use* of imagination to an end. In art, imagination may be a wellspring or a tool but not an end in itself.

§

It may have seemed unfair to set the very differently oriented Tolkien against such powerhouses as Gray and Batchelor, but in the field of romantic adventure he has his own ascendancy. He must at least be included in the list of great world-creators of the written word. That line goes a long way back in literary history, at least as far as the comedies of Aristophanes, which are still read, but the modern reader rarely ventures much further back than the savagery of Swift's *Gulliver's Travels*, which relies on exaggeration rather than *a primo* creation. For most of us the purely imaginative begins in the nineteenth century with Carroll's *Alice in Wonderland* and here, in one of the most frothily conceived (it must seem) of all stories, the writer's imagination is reined more tightly than in almost any other work of fiction.

It says much about the special qualities of imagination as the progenitor of hard thought, and about the subconscious springs of what we term fantasy, that the origin of *Alice* was a spoken tale, delivered impromptu and only later committed to writing. It is hard to believe that Carroll was thinking of the paradoxes of visual relativity (a conception familiar to the classic Greeks) when he spoke of Alice swallowing the contents of a bottle labeled *Drink Me*, but he certainly was thinking of them when he came to transfer the incident to paper. The process of rationalization, of seeking out meaning, was at work by then, and every one of the imaginative jokes in *Alice* is a commentary on philosophy, an aside on the quirks of human nature, or a mathematician's dig at systems of logic. *Alice*, possibly the best known and best loved of all "fantasies," turns out to be no fantasy at all but an intricately constructed set of Russian Dolls, holding meaning within meaning. Imagination "on the loose" has here been caught and tamed as possibly nowhere else in our literature.

I do not know what might be said of the famous American *Doctor Doolittle* and *Oz* books, never having read them (there simply isn't time for all the things one would like to sample) but I do know James Branch Cabell's "Don Manuel" series, beloved by the late James Blish and the cornerstone of a specialist fan club which has published its own magazine for half a century. For most people Cabell means *Jurgen*, the best known of the novels, though there are in fact fifteen of them, forming an evolving chain of philosophic argument, highly fantastical, with two books of essays which act as Foreword and Afterword. Books of essays are not written to bolster "imagination on the loose," nor are magazines published to embalm such froth, yet Cabell's books are replete with knights and damsels, magicians and shape-changers, gods and godlets and adventures both in and out of this world—and the whole adds up to a sly but genuine philosophic statement revealed in the final volume. It is the discipline that counts and confers longevity.

Coming closer to the present, *The Lord of the Rings* seems to tower over the field, and certainly over its painful imitators. Why, is not easily discerned. As a work of imagination it is, outside of the linguistic basis, almost wholly derivative (the Ents and the Ring-Wraiths are its most original ingredients), the verse is rather plodding stuff, the social attitudes are feudal, the psychology superficial—and the whole thing is charming. Perhaps the generally understated prose (supposed for some reason to be typically English, which is nonsense) carries one effortlessly along; perhaps the sense of building drama, which is never relaxed, exerts its own hypnotism; whatever the reason, *The Lord of the Rings* is eminently readable and (though there are dissenters) gripping. What it is *not*, is imaginatively "on the loose"; it is calculated to the last word. In one or two places it slyly transcends physical possibility—for instance, in Gollum's passage head-first down a vertical cliff face—and in these the diversionary stops of expertise are pulled out to suspend incredulity, but on the whole this is highly professional fantasizing with imagination firmly between the shafts and never allowed to gallop.

Immensely popular, too, is Ursula Le Guin's *Earthsea* trilogy which began, according to her own account, with the idea of the floating islands which do not appear until the third volume. The rest was added by the novelist rather than the dreamer. That it is a *deliberate* collation of plot and idea does not make it a lesser work than others of its genre, rather the reverse; it is a superior product wherein artistry counts because it disciplines imagination.

The mention of artistry brings me to confess defeat by the double "Thomas Covenant" trilogy from the immensely successful Stephen Donaldson. I ploughed through a hundred and twenty pages of one of them (I can't even recall the title) before I decided that his stolid ten-words-where-one-will-do style, allied to what seemed a ragbag of all the current "heroic fantasy" concepts, sent me in search of something less second-hand; even the "imagination" seemed not his own. Perhaps I have missed something worthwhile—but, as one who has read and loved most of the canon of enduring fantasy, I think not. That several million readers love the Donaldson baby will not persuade me to kiss it; it seems to be "fantasy" with neither imagination nor style.

And so we come to the real wasp in the shower. It is a sour joke that the great imaginative lines of descent, science fiction and heroic fantasy, continue to breed on each other's common-places while the truly original and powerful imaginative writing is being produced, with wit and panache, by writers whose origins and preoccupations are firmly in the classic mainstream of fiction.

THE LEVER OF LIFE
CORDWAINER SMITH AS ETHICAL PRAGMATIST

by Terry Dowling
[1982]

> This is the task of man always...not to illuminate the ancient truths, the ancient truths of the unconscious, the ancient intimations of the soul, but...to make them immediate and contemporary, to give them a meaning in the here and now.
> —Laurens van der Post, citing Jung. BBC television program: *The Story of Carl Gustav Jung*

> Ever. Never. Forever. Three worlds. The lever of life upon times. Never, forever, ever....
> —Old Norstrilian Poem

> "Fathers and teachers, I ask: 'What is hell?' I maintain that it is the suffering of being unable to love."
> —Father Zussima in *The Brothers Karamazov*

There is a broad refrain that runs through the late Paul Linebarger's Instrumentality series; a refrain that is a central motif in almost all the stories he wrote as Cordwainer Smith. This is the recurring, connecting theme of winning and losing, of triumph and celebration and loss as part of an unending cycle fundamental to the phenomenon and spirit of our humanity. The Instrumentality stories are built solidly upon this cycle. Out of the chaos of the Ancient Wars, mankind wins through to a new utopian future under the supervision of the Instrumentality, a victory of dubious value for a humanity that is "dying of perfection" (N/163) prior to the Rediscovery of Man.[39] Rod McBan wins the Earth and loses it again. He is prepared to "win or fail" (N/197) in the Hate Hall of the Department Store of Hearts' Desires, and so wins something of far greater value than a world or a fortune. On Pontoppidan, a still-unfulfilled Casher O'Neill is told: "You can't win now" (Q/32), even at the outset of his struggle to liberate Mizzer. Jestocost loses C'mell but wins a future for the underpeople. The martyred dog-girl, D'joan, loses her life to the same end; and so it goes *(see appendix)*.

There are references aplenty to take up this refrain, whether it be the "I Loved You and Lost You" song from "The Dead Lady of Clown Town":

> I knew you, and loved you
> and won you, in Kalma.
> I loved you, and won you,
> and lost you, my darling! (B/160)

or the poem about the "testing" of the Norstrilian young recalled by Rod:

> Out in the Garden of Death, our young
> Have tasted the valiant taste of fear.
> With muscular arm and reckless tongue,
> They have won, and lost, and escaped us here.
> (N/7),

or a determined remark made by T'ruth, the turtle-girl guardian of Murray Madigan's estate on the storm planet, Henriada:

---

39. The page references cited are to the editions coded in the text as indicated at the end of this study.

"I'm not going to lose, Casher. I'm going to win."
(Q/108)

Quotes from the text simply highlight the richness of this thematic refrain. What becomes important is the exact sense in which we are to regard this pattern of conflict, defeat, and victory. What is it to win, from Smith's point of view? What is it to lose?

To discover this, we must remember that Smith was a true humanitarian; a person who was deeply sympathetic to Christianity—largely because, unlike many other world religions with their "fatalism and indifference to human life" (B/xv), it put life and love before all else. His own faith appears repeatedly as the Old Strong Religion, though it must be remembered that Smith goes beyond merely advocating to others his own beliefs or one body of doctrine. The universe of the Instrumentality (where organized religions become strictly limited to their worlds of origin) may be essentially a neo-Christian universe, but at the same time it is more than that. Whatever was gained by Linebarger from his High Church Episcopalian upbringing must be seen in the light of a subsequent, equally dynamic involvement with other similar bodies of religious teaching and philosophical thought. In his capacity as a social scientist and a US adviser in Asia, he was continually exposed to Eastern philosophies. By his work on psychological warfare, he knew well the power of belief and the fundamental motivating forces in man that directed him along one path and not another. From such an interaction, from such a specialization in the mainsprings of ideology and human need, Linebarger distilled a unique insight. Consequently, writing as Cordwainer Smith, we see him as a synthesist—a syncretist who saw the best of man's beliefs through all of history, whether it involved the worship of Christ or of Aten.

The plight of the underpeople, the teachings of D'joan, E'telekeli, and T'ruth, the subject matter of so many of the Instrumentality stories, may all reflect a concern with a traditional Christian faith, surfacing here and there throughout man's future with its ideals and values, its humanizing, civilizing force intact, but it is rather as J.J. Pierce has observed, that Smith "became obsessed with the sanctity of life on any terms, as something too precious to sacrifice to any concept of honor or morality—Oriental or Occidental" (B/xv-xvi). While Linebarger himself was brought up as a High Anglican and was "devoutly religious" (B/xiv), as Cordwainer Smith he has no "vested interests" in Christianity. The constants acted and re-enacted in his Instrumentality stories show him as a synthesist and a natural "Jungian" writer and thinker.

1: The Nature of the Struggle

"Sweet are the uses of adversity,
Which, like the toad, ugly and venomous,
Wears yet a precious jewel in his head."
—William Shakespeare, *As You Like It*

The stories set within the Instrumentality framework are always concerned with struggles that are inevitably:
(a) Man against himself;
(b) Man against his universe;
(c) Man against ideas;
(d) Man against death;
(e) Man against loneliness and fear;
(f) Man against the unknown.
Any given Smith story will involve most if not all of these areas.

Man Against Himself

"I think therefore I am...I think!"
—Anonymous

This first area of conflict does not refer to the basic physical, political, or ideological conflicts of one sphere of interest against another (as presented in "War No.81-Q" or "Golden the Ship Was—Oh! Oh! Oh!"), but rather it refers to a confrontation between the individual, his notions of his own humanity, and the reality containing him.

In the Instrumentality series we are given constant crises of self; recurring semantic, philosophical, epistemological, and ontological crises, such as: What is life? What is being? What is human? What is real? What is self? These are the basic identity conflicts of any sensitive, sentient creature. Smith, of course, approaches these questions as a poet and not as a scientist, but he is a most intelligent and self-aware poet, capable of strict scientific and philosophical disciplines. These debates with self and others are very important to the philosophy of love and tolerance practiced by Linebarger the private man. Typically, they go like this. Elaine asks the Traveler's Aid:

> "...are you a person or are you a machine?"
>
> "Depends," said the voice. "I'm a machine, but I used to be a person.... So what do you say? Am I me or aren't I?" (B/136)

In "Think Blue, Count Two" Talatashar asks the "illusory" captain about Sh'san:

> "But what *is* he? Who *are* you?...Are you imaginary? Are you real?"
>
> "That's philosophy. I'm made by science. I wouldn't know...." (I/115-116)

So too does Lord Sto Odin question his two robot companions:

> "I am alive?" the Lord asked.
> "Yes," said both the robots.
> "You are dead?"

"We are not dead. We are machines, printed with the minds of men who once lived." (B/221)

And if they "are not dead," there is the suggestion that they *are* living.

As this debate continues, there comes a pointed warning, as relevant today as in this far future time:

> "You are machines, nothing more, are you not? Are you not?" His voice shrilled at the end.
> Said Flavius, "Nothing more."
> Said Livius, "Nothing more. And yet–"
> "And yet what?" demanded the Lord Sto Odin.
> "And yet," said Livius, "I know I am a machine, and I know that I have the known feelings only when I was once a living man. I sometimes wonder if you people might go too far. Too far, with us robots. Too far, perhaps, with the underpeople too. Things were once simple, when everything that talked was a human being and everything which did not talk was not. You may be coming to an ending of the ways." (B/229)

Man is complicating his own environment, his own philosophical traditions; the "ending of the ways" is near indeed. The old hard-and-fast yardsticks have already become useless. People can be printed onto machines (the Lady Panc Ashash, Flavius and Livius); machines can be fashioned about the brains of animals (owl-brained little Harry Hadrian, the gun-watching robot, for example); animals can be made to resemble humans (D'alma, D'joan, C'mell); men become both wild "animals" (Talatashar, Benjacomin Bozart) and nonhumans (the klopts of Arachosia). The reflective and apprehensive dialogue between Sto Odin and his robots is as rigorous as Smith's debates get. The dilemma is there: what constitutes a man? humanity? Such questions are not to be answered easily. Certainly they are never fully answered within the Instrumentality stories as we have them, although an answer seems to be forthcoming at some inevitable stage of future growth.

It is enough that any thinking creature be brought to this philosophical impasse. He will then be directed to a new examination of those age-old "big" questions; his awareness will be fine-honed, and he will acquire a new respect for life in general. We cannot go any further. Our own confusion over these questions is highlighted by the equally paradoxical remarks of a psychically motivated warden like Sh'san, summoned by Veesey to save the crew and passengers of her sailship:

> "I do not exist," said the stranger, "but I can kill you, any of you, if I wish." (1/109)

It is reinforced when the "lost art of fighter replication" (Q/87) is used against the insane Go-Captain, John Joy Tree:

> Tree whirled around. "You're not real," he said.
> Image-Casher stepped around the console and hit Tree with an iron glove. The pilot jumped away, a hand reaching up to his bleeding face. (Q/86)

This dilemma of identity and reality is compounded further in "Think Blue, Count Two" when that other "temporary, artificial personality" (I/115), the captain, is questioned about his immediate creator, Sh'san. Awe-struck, the "ghost" captain replies:

> "He is the thinker of all thinkers, the 'to be' of being, the doer of doings. He is powerful beyond your strongest imagination. He makes me come living out of your living minds. In fact," said the captain with a fine snarl, "he is a dead mouse-brain laminated with plastic and I have no idea at all of who *I* am. Good night to you all!" (I/116)

In other words, Sh'san is a "relative god," all-powerful within a certain set parameters. It is a most wonderful evasion, for Sh'san can be reduced mechanistically, functionally, scientifically—contained and explained by theories and techniques—while at the same time he continually eludes complete understanding. As with the robots and the underpeople, the ends often transcend the means producing them.

Thus we are to remind ourselves not only that our own gods may be quite relative to our finite world-view and life-experience, but also that while we can reduce ourselves mechanistically to an intricate set of interlocking systems and electrical impulses, we too are beyond easy quantification: the knowns quickly falter in the face of the unknowns. This is a proper and healthy attitude.

In a "fringe" Instrumentality story like "Nancy" (there is only one connection, a single reference to the Up-and-Out) the same crisis of self, existence, and reality-perception exists. A space-pilot is infected with a *sokta* virus which gives him an illusory female companion—a Nancy—who is "more real than life itself" (I/196). Elsewhere the same crisis of reality versus illusion occurs in an unrelated story, "Western Science Is So Wonderful," when an American challenges a Martian visitor with: "You're not are you? You can't be. Or can you?" and is answered: "What is real, darling?" (I/172). The point, once again, is that it is correct for man to be in awe of the miracle of existence, and that we must be careful to avoid dogmatic assertions and rationalizations about things we cannot ultimately understand in our present condition.

Man Against His Universe

"The only real danger that exists is man himself. He is the great danger, and we are *pitifully unaware* of it."
—Carl G. Jung

"It's a lot of work to be human and it's work which must be kept up or it begins to fade." (Q/30)
—Philip Vincent, Hereditary Dictator of Pontoppidan

Another major area of conflict in the series is between man and his universe. Space is not kind to man. It is an ordeal, cruel and deadly, and all the transits between the worlds of men are hard-won. In "Scanners Live in Vain," in the early days of space colonization (c.6000AD) when huge sub-light sailships were used to cross normal space (presumably Space One), we learn of "the great pain of space" (B/6), an actual physical pain:

> which started quietly in the marrow, like an ache, and proceeded by the fatigue and nausea of each separate nerve cell, brain cell, touchpoint in the body, until life itself became a terrible aching hunger for silence and for death.... (B/20)

We learn too that "People who went to the Up-and-Out had to pay the price for space" (B/4). Initially this price is met by the scanners, the scanner-pilots, and the habermans who man the ships which carry cryogenically-suspended colonists between the stars. With the discovery of Space Two and "planoforming" (c.8000-9000AD) there are the Go-Captains and the pinlighters (playing their "game" of "Rat and Dragon" with that enemy "out there *underneath space itself* which was alive, capricious and malevolent" (B/70)); and later we hear of the more lethal Space Three, "where so many travelers had gone in and so few had come out" (Q/112-113).

But whether it is Space One, Space Two, or Space Three, or such space-borne enemies of Instrumentality-governed humanity as the Arachosians, the chicken-people of Linschoten XV, Raumsog and the Bright Empire; hostile planets like Arachosia, Paradise VII, Amazonas Triste, Henriada, the Solid Planet and Shayol; the sheer physical realities of coming to grips with an inimical cosmos serve to bring out the best and the worst in man; wearing him down, driving him insane, exposing his darker qualities one minute, ennobling him through trial and suffering the next.

Smith uses space, with its "real or imagined horrors" (Q/163), to examine the various aspects of our humanity; and understanding and celebrating our humanity is Smith's greatest priority. One ancient lord is quoted as saying: "We must be people first and happy later, lest we live and die in vain" (B/211). Space stops man from being "people first," and so this is the level at which man must confront it.

By the nature of this confrontation, space too becomes the place of self-discovery, of expiation and sacrifice, of nobility, reaffirmation, and endless promise—one of the settings in which we may discover what being "people" means. Space is where man meets himself. Apart from the very real dangers of "Rats/Dragons" and the "wild unformed life" (Q/158) living in space itself, it is where we confront all our hidden evils—the worst aspects of ourselves. In a story like "Think Blue, Count Two"—a veritable moral and philosophical progress if ever there was one—an important distinction is made:

> Space never committed crimes. It just killed. Nature could transmit death, but only man could carry crime from world to world. Without the boxes, they looked into the bottomless depths of their unknown selves. (1/101)

So, when we hear of how the Storm Planet, Henriada, is "located within a series of bad pockets of space" (Q/68), we know that this is firstly a physical reality, for the Big Nothing is far from empty (thanks to the discoveries made by Colonel Harkening, Rambo, John Joy Tree, Samm and Finsternis); but we also come to understand that it comes to be a "Nothing" for the human spirit. We realize that such regions are "bad" because man is tormented there by the very facets of his own humanity, a humanity that is stretched thin, twisted and tested to the limit.

Aware of this awful dehumanizing role played by space, Trece thus says to Veesey:

> "The little boxes protected us from ourselves. And now there aren't any. We are helpless. There isn't anything here to protect us from us. What hurts man like man? What kills people like people? What danger to us could be more terrible than ourselves? (I/101)

Death in Smith's stories is never the terrible end we often make it, as we shall see presently. It is the "how" and "why" (rather than the "what") of it that matters. To survive space, the terrible Up-and-Out, man must ultimately survive himself. And again, to do that, he must fathom the depths of his humanity and draw on courage and sacrifice and love: he must re-establish his priorities and find a new purpose for being man.

§

In all of the actual "space travel" stories in the series—"The Lady Who Sailed the Soul," "The Game of Rat and Dragon," "The Burning of the Brain," "Drunkboat," "Think Blue, Count Two," "Scanners Live in Vain," etc.—the transits are generally shown to involve self-sacrifice and a richer understanding of loving and giving. For these journeys through danger, death, and the naked evils of self to be successful, man must resort to his better self, his higher qualities. Perhaps this is why Smith's stories suggest legends and myths: they resonate with the struggle, both inner and outer. When man loses this struggle, it is because he has lost his humanity, his vital sensitivity to life. This is the terrible loss Sto Odin recognizes in "Under Old Earth" when he speaks of mankind being killed "with a bland hopeless happiness" (B/214), or that Philip Vincent refers to on Pontoppidan when he recalls the long ago Dark Ages when "*people lost people*" (Q/30). By going through space to fulfill the destiny of man, people stand to lose what it is that makes them people. To lose, in Smith's worldview, is to be shut off from hope and love, to be without an insight into the true essence of what it is to be fully human.

Unlike the Christian polarization of good and evil into extremes, Smith recognizes—again in the Jungian way: acknowledging the value of archetypes such as the shadow—that this vying of good with evil is a necessary and vital melding, beyond morality. Benjacomin Bozart is not censured by the narrator of "Mother Hitton's Littul Kittons" as a bad man, but rather is explained:

> He was no more "wrong" than a shark approaching a school of cod. Life's nature is to live, and he had been nurtured to live as he had to live—by seeking prey. (B/258)

Often it is ignorance and fear, propaganda or social conditioning (as on Viola Siderea) that leads to cruel unjust acts. Smith has the post-Rediscovery narrator of "The Dead Lady of Clown Town" speak of the need for a seasoning of anger and hate with our better qualities to preserve vitality in the race:

> We today know that variety, flexibility, danger and the seasoning of a little hate can make love and life bloom as they never bloomed before.... (B/193)

It is Smith as ethical pragmatist, as again the Jungian "healer," who has Jean-Jacques Vomact express the Instrumentality's Rediscovery of Man program as being: "To make life dangerous enough and interesting enough to be real again" (N/123). There is no tonic like loss and adversity. When man rediscovers himself, he is brought face to face with pain and suffering and death; with the harsh realities we find still rampant in the earlier stories set in the pre-Rediscovery period. Surviving space is therefore a raw test of man and his ability to stay civilized. As Philip Vincent tells his council:

"We are judging space. What happens to a man when he moves out into the Big Nothing? Do we leave Earth behind? Why did civilization fall?" (Q/29)

It is not easy for man to remain kind and noble and civilized among the stars, nor does he always succeed. We witness the klopts; we see Talatashar before the wardens come to his aid; and we hear of the fate of the *Old Twenty-two*, whose crew "began making up evil from the people-insides" (I/103).

If man fails, it is because his humanity has failed. Space is deadly, but mainly because it does test all that man needs most to stay man. It tests us just by being itself. By fulfilling its own nature, it threatens to undermine our own. If man cannot survive such an acid test, then he does not deserve to.

Man Against Ideas

It hardly needs mentioning that "man" in Smith's universe comes to signify any sentient, self-aware being capable of love and self-sacrifice (though this is a truth not generally accepted by organized humanity in the Instrumentality stories). In the Hate Hall, a voice *spieks* to Rod and asks:

> *Rob McBan is a man, man, man*
> *But what is man?* (N/198)

Whether related to a true human, a machine, a synthetic phantom warden like Sh'san, a "hominid" (adapted humans from other worlds) or a "homunculus" (animal-derived under-person), the debate over what constitutes humanity comes up against barriers of ideology and social convention.

Smith repeatedly makes his most "human" and attractive characters non-human (C'mell, D'joan, B'dikkat, even the unmodified cat Griselda on Xanadu) and so continually tests these prejudices and conventions. Stories like "The Ballad of Lost C'mell" and "The Dead Lady of Clown Town," and parts of

Norstrilia concern revolution by coercion, no matter how generally non-violent. C'mell works with Jestocost and the powerful E'telekeli to win time for the underpeople in their centuries-long struggle against the amazingly hidebound attitudes of the Instrumentality. D'joan, Elaine, and Hunter, working with the mechanical imprint of the Lady Panc Ashash, have already begun this long progress towards a new status by their passive love-revolution on Fomalhaut III. Jestocost, as a member of the Instrumentality, becomes a champion of justice. Like Smith, he too is a pragmatist:

> He did not think that mankind would ever get around to correcting ancient wrongs unless the underpeople themselves had some of the tools of power—weapons, conspiracy, wealth and (above all) organization with which to challenge man. He was not afraid of revolt, but he thirsted for justice with an obsessive yearning which overrode all other considerations. (B/319)

Though it remains a tale of revolution, "The Ballad of Lost C'mell" is pre-eminently a story of unrequited love, and in this there is an even more provocative revolutionary issue, namely the social and moral dilemma of a relationship between a human and a cat-derived girlygirl. In the far future it is not uncommon for humans and underpeople to enter into close physical relations, an idea advanced long before Harlan Ellison was outraging the public with his *Dangerous Visions*. A desperate Earth government hopes to appease Rod McBan by providing him with girls "of all shapes, sizes, smells and ages—all the way from young ladies of good family down to dog-derived undergirls who smelled of romance all the time...." (N/2).

Smith plays it safe here. Seduction is permitted, provided there is no actual consummation—or at least that is the *legal* and *official* position regarding the use of girlygirls and female servants of animal extraction. But when we witness the advances made on C'mell by Tostig Amaral, we realize that such conduct may not be uncommon.

And while there is no interbreeding between the different species of under-people for physiological and genetic reasons (N/155), C'mell embarrasses some soldiers high on Earthport by suggesting that "she might be a mixed type, part human and part animal" (N/149). This could mean merely a scientific rather than an illicit sexual origin, but however we interpret clues like "mixed," the connection is deliberately made and flaunted. Such a provocation, made about such a hedonistic age, is no accident. Smith is purposefully toying with one of our own society's most fundamental taboos. The parallels with contemporary and historical racialist attitudes are obvious; and just as the differences of color and physiological type are as artificial as the barriers of ideology, so too do the differences become immaterial here. The love of T'ruth for her cataleptic master, Murray Madigan, is beyond reproach regardless of her sexual ministrations to him; while Rod's caring for C'mell "because he sensed in their whole relationship a friendliness much more fervent than sex itself" (N/176) shows Smith's position most clearly. These are conscious, consenting creatures who share a full awareness of life and its common bonds between them.

It is immaterial that the C'mell/Jestocost relationship remains unconsummated, for there are better victories in Smith's credo of love. Jestocost likes C'mell "as a being, not as a girlygirl" (B/332). It is this "equality"—the equality that has such a creature chosen for reasons above and beyond her functional, designed role—that is important. The major point is that we feel as a certain "off-Earth prince" felt:

> "Funny, C'mell, you're not even a person and you're the most intelligent *human being* I've met in this place. Do you know it made my planet poor to send me here? And what did I get out of them? Nothing, nothing, and a thousand times nothing. But you, now. If you'd been running the government of Earth, I'd have gotten what my people need, and this world

would be richer too. Manhome, they call it. Manhome, my eye! The only smart person on it is a female cat." (B/327—my italics)

Here in this one paradox-ridden remark is the essence of man's struggle with ideas, as well as an inkling of the shift in attitude that shall lead on to that "ending of the ways" foreseen by the robot Livius. Were man able to let himself be guided more by his heart and feelings and less by his over-rationalizations (his protocol and conventions) these dilemmas would cease to exist, and the whole issue raised by Livius about the tests for humanity would be relegated to its proper place: an unanswerable mystery requiring tolerance and understanding. Perhaps it is important that Jestocost, with his sense of justice and his commitment to humanity, relies on instincts and ideals rather than intellect:

> His mind was quick, too quick to be deeply intelligent. He thought by gestalt, not by logic. (B/320)

We too must act with all our faculties; with ourselves in balance.
Smith emphasizes this "Jungian" need for a balanced self — the fully "human way"—when he has Martel survey his own fellow scanners at the emergency meeting called to decide on the fate of Adam Stone. Martel is "cranched"—temporarily restored to a feeling, sensation- and emotion-rich mode of existence and reality-perception. Once again, he sees things with the balanced view available to ordinary men, with the added incentive of cherishing such precious, fully human moments because they are so rare.

> Had he been haberman, he would have thought only with his mind, not with his heart and guts and blood. (B/27)

That is, not with his full humanity. He realizes too just how dangerous it is to be unbalanced and "dehumanized" this way, and later says:

> "If the others were all cranched, as I am, they would see it in a human way, not with the narrow crazy logic which they used in the meeting." (B/28)

Important here is the connection Smith makes between being fully human and true freedom. They go together, one the automatic result of the other. Away from "the narrow crazy logic," being human and free to choose, Martel discovers the truth of this: "With real freedom, he began to think of what he still might do" (B/28).

What bitter irony it is that the scanners cannot see beyond the preservation of their code and their way of life, cannot see positive alternatives, because they are constantly being cut off from their full humanity *for the good of humanity in general*.

The other deadly idea which prevails in this future society is the sinister belief nursed by the Lords and Ladies of the Instrumentality that they are automatically working in humanity's best interests. In spite of its victories over Raumsog, the Arachosians, even the duck-like Apicians,[40] the Instrumentality is a very real threat to man, bringing him through "a nightmare of perfection …to the edge of suicide" (B/283). It has always been guided by "the old philosophy—if you see wrong, right it" (N/163), never thinking, never realizing as Jestocost does (and as the wise and aging Lord Crudelta does) that suffering and having things go wrong are as much blessings for our humanity as are an appreciation of the beauty of life or an awareness of the value of true friendship. Shared adversity is a stabilizing and ennobling thing for any community just as it is for any individual. Hence the significance of Rod McBan's comparison of

---

40. A rum victory, this: "From Gustible's Planet" is, by its tone, the only distinctly anomalous tale in the canon, less integral even than the tenuously-linked "Nancy."

the rich vitality of an ever-threatened, harsh Norstrilia with that of an over-populated, newly-awakened Earth, recovering from its centuries-long malaise—from the misguided caring that was in fact the worst possible neglect. Hence the importance of the dissolute Lord Tedesco's finding pleasure in service, a pleasure "greater than any he had ever experienced before" (B/122). For these things show ideas and assumptions on the turn: duty and service become their own rewards; an awareness is growing that humanity must be earned and won and deserved—it is not an automatic right of birth.

The Instrumentality has been responsible for this "fool's paradise." It has known that man is his own worst enemy; what irony that it should also be the "enemy within." When we are told that:

> Earth won and the others lost, because the leaders of Earth never put other considerations ahead of survival (B/114)

we realize just how unimportant survival could become without these "other considerations"—things like self-respect, freedom, personal honor and an individual sense of purpose. In "Alpha Ralpha Boulevard" Maximilien Macht tells Paul and Virginia:

> *This is what the Lords of the Instrumentality never let us have. Fear. Reality. We were born in a stupor and we died in a dream. Even the underpeople, the animals, had more life than we did. The machines did not have fear. That's what we were. Machines who thought they were men. And now we are free.* (B/301)

What irony, too, that the underpeople, hunted and killed for the slightest misdemeanor, are seen as having more *life*.

This threat posed by the Instrumentality does not disappear with the Rediscovery of Man, for the Instrumentality is a repressive elite. Even by the time of Rod McBan's arrival on Mars, there is little effective freedom of expression. Jean-Jacques Vomact has been banished from Earth—charged with revolt against the Instrumentality—simply because he produced more than the stipulated number of issues of a newspaper.

> "People can say anything they want on Earth, and they can print up to twenty copies of anything they need to print, but beyond that it's mass communication. Against the law." (N/124)

Given the ferocity with which the Instrumentality protects itself, such rulings are expedient to this end, as is the prohibition of the dissemination of religions and ideologies between the different worlds of man. But such caution, even when amply justified, stands to make such a body overzealous and over-prescriptive in the public interests they allegedly serve, allowing the Pleasure Revolution and an almost unnatural cultural homogeneity to draw mankind into decadence. It is only by the actions of the Jestocosts and the Sto Odins of the day, by the foment of ideas provoked by the aspirations of the underpeople, that the race is saved.

Man Against Death

"O death, where is thy sting?"
—I Corinthians XV:55

Related to the struggle with an inimical if oblivious cosmos is man's confrontation with what we conventionally call the "final adversary"—death. Death is "the long bleak dark" (N/187), the "private, everlasting night" (N/145)—the "final shock" and the "dark forever" (N/191) of the Judson poem seen by Rod McBan when he goes to visit the Catmaster.

Smith would have us see death in a special way. It is indeed "a very private affair" (N/211) but, again in a Jungian sense, there are important qualifications to its tyranny. It is not the ultimate isolation, as we shall see presently, and it is just one more facet of nature. "Death is not bad, soldier. It just comes badly," says the rat-woman to the human soldier who is about to kill her (B/196).

The worst threat that such a state poses for man is that it might separate him from life before he has achieved self-fulfillment, before he has discovered that death does not matter. Death alters things, but need not finish them; and there are always fates far worse—like a second-rate, unfulfilled life such as that lived by those under the pre-Rediscovery Instrumentality. In Smith's stories, death is constantly being qualified in its role as the great leveler; it is contained and reduced by factors that transcend death.

It is important to note that death is not defeated by a divine being with a promise of eternal life, or even some celestial union of souls. Death is defeated simply by an attitude—one directly related to self-fulfillment. The old mouse-woman, Baby-baby, explains to Elaine how:

> "Death is a *when*, not a *what*. It's the same for all of us. Don't be scared... you may find mercy and love. They're much richer than death, if you can only find them. Once you do find them, death won't be very important." (B/152)

Nor is it important whether the horse on Pontoppidan lives or dies after its spectacular climb out of the Hipsy Dipsy and its own personal "rediscovery" of man: "After all, he has already had his great triumph" (Q/29). This same "enlightened" attitude is echoed by the bear-man Orson: "There is no death. Not for love." (B/1 98).

In that beautiful moment at the end of "The Lady Who Sailed *The Soul*," Helen is seen dying happily, believing "that if they could conquer space, they might conquer death as well" (B/66). If space is a place where man is exposed and death exerts its terrifying dominion, then the conquest of space—as a process of fulfilling man by teaching him about his humanity—is also a fitting conquest of death, in spite of the pain, in spite of the personal suffering. Rather than being the great and final unknown of most human cultural traditions, death marks the change-over point, a point of transition and quite possibly of some as-yet-unknowable metamorphosis.

Man Against Loneliness and Fear

"But none shall triumph a whole life through:
For death is one, and the fates are three.
At the door of life, by the gate of breath;
There are worse things waiting for man than death."
—Swinburne, "The Triumph of Time"

The conflict with death is also related to the struggle against loneliness and fear. This is yet another crisis of self that haunts all conscious life. Aggravated by the vast solitudes of space, and exacerbated by the inevitability of death and the prospect of being forever alone, it is relieved only by love, empathy, and companionship, by self-realization and—ideally—self-fulfillment.

We hear of synthetic companions being given to man in space, or made by him out of desperation simply to stave off this loneliness: Suzdal's "hypnotics and cubes to provide him the semblance of company, a large crowd of friendly people who could be convoked out of his own hallucinations" (B/96), as well as his turtle-men; Gordon Greene's *sokta*-induced Nancy in "Nancy"; and the party-companions summoned by a lonely spaceman in "The Good Friends."

Even in an age when there can be the telepathic sharing of one's subjective experience of life with others, it is being alone, without friendship, without love that is the ultimate agony and loss. When the council on Pontoppidan considers the fate of Perino's near-immortal horse, the Hereditary Dictator points out just how insignificant a loss death can be:

"If we kill that horse, gentlemen, we will not be doing the horse a great wrong. He is an old animal, and I do not think that he will mind dying very much, now that he is away from the ordeal of loneliness which he feared more than death." (Q/29)

Just as Helen America, D'joan, Laird, and even Jestocost all attain a triumph in death by not dying alone, so does this aged and unmodified creature.

Man Against the Unknown

"All the thousands and tens of thousands of gods are all one god."
—Chinese proverb

"Some people might call it a god. I call it nothing."
—Paul, regarding the Abba-dingo

"The pattern of God exists in every man."
—Carl Gustav Jung

"God is where he has always been—around us, near us, in us."
—Maximilien Macht in "Alpha Ralpha Boulevard"

This brings us to the ultimate sphere of conflict: man against the unknown. As a finite creature in an infinite universe, man is continually being brought into confrontation with things beyond his ken. We have the inability of either the humans or the "illusory" guardians of "Think Blue, Count Two" to explain the true nature of the "ghosts" (Sh'san, Tal's mother, Marcia and the captain) when they appear (I/115). In "The Colonel Came Back from Nothing-at-All" we have Colonel Harkening's space-being—"*some gigantic form of life immensely beyond the limits of human imagination*" (I/128). There are the visions and nightmares of Space Three, the "wild unformed life" (Q/158) detected and destroyed by Folly, Samm, and Finsternis; the weeping two-headed elephants and their "unimaginable ships" (Q/168) discovered by John Joy Tree (again with the assertion that such things are beyond our imagination); and in "Under Old Earth" we learn of the Douglas-Ouyang entity—"A power which had tried to find friendship with man, but had found the wrong man and the wrong friendship" (B/256).

§

Smith clearly opts for a marvelous universe, purposely beyond the limits of the human imagination. As we have already seen, there is a double process at work in most of the Instrumentality stories—an expanding out to touch on issues of ultimate meaning and the nature of being, and then a contracting away from rigorous scientific enquiry to a respect for all aspects of life and the simpler ethical abstractions of love and charity.

This process is well illustrated in "The Colonel Came Back from Nothing-at-All" (re-worked and later published in a different form as "Drunkboat"). Colonel Harkening, the first human to undergo a planoform jump, is lost in the Big Nothing of space. Later he re-appears, naked and virtually comatose, without his tiny chronoplast chamber, and is discovered to be in mental contact with a vast non-human intelligence from which he must be rescued by a team of doctors and a little girl telepath.

From the first, the nature of this encounter is presented as being with a distinctly God-like being. Smith prepares us for this by making his telepath a member of the Post-Soviet Orthodox Eastern Quakers; someone with a pronounced religious bias. She says to the doctors:

> "I want you three to wear the helmet of the pin-lighters and ride with me into hell itself. That soul is lost... lost to the mercy of God and to the friendship of mankind." (I/126)

The irony is that when they set off on their "crusade" to win Harkening back from "all the terrors of the Up-and-Out" (I/121), they discover him to be communing with an awesome entity which *could* be a deity—but which turns out to be just another physical phenomenon. Thus there is a revelation, but hardly an epiphany. When at last they return to Earth with all that they have learned and accomplished, they realize that "The world was better, but not much the wiser" (I/129).

This is a fundamental dictum for Smith's Instrumentality stories. There is a constant counterpoint in this double process of discovery and wonder. We become wiser, but only wise enough to realize that we are not so very wise at all in the face of an infinite universe and ultimate meanings. The struggle to know continues. As is the case with the return of the Vom Acht sisters or the Rediscovery of Man, life may become better, but man remains man, fallible, striving, nursing his own best and worst features within himself.

And there are still miracles, even if they are subjective and phenomenalistic ones—miracles that cannot be adequately communicated to the world in general. Gordon Greene does find his Nancy, who is "more real than life itself" (I/196), even though she is a drug-induced reality, and Helen America remains convinced that Mr. Gray-no-more came to her even as she journeyed across space to join him on New Earth.

> "You did so come to *The Soul*," she said. "You did so stand beside me when I was lost and did not know how to handle the weapon."
> "If I came then, darling, I'll come again, wherever you are...." (B/66)

As we have already seen in man's conflict with the nature of being and death, there are no easy answers. We might say that Colonel Harkening's space-being, though awesome and unknowable and seemingly absolute, is one more phenomenal fact in a vast phenomenon-filled cosmos. It is just another "relative" god when seen from anything like a clinical over-view, just as Commander Suzdal is an absolute God to the Cats of Catland, or Murray Madigan is T'ruth's "god" (Q/91) or humans are "gods" to the underpeople (N/247). The revealed gods of Smith's universe—Christian and non-Christian alike—are relative gods, forever contained and "accounted for." But whatever their form or limitations, such gods do point to a direction which the human spirit would take; they do reflect a longing that is vital to our nature.

Thus, offsetting Smith's orthodox Episcopalian background we have this expansive viewpoint which sees all man's gods as merely reflections of a yearning for meaning—a yearning which, properly manifested, becomes a celebration of the vital and noblest sides of humanity. Any absolutist idea of god is always qualified by what man is and what man needs his god to be. When Sto Odin asks his robot servant, Livius, "What do you call a god?," the robot answers: "A person or an idea capable of starting wholly new cultural patterns in motion" (B/218). Consequently, in a man-created-god inversion, the pharaoh Akhnaton is described as a ruler who "invented the best of the early gods" (B/219), a very revealing behavioral and cultural observation by Smith. (Of course, this *is* a robot talking, supposedly divorced from spiritual imperatives, but Smith has always given great wisdom to his artificial constructs, whether it be T'ruth, D'alma, the Lady Panc Ashash, Sh'san, or Livius, printed with the brain pattern of "a psychiatrist who turned into a general" (B/216).)

By Libius's same definition, Christianity too becomes a projection of human needs—an institutionalization of mankind's desires for an answer to life and for a higher meaning.

This same "miraculous" dimension also intrudes in such things as the visions, the nightmares, the awesome powers experienced by Artyr Rambo in Space Three en route to his Elizabeth, or in Lavinia's inexplicably precise vision of a trans-formed Rod with C'mell on Earth. Though this last wonder has the pseudo-scientific agency of stroon-laced honey from

Paradise VII for an empirical basis, it nonetheless smacks of the paranormal, even in Smith's already amazing universe of tele- paths and visionaries. Occurring alongside the appearance of wardens like Sh'san and the marvelous architectural and teleki- netic feats of the Daimoni, this "paranormal" aspect adds a rich edge to the possibility of anything and everything taking place. Regardless of the source or the cause, the appropriate attitude in such an infinite universe has to be one of infinite wonder, faith, and reverence.

2: The Nature of the Victory

There is a simple equation that may be applied to the Instru- mentality canon:

Love—is the measure of our humanity
　is the key to our humanity
　is the way to truth
　is knowing yourself and all life
　is sacrifice
　is the way to defeat death
　is the way to transform life
　requires/leads to understanding and self-fulfilment
　transcends all.

The winning that takes place in the areas of conflict we have mentioned, comes down to a simple awareness that this equa- tion holds true. Victory without love, without mercy and kind- ness and denial of self, is no victory at all, regardless of personal, economic, or material gain.

The Different Kinds of Love

In Smith's writing, love covers all the traditional classifi- cations—*eros* to *agape*—involving sympathy and empathy, selfishness and self-denial, the sacred and the profane. Smith's heroes and heroines—Jestocost, Hunter, Sto Odin, D'joan C'mell, Santuna—are all champions of ideals, all fallible, all capable of immense giving and sacrifice.

To classify and illustrate these aspects of love, we might say that the Instrumentality stories deal with the love of:

(a) Man for woman; woman for man;
(b) Man for an ideal;
(c) Man for humanity and all life;
(d) Man for a universal spirit.

We are never given the lower "survival" love of man for self except as a passing contrast to highlight one of the other forms of positive love.

The first kind of love is at the center of nearly all of Smith's best stories. Most often we have tales of great loves involving a quest, or trial, or ordeal: a conventional love relationship under stress which serves to elevate it so that it touches on other kinds of love, overlapping inextricably with them. Many such stories, by the nature of the love-adventure being recounted, take on the status of myths and legends, with that delightfully Jungian archetypal quality we have mentioned, making them rich with wholeness and healing and fulfillment. Such love stories include those of: Martel and Luci; Rambo and Elizabeth; Helen America and Mr. Gray-no-more; Carlotta and Laird; Juli and Laird; Dobyns Bennett and Terza Vomact; Magnus Taliano and Dolores Oh; Paul and Virginia; Rod and C'mell and Lavinia; Elaine and Hunter; T'ruth and Murray Madigan; T'ruth and Casher (her "might-have-been"); Casher and Calelta; Samm, Folly and Finsternis; Veesey and Talatashar; Lady Da and Mercer.

These relationships are set in frameworks of crisis and self-discovery, and they lead on to other forms of loving and kindness. It can be argued that some of these loves are less integral than others (for example, Rogov and Cherpas, Santuna and Sun-boy), but as they provide a structure of emotional and spiritual involvement—illustrating sacrifice, patience, loyalty, charity—they tend nonetheless to lie at the basis of the different kinds of love interrelated with them.

Furthermore, these love-adventures display in miniature the qualities man should apply in all his dealings with his fellow beings. For example, Martel loves Luci—but he also loves humanity enough to defy his fellow scanners to save Adam Stone. He abandons his duty to the code of the scanners in order to fulfill a higher duty to all of humanity. Jestocost, though we are told he has "little love, no fear, freedom from ambition and dedication to his job" (B/318), nevertheless (by whatever passion of government and sense of propriety moves him) truly believes in justice and the rights of the underpeople. He genuinely serves life. And love is such an infinite, transcending quality, that even the little of it he possesses is enough to work the necessary miracles. On his death-bed, after a life in which only "justice mattered," only "the perpetual return of mankind to progress" mattered (B/330), Jestocost's final questions in the face of death turn not to a cosmic creator, nor to any of the religions thrown up by the Rediscovery of Man, but rather his "death-bed conversion" would seem to be to love:

> *I have helped your people.*
> "Yes," came back the faintest of faraway whispers, inside his head.
> *I am dying. I must know. Did she love me?*
> "She went on without you, so much did she love you. She let you go, for your sake, not for hers. She really loved you. More than death. More than life. More than time. You will never be apart."
> *Never apart?*
> "Not, not in the memory of man," said the voice, and was then still.
> Jestocost lay back on his pillow and waited for the day to end. (B/337)

Thus selfless love ennobles, and allows one's better self to grow. It cuts across the worst parts of man and touches on the best—nobility and dignity, those higher abstracts in our nature. When the "witch" Elaine first comes upon the forbidden door leading down to the Lower City of Kalma, we are told: "She was not yet frantic, not yet desperate, she was not yet even noble" (B/133). She has yet to experience Hunter, D'joan, and the underpeople in the Brown and Yellow Corridor. She has yet to have the experience that will provide the basis for her achieving a Blakean "innocence through experience."

And, of course, while the "ultimate" loss always seems to be death itself, we are to remember that there is no final grave in a Smith story. Death remains the great cheater, but it too is constantly cheated of its prey. In *Norstrilia* Smith quotes from "A Forsaken Garden," a poem by the pre-Raphaelite poet Algernon Charles Swinburne. Swinburne is an interesting choice for Smith to make, for, like the E.C.Z. Judson verse quoted earlier in the same novel (dealing with the closeness of "the tideless river" and "the dark forever" (N/191)), Swinburne's work also shows a preoccupation with the transience of life and with that final terrible confrontation with death, but in contrast to the Judson extracts the Swinburne verse promises a victory. In poems like "The Triumph of Time" and particularly "A Forsaken Garden" there are both fearful questions ("What love was ever as deep as a grave?") and others that suggest hope ("Or they loved their life through, and then went whither?/And were one to the end— but what end who knows?").[41] But there is also the paradoxical solace, the reassurance that after death there is no longer the fear of death ("Here death may deal not again for ever"). By making that terrible crossing, we are free of it; death is defeated at its moment of triumph. Moreover, it is a crossing to be made with love if the victory is to be won, for as T'ruth tells Casher O'Neill: "Love is the only end of things" (Q/97).

Consequently, as an act of faith in the transcending power of

41. Cecil Y. Lang, ed., *The Pre-Raphaelites and Their Circle* (1968), 383.

love over death, Laird willingly dies to be with Juli Vom Acht *and* his first love, Carlotta, in "The Queen of the Afternoon," sacrificing youth and vitality:

> "My darling and last love," he said, "I will be losing you twice. I cannot bear it. I have asked the physician for medicine to counteract the rejuvenation. In an hour I shall be as old as you. We are going together. And somewhere out there we will meet Carlotta and we will hold hands, the three of us, among the stars." (I/70)

So too does Helen America meet death happily:

> She believed that if they could conquer space, they might conquer death as well. (B/66)

Such attitudes contain the same transcending note of triumph as C'mell's love for her "renegade" Lord. Once again, the Jungian note is clear. If the psyche "isn't entirely confined to space and time" as Jung says,[42] then death is truly an interruption and not an ending. How true are those words from "A Forsaken Garden," quoted to Rod by the great bird-man, E'telekeli; for in the face of such prospects "Death lies dead" indeed (N/249).

Death, then, remains the penultimate rather than the ultimate loss. The ultimate uttermost losing, as we have already seen, is the inability to feel and know love—the loss of love which is the loss of one's very humanity. This one fact lends new substance to the *I Loved You and Lost You* song sung by Hunter to Elaine, completing the circle, the equation of true loss—to "know" before winning and losing.

> I knew you, and loved you,
> and won you, in Kalma.

---

42. Laurens van der Post citing Carl Jung, BBC television program, *The Story of Carl Gustav Jung* (1975).

I won you, and loved you,
and lost you, my darling! (B/160)

It is a refrain taken up by Sto Odin, a seemingly less likely candidate, when he reflects on friends long dead:

"...they were here, and they loved me, and they knew me, and now they are dead." (B/221)

It is an isolation from love that is feared here; that is what gives death its sting. And if loss of love means the loss of humanity, then, conversely, the gaining of love means the gaining of humanity. It is the greatest of all weapons, making all the conflicts—with space, with death, with ideas, with fear—end in victory. When a jealous and hurt Casher O'Neill is confronted with T'ruth's total life-commitment to the cataleptic Murray Madigan, he questions it as a waste:

"But what for?" asked Casher, a little crossly....
"For life!" she cried, "In any form, in any way...."
"What's the use of it?" insisted Casher.
"I can tell you, man, what the use is. Love."
"What did you say?" said Casher.
"I said the use was love. Love is the only end of things. Love on the one side, and death on the other. If you are strong enough to use a real weapon, I can give you a weapon which will put Mizzer at your mercy. Your cruiser and your laser would just be toys against the weapon of love. You can't fight love." (Q/96-97)

Similarly, the revolt of the underpeople on Fomalhaut III (which so severely tests the established definitions of humanity held by the Instrumentality) is a revolution through an understanding of what love is and what it can do. D'joan (now called Joan) says:

"Love is knowing yourself and knowing all other people and things." (B/205)

And again:

"Love is for life itself, and we have life." (B/180)

Baby-baby corrects a misunderstanding Elaine, and describes the sort of love they have discovered for themselves as "Love for life. Love for all things living" (B/152). When the robot soldier asks his crucial question, the mechanical Lady Panc Ashash provides the inevitable answer:

"You mean I'm *alive*? I *exist*?"
"With love, you do," said the Lady Panc Ashash.
(B/186)

She continues with: "You are not really escaping two human commands. You are making a choice. You. That makes you men." (B/186)

This final qualification is an important one. It is no programmed, preconceived concern for life which is being talked about here; no inbuilt rearing. It is contingent on choice, and on a choice that means self-denial (and in the case of the robot sergeant and his troops, self-destruction). This moment of confrontation in "The Dead Lady of Clown Town" is an ideological, ontological, and poetic climax. It works beautifully in context, and ends up making the robots and underpeople, newly awakened to love, seem so much more human than the human citizens whose daily routine has been disturbed by this incident. It is with savage irony that we are told: "The street had filled full of real people" (B/190), for these are the ones who have lost; they represent humanity locked in its "nightmare of perfection" (B/283), being seriously imperiled by the "bland hopeless happiness" (B/214) maintained by a decadent pre-Rediscovery Instrumentality.

There can be no real happiness without loss, trial, and sacrifice. And just as mankind will later attain a "real" life under the Rediscovery, so too do the underpeople yearn to be given "real life" (B/150)—that is, a life in which they are loved as sentient creatures and as having dignity.

The Glory and Affirmation of Man

Smith makes a religion of love and of life itself. All vitality, all Nature, is good (and is contained by its own natural justice), whether it be the life of a natural predator like Benjacomin Bozart, that of the lowliest underperson, or even that of some unchanged birds high on Alpha Ralpha Boulevard. When the cynical, jaded Jean-Jacques Vomact tells Rod that his servant Eleanor—disguised to look like Rod—will probably be killed, adding: "That's what you bought her for, isn't it? Aren't you rich enough?," Rod answers: "No, no, no... nobody is that rich" (N/127). If life alone is of such immense value, life enriched by love is invaluable. Only creatures who deny and abuse their natures, who are "contaminated" (N/199) by their own conscious actions, are the exception to this rule of life.

The Arachosians, for instance, are "not men" but "enemies" (N/199) (unlike the chicken-people of Linschoten XV, who are misguided and motivated by fear), not because of the cruel fate on Arachosia that has left them mutated into hermaphroditic klopts, but because of their willful acceptance of such a lot. By making a virtue of their grim situation, embracing a code of hatred for beauty and anything not their own twisted brand of normal, they have sunk through deprivation to depravity, sacrificing dignity and forsaking even the very idea of being human. The idea that can transform animals and machines into something more can work the other way, transforming careless men into something less. As with the robots outside Clown Town, just as choice makes us men, choice can also "unman" us. Along with hope and love, choice is the distinctively human way. Through the very act of choosing, even when the choice is not well-made (as in the case of the Arachosians and of Suzdal's folly—a bad choice followed by an irresponsibly good one—and mark the tone of approbation taken by the narrator for the "human way" behind Suzdal's freely-chosen solution to it):

> It is the pride of the Instrumentality that the Instrumentality allows its officers to commit crimes or mistakes or suicide. The Instrumentality does the things for mankind that a computer cannot do. The Instrumentality leaves the human brain, the human choice, in action. (B/109)

With this love for all life there is also an appropriate respect for the unique individuality of each "sentient" thing. C'mell tells Rod:

> "You're not in the world just to own a piece of property or to handle a surname with a number after it. You're *you*. There's never been another you. There will never be another one, after you." (N/170)

And, in the same vein, reinforcing this focus, she later pleads with him:

> "Please make a trip with me, Rod. One last dangerous trip for you. Not for me. Not even for mankind. For life, Rod." (N/234)

When he descends into the Downdeep-downdeep, confronts E'telekeli, and has the true loving custodianship of the underpeople revealed to him, Rod willingly uses his wealth to set up the One Hundred and Fifty Fund, not for man, not for the underpeople, but for life itself. He realizes that the underpeople, who are becoming "the masters of men" (N/241) by "fixing up" the new cultures revived and needed for the Rediscovery of Man, are blessed by the same life-awareness and life-reverence. As C'mell says:

> "They make the same basic choices between power and beauty, between survival and self-sacrifice, between common sense and high courage." (N/237)

These crucial choices highlight the best and most noble aspects of man; reaffirming yet again Joan's teaching that:

> ...whatever *seems* human *is human*. It is the word that quickens, not the shape or the blood or the texture of flesh or hair or feathers. (N/211)

When Rod's money is wanted "to improve the race of man" (N/248), we are aware that there is a common destiny that these improvements will help make possible, and we are aware of how encompassing the term "man" now is. An "ending of the ways" is brought still closer.

Just as Joan becomes the mouthpiece for Smith's basic precepts for life, so too does the eagle-man, E'telekeli, become a speaker of truths and a virtual prophet-figure. His words to Rod are a synthesis of the great religious teachings, re-located into a new time and given a new application, but within the same general focus of ministering to life. He says to E'lamelanie:

> "True men are not free either.... They too have grief, fear, birth, old age, love, death, suffering and the tools of their own ruin...." (N/210-211)

And in referring to the men of the Ancient World:

> "They had all forgotten that humanness is itself imperfection and corruption, that which is perfect is no longer understandable...we must never be so foolish enough to look for perfection in this life." (N/211)

Similarly, he declares:

> "Freedom is what you do...." (N/211)
> "Great beliefs always come out of the sewers of cit-
> ies, not out of the towers of the ziggurats." (N/211)
> "We know that everything which loves has a value
> in itself." (N/212)
> "It is not necessary to do your duty joyfully—just
> to do it." (N/212)

The presentation of E'telekeli is almost overdone, for Smith surrenders the lyrical, restrained richness of a shorter work like "The Dead Lady of Clown Town" for a much more concentrat- ed, traditionally Christian presentation of the Holy Insurgency. But the latter day "Christianity" (characterized once again in its clandestine guise by the Sign of the Fish, and waiting for its Promised One) is of utmost importance simply because at its center lies the true mystery of a god of love. It is an agency of reverence and caring whereby people and underpeople might "mingle in complete comradeship" (N/219). When T'ruth refers to Casher's "most important weapon in the fight" for freedom on Mizzer (Q/71), and then produces her crucifix, it is of "the ultimate and undefeatable wisdom of the Sign of the Fish" that she is speaking (Q/114): the wisdom that sees love as the basis of any life-experience and certainly of any god-experience.

Balancing this, we are to remember how stringent the Instrumentality is in policing the dissemination of organized religion, for that too is a crucial aspect of Smith's attitude. In its custodianship and monitoring of human affairs, the "trans- planting of religion" is one of the Instrumentality's "hostile obsessions" (Q/73). Most of the precautions taken by this pragmatic and quasi-mystical authority are intended, first, to preserve and maintain its position, and then to make sure "that fanaticisms did not once more flare up between the stars, once again bringing wild hope and great death to all the mankinds" (Q/73).

But while this is a sound measure for government, the Instrumentality tends to overlook the spiritual mainsprings of such phenomena for the business of "keeping house." Quite rightly, the spiritual experience is (at least initially) a solitary thing, and Smith is continually celebrating this ennobling and uplifting force in man, exploited and distorted by religion, but pure and transforming in its solitary inception within each individual.

Restoring this vital and healing perspective to a view of our humanity, it is up to figures like E'telekeli to remind Rod that "mankind has moments of enormous passion which will come again and in which we will share" (N/212). And while E'telekeli acknowledges a higher power as something which the underpeople "love and cherish" because they "need it more than do the people on the surface," he reminds Rod and us that "the higher power and the large problems still wait for all men, whether men like it or not" (N/211-212).

The Christian cast to events in Downdeep-downdeep is later freed from polemics and dogma when the motives of the underpeople are revealed:

> "We are afraid that Man himself will die and leave us alone in the universe. We need Man, and there is still an immensity of time before we all pour into a common destiny.... We are the creatures of Man. You are gods to us." (N/247)

In turn, by implication, it is the faith of man and underpeople alike to worship the power that created all life, whatever it may be. Once again, the truths that are the motives in this ultimate self-sacrifice are pointed out to Rod by E'telekeli:

> "Men are evil when they are frightened or bored. They are good when they are happy and busy. I want you to give your money to provide games, sports,

competitions, shows, music, and a chance for honest hatred." (N/249)

And behind it all, behind the joint plan of E'telekeli, Lord Jestocost, and the Lady Alice More (the architects of the Rediscovery, who comprise this steadily-working "lever of life upon times" (N/262)), there is the simplest motive:

> "We are just altering the conditions of Man's situation for the present historical period! We want to steer Mankind away from tragedy and self-defeat. Though the cliffs may crumble, we want Man to remain." (N/249)

The implication too is that man cannot endure (or even remain man) unless he grows and develops; nor can he hope to grow without the spiritual awareness that is natural to him.

Also, Christianity is a blueprint for civilization. It is "the mystery behind the civilization of all these stars" (Q/129), for it has been the one agency which has kept man truly human. Early in Casher O'Neill's progress, on the Gem Planet, Pontoppidan, Philip Vincent and his daughter, Genevieve, remind us of how *"people lost people"* (Q/30) during the Dark Ages, and of how civilization ("a woman's choice first, and only later a man's" (Q/30)) is not a first nature condition for man but rather a second nature condition, learned and mastered through conscious choice, self-control, and the achievement of nobility. Philip Vincent says, in commenting on how civilization is an ancient "lady's word":

> "To be 'civilized' meant for people to be tame, to be kind, to be polished. If we kill this horse, we are wild. If we treat the horse gently, we are tame." (Q/30)

But not weak!—for tameness means the potential for wildness held in check. The storms of our first nature all rage within, as a personal and private conflict. Each of us, alone, must win for ourselves the name "civilized." "Lady" and "gentleman" are no idle terms in Smith's universe: to be these things represents a hard-won victory over self.

And what better "civilizer," what greater incentive for civilized behavior, than the notion that there exists a power which sanctions this ability to discriminate, to choose, and to grow through self-understanding? When Casher O'Neill sought victory over Colonel Wedder—a just vengeance through violence—he was pursuing Francis Bacon's dictum that revenge is "a kind of *wild* justice." The "tame" justice of a civilized man involves the self-restraint that can perceive an alternative way; employing non-violence and forgiveness, though again in a balanced fashion. Casher is "wild" enough to choose love as his weapon, because he sees that it will do the good. Though his "healing" of Wedder is dependent on the vast mental powers passed on from Agatha Madigan, Casher's self-denying love is the ultimate force and reason behind those gifts enlivened in him.

The Word That Quickens

When the heretic pharaoh Akhnaton is described by the robot, Livius, as "one of the first and greatest of the more-than-ancient kings" (B/228), the love-credo of Smith's Instrumentality canon is augmented yet again. In conventional terms, Livius's words about Sun-boy's namesake are not altogether true. As ruler of Egypt during the ill-fated Amarna period, Akhnaton was quite ineffectual: he lost provinces, his pacifism and monotheistic practices caused only trouble for Egypt, and his reign ended in blood and violence. But these negative aspects are those of that eternal struggle between the best and worst in man seen in "Think Blue, Count Two." In terms of love, mercy, nobility, and the courage to stand against opposing ideas, Livius's description of Akhnaton validly describes the first religion of love—the worshipping of one benign universal creator and life-source. This praiseworthy, love-based monotheism is later taken up by Christianity with its God-Nailed-High, though there is never any general endorsement by Smith of any one faith over another beyond such a foundation in love.

Love requires tolerance, and it is no accident that the taking of organized religion from one world to another is regarded by the Instrumentality as one of the few major crimes. Smith sees that it is in the exploitation of one's individual views by another (whether of moral codes, political beliefs, or god-perception) that most of history's greatest crimes have been committed. Within an attitude of love and tolerance, Smith has D'joan say:

> "...it is the duty of life to find more than life, and to exchange itself for the higher goodness." (B/191)

Smith's stories inevitably chronicle such moments of exchange, leading individuals through self-discovery to the point where they discover answers for themselves. So important is this one dictum, that Smith has it later re-stated by the narrator himself:

> "It's the mission of life always to look for something better than itself, and then to try to trade life itself for meaning." (B/208)

Such a mission is an individual one, the individual alone knowing when meaning has been attained.

But, whilst Smith would have us remember that mankind might get better, but not much wiser, it is clear that this is a case where travelling hopefully is better than arriving. The establishment of the Instrumentality after the Ancient Wars appears to be an act of progress offering a wonderful future for the race, though it did lead an unsuspecting humanity to "the edge of suicide" (B/283) before the Rediscovery of Man. The winning of rights for the underpeople begun in "The Dead Lady of Clown Town" is only a "relative" victory too. By the post-Rediscovery "Ballad of Lost C'mell" the underpeople have many new rights (they can earn money and hold property) but they are still second-rate citizens and they are mere "property" themselves. Jestocost is still seeking "a little more justice" for them (N/133) at the time of Rod McBan's journey to Earth, and we witness the contempt displayed to Rod on Mars by Dr. Vomact when he considers the ease with which Rod impersonates a cat underperson.

Thus we have yet to see the true emancipation of the underpeople, and this reminds us that there are not always simplistic, spectacular transformations in any society, no matter how enlightened. We must keep in mind the fact that even the Rediscovery-envitalized Earth of Rod McBan's day has "the vitality of the cesspool, of the compost heap" (N/178). Man still has a long way to go. There is, as well, the natural conservatism, the traditional views that must be changed and conditioned, as well as fear and avarice and the darker qualities of man's nature. Not even love can eradicate all these obstacles immediately.

Love, after all, must happen within each individual as a personal experience, before the love-equation can be made manifest; and one person's love-experience is always a notoriously provocative thing, causing a host of adverse reactions in the not-yet-converted. The beautiful things that make us truly human surface unevenly in any society as in any individual. (One need only recall the persecution of Christ or St Joan, Gandhi or Martin Luther King.)

It is important, too, that innocence, even the innocence of an Akhnaton or a Buddha, is not as out of place as it first seems. Rod displays the same naivety as such men when he regards the wonder of Earth for the first time and says, with ingenuous wisdom: "When people have such a wide, wet, beautiful world, all full of life, why should they kill me?" (N/142). It is no easy question to answer. The fault is not with Rod, it is with ourselves. We have our priorities wrong. Rod's words, the wonderful wisdom underlying the vision of Akhnaton, even the sheer joy displayed by the little gun-watching robot, Harry Hadrian, when, relieved of duty, he asks, "Can-I-go-wait-in-the-garden-and-look-at-the-live-things?" (Q/105)—these are intimations of a true and healing humanity and of how we should go about finding it.

Jung has alerted us to the danger of failing to see our vital priorities, claiming that in our present-day age "we are courting disaster"[43] through spiritual atrophy and neglect of our humanity; just as Smith is alerting his questing heroes and Lords. Like Jung, who says that any change must begin with the individual, Smith believes that each of us must, through self-realization, come to an understanding of what is best for us as a race. The "word that quickens" (N/211) is the word *human* (potentially, going even further, *life*) and the whole vast healing enterprise of the Rediscovery of Man is a rediscovery of self, the objective being a better, more complete humanity.

The Uttermost Mission

"To know one's self is to know others,
for heart can understand heart."
—Chinese proverb

Even at his most pragmatic and ruthless, Smith was a pro-Jungian thinker and writer. His whole life conforms to the creed of helping and healing; of close spiritual contact with all life. We see this in the repeated articulation of the archetypes; in his acceptance of the collective unconscious and his yearning for a higher meaning; in the creation and relocation of the great myths; in the rich patterns of symbols by which this is done. Of all the modern psychological and spiritual thinkers, it was Carl Jung who pointed out that it is the individual's paramount obligation to discover and realize his own unique self. To do anything else was to cause tension and conflict between the various aspects of that self; psychic storms that reflected the lack of cohesion and adjustment in the personality—the lack of personal fulfillment.

---

43. Carl G. Jung, ed., *Man and His Symbols* (1964), 101.

Little wonder, then, that the turtle-girl, T'ruth, should say:

> "You are right...about each of us being what she has to be. Isn't that liberty itself? If we each one must be something, isn't liberty the business of finding it out and then doing it—that one job, that uttermost mission compatible with our natures? How terrible it would be, to be something and never know what!" (Q/65)

So it is self-realization, the fulfillment of our natures, that is vitally important.

In this struggle, death is immaterial. Even the horse on Pontoppidan—its thoughts monitored by the dog-woman tele-path, D'alma—can discriminate:

> "Do you know what dying is?"
> Thought the horse promptly: "Certainly. No-horse."
> "Do you know what life is?"
> "Yes. Being a horse." (Q/26)

In other words, fulfilling his nature, being everything he can be. When Casher asks, "Do you want to die?," he is given the answer: "To no-horse? Yes, if this room, forever, is the end of things" (Q/27). When asked what it would prefer, the horse's answer is quick: "Dirt beneath my hooves, and wet air again, and a man on my back" (Q/27). In short, true to its nature, the horse wants fulfillment in terms of a horse life-view: it is totally itself. This recalls the truism in D.H. Lawrence's poem, "Lizard": "If men were as much men as lizards are lizards they'd be worth looking at."[44]

Death is no enemy when it provides relief and a release from what is not natural. Indeed, for the fulfilled—as with Laird, Jestocost, Sto Odin and D'joan—it can be a blessing: the moment of transfer and transcendence. Life to us, as for the

---

44. D. H. Lawrence, *Selected Poems* (1950), 156.

horse, is a fulfilling of one's nature. T'ruth tells Casher:

> "That's what life is, isn't it? Doing what you have
> to do in the first place. We're lucky people if we find it
> out." (Q/101-102)

The Meek Shall Inherit

Having considered a wide array of themes and stories, it will
be useful to conclude by examining a single story—showing the
patterns of winning and conflict and victory, and attainment-of-
love-and-humanity at work, in a set piece.

This story is "On the Sand Planet" (1965)—the third part of
Quest of Three Worlds and the next-to-last Cordwainer Smith
story published before Linebarger's death in 1966. Along with
the final story published in his lifetime, "Under Old Earth"
(1966), it is perhaps the most elusive and potentially most difficult story in the Instrumentality canon, reflecting the same
growing mystical dimension as that final tale of the Lord Sto
Odin's descent into the Gebiet—a mystical dimension always
present in classical Instrumentality stories but never before so
strongly displayed.

Here, in Casher O'Neill's return to Mizzer, we have a real
spiritual progress—a pilgrimage laden with private sanctions
and personal revelations. Though it has a pronounced Christian
cast to it (through the various devotional references—which
account for much of its difficulty) the story also bridges the gap
between the great religious teachings of East and West, synthesizing the best of human beliefs. By the time Casher returns to
the desert planet, Mizzer, through Space Three, he has learned
from T'ruth the lesson of the Old Strong Religion: that the meek
(but not necessarily the weak) shall inherit, and that love is the
greatest weapon. From the moment he defeats Colonel Wedder
by changing him from within, making him "more human"
(Q/122), there is only one task left for Casher—the "uttermost
mission" anticipated by T'ruth: "I have to find out who I myself

may be" (Q/124).

The crisis that Casher feels once he has won is crucial, for it challenges the whole point of committing oneself to the struggle in the first place. Even though he has done what "he had to do" (Q/125), even though he has done "what is right" (Q 125), and can anticipate a continuing self-discovery when he speaks with his mother, Trihaet ("I have done what I had to do and much later perhaps, I will come back and see you again. When both of us know more about what we have to do" (Q/126), he is confronted, for a moment, with one of the most terrible fears a person can have: the prospect of a purposeless life. Like Christian in *Pilgrim's Progress*, Casher has entered the Slough of Despond:

> *Where do I go now?* thought he. *Where do I go when I've done everything I had to do? When I've loved everyone I wanted to love, when I have been everything I had to be? What does a man with a mission do when the mission is fulfilled? Who can be more hollow than a victor? If I had lost, I could still want revenge. But I haven't. I've won. And I've won nothing.... Where do I go when I have nowhere to go? What do I become when I am not ready for death and I have no reason whatsoever.* (Q/128-29)

These questions are, of course, asked in a moment of self-doubt, when one can see the future only in terms of a completed past, which is nearsightedness in the extreme. The points raised by Casher's questions are simply not true. From the moment Casher asks them, the rest of "On the Sand Planet" shows how pointless and unfounded his misgivings are. He has not yet loved everyone he has wanted to love, for he has not yet met Calelta. He cannot have won "nothing" when he has won—through love—a non-violent peace for the whole world (a victory that is another stage in his continuing growth), or when he has won the self-awareness that brings him to such a point of crisis as his present one. A less civilized (wild) or a more civilized (tame) person would not have had these doubts, but Casher is a true man, balanced between the tame and the wild, still raw with his own inner progress-through-adversity.

Nor can he have truly fulfilled his mission when the "uttermost mission" is not yet completed (it cannot have been, for such a task can never end with such despair; that alone is an assurance that the progress is far from over). How can any *real* person ever say that he has been all that he had to be and so lacks a reason for living? Casher has forgotten himself.

But this is the black night of the soul, and from this point Casher moves toward a real victory—over fear and loneliness, over ideas and self. (He has already shown compassion and courage and remained human among the stars.) Later, motivated by the mystery of the First, Second, and Third Forgotten Ones, he begins his real progress "to find himself again" (Q/133). Ironically, this brings the quest full circle, for Casher ends up understanding the happiness of the slatternly dog-woman, D'alma, and being able to answer the questions raised when he first met her on Pontoppidan:

> Work had been her life and she had had plenty of it. Casher O'Neill felt a twinge of envy when he realized that happiness goes by the petty chances of life and not by the large destiny. This dog-woman, with her haggard face and her stringy gray hair, had more love, happiness and sympathy than Kuraf had found with his pleasures, Colonel Wedder with his powers, or himself with his crusade. Why did life do that? Was there no justice ever? Why should a worn-out old underwoman be happy when he was not? (Q/25)

True to the mystery of the Three Forgotten Ones by which Casher's particular progress is directed, D'alma demonstrates just how "the meek shall inherit." Casher's reflections about her are truer than he knows. When he considers that "work had been her life and she had had plenty of it," the ambiguity is clear to us: she has had plenty of life!

By the end of "On the Sand Planet" Casher O'Neill has left behind the City of Hopeless Hope (where all forms of organized religion are carried out) just as he has left behind the City of the Perfect Ones (where the Jwindz dwell in their sterile perfection). Both are cities that "stay away from life" (Q/141). He has even left Kermesse Dorgueil, the city where all happy things "come together" (Q/140), but "where the man and the two pieces of wood never filter through" (Q/140). Though a veritable Mecca for thousands from all over the human universe—even known and cherished by some ex-Lords of the Instrumentality as an ultimate, civilized goal and a haven of true peace—it is not enough. Given the great wisdom and controlling benevolence of the Instrumentality, Kermesse Dorgueil is an enlightened and working concern. As Howard says: "We have nothing here but simple and clean pleasures; we have only those vices which help and support" (Q/141). To be sure, it is "a very civilized place" (Q/141), but it is too tame, lacking something of the "wild" first nature that makes man human. Folly later reminds us of the necessary balance, the paradox of what it means to be human; she tells Samm:

> "Life always trembles on the edge of disappoint-ment. If we hadn't been vital and greedy and lust-ful and yearning, if we hadn't had big thoughts and wanted bigger ones, we would have stayed animals, like all the little things back on Earth. It's strong life that brings us so close to death." (Q/153)

This is Smith as ethical pragmatist again, the same informed idealist who excused the behavior of Benjacomin Bozart but not the Arachosians.

So, Kermesse Dorgueil, idyllic and refined, is nonetheless unbalanced, and so not altogether human. Again, the uttermost quest remains: to fulfill our natures, to be what the "word that quickens" would have all sentient life be—human. About to move on from Kermesse Dorgueil with Calelta, Casher says:

> "I am looking...for something which is more than power between the worlds. I am looking for a sphinx that is bigger than the sphinx on old Earth. For weapons which cut sharper than lasers, for forces that move faster than bullets. I am looking for something which will take the power away from me and put the simple humanity back into me." (Q/146)

Smith makes Casher reject those centers where there are the hidebound, death-oriented religions, or the enlightened, atheistic (but sterile and foolish) humanists, or the elegant, dignified, and tolerant vitalists, and moves him on to a more personal and esoteric Adam and Eve rebirth with Calelta. He opts for simplicity and exuberance and new untainted beginnings, full of innocence through experience—the next stage in an unending cycle of hope and renewal, with victory made all the more sweet through loss and suffering.

The terms of expression by which Casher understands what is needed to draw nearer to a final victory are mystical:

> "I am looking for something which will be nothing, but a nothing I can serve and can believe in." (Q/146)

> When they reach the Quel of the Thirteenth Nile—
> "The final source and the mystery" (Q/147)—Calelta observes that this is their destination.

> "But this is nothing," said Casher.
> "Exactly. Nothing is victory, nothing is arrival, nowhere is getting there." (Q/147)

This is a baffling reply from Calelta, tapping the vast mysteries of the Orient—from Zen to Taoism—that were as much a part of Smith's understanding of life as were the Christian mysteries. While Casher—operating in terms of his own spiritual imperatives—feels that their goal is there, where he feels "The presence of the First Forbidden One, the Second Forbidden One and the Third Forbidden One" (Q/148), Calelta—oddly in command of the situation and very much reflecting the archetype of an all-knowing Earth Mother—tells him:

> "We're Adam and Eve in a way. It's not up to us to be given a god or to be given a faith. It's up to us to find the power and this is the quietest and last of the searching places. The others were just phantoms, hazards on our route. The best way to find freedom is not to look for it, just as you obtained your utter revenge on Wedder by doing him a little bit of good.... You have won at last the immense victory that makes all battles seem vain." (Q/148)

It is by her words as traditional "civilizer" and "humanizer" that we are taken away from a merely neo-Christian resolution for Casher's quest to a private, nonpartisan, mystical resolution. As true humans, they await a revelation from that higher power to which their humanity has exposed them. How ironical are Casher's earlier thoughts, when he thought that he had "nowhere to go," for the searching individual need not go anywhere: the place of his revelation is within himself.

Later, in "Three to a Given Star," we hear of Casher and Calelta again, doing their great service for life, happy and fulfilled, themselves now an example and an agency of fulfillment for others. This happy state, achieved through self-fulfillment, through being human, is sustained in this story. When the huge mechanical body of Samm is left *to stand forever as a monument of human victory*" (Q/171), it is a monument to "humanity" the concept—rediscovered by those three "re-born" ones, whose self-realization has made them fit to be truly human again. Ellen/Folly says, echoing Casher and Calelta, "I have had to come to the end of the stars to get what I wanted, to be what I could become" (Q/174). Alma/Finsternis makes a similar remark: "Where else could I turn out to be me?" (Q/174).

An Ending of the Ways

"One generation opens the road upon which another generation travels."
—Chinese proverb

To conclude, then: the winnings, so wonderful and pure in their telling, are largely private things—amplified out into the larger world, but nevertheless often only initially "relative" victories, just as the losses are relative. The cycle continues; the struggle continues; for this is the lot of creatures forever at war with themselves—individuals experiencing their individual fulfillments and being able to share something of these experiences with others.

And while we are told that "centuries passed before mankind finally came to grips with the problem of the underpeople and decided what 'life' was within the limits of the human community" (B/193), it is not this final never-recounted victory that is so very wonderful, but the fact that the struggle is made at all, by creatures forever striving, forever hoping, through love and true caring and a sense of justice. We are tantalized by an entry in J.J. Pierce's Timeline referring to the never-finished, projected series *The Lords of the Afternoon*, which states: "Common destiny of men and underpeople; religious climax" (B/ix), for this suggests the wonderful victories and resolutions in store, so often hinted at in the stories we have to hand.

We already have such promising relative victories in the appearance of a person like T'ruth, for she is "the first of the underpeople really and truly to surpass humanity" (Q/103). Meeting such positive developments halfway, we find changes in the Instrumentality itself—suggestions that this nobly-motivated but sometimes fallible institution is once again firmly and wisely in control of the affairs of all humanity, well on the way to achieving the "common destiny" of men and under-people, and the religious "climax" (B/ix)[45] referred to by Pierce: the "ending of the ways" foreseen by the robot Livius. For instance, when Casher rejects the three cities that lie beyond the Ninth Nile, even the city known and sought by so many citizens of the Instrumentality-governed universe; when he has gone beyond the Deep Dry Lake of the Damned Irene to the "Shrine of Shrines" (Q/143) that is in fact no church, nothing more than just a place (a goal that is to be made meaningful by an inner revelation)—it is then that Calelta, an ex-Lady of the Instrumentality, says:

> "I was once Instrumentality, my Lord, and I know that the Instrumentality likes to do things suddenly and victoriously. When I was there we never accepted defeat, but we never paid anything extra. The shortest point between two points might look like the long way around; it isn't. It's merely the cheapest human way of getting there. Has it ever occurred to you, that the Instrumentality might be rewarding you for what you have done for this planet?" (Q/149)

This important revelation comes at the very end of "On the Sand Planet" and is never challenged or undercut. It is a final reassurance that mankind is in safe hands, in the hands of "the oldest servant of mankind, the Instrumentality itself" (N/272).

Once again that ruling body is benevolent and effective, tolerant and just; the good and faithful custodian of humanity (as an idea as well as a physical fact). Now, more than ever before, it conforms to the distinct religious connotations of the word "instrumentality" (noted by J. J. Pierce when he says that "in Roman Catholic and Episcopalian theology the priest performing the sacrament is the 'instrumentality' of God

---

45. In view of the City of Hopeless Hope, "spiritual" would be a better term here.

Himself" (B/xiv-xv). Its chosen members (who are "called" to service—to a life of sacrifice—as Eleanor is called in *Norstrilia*) are "the instruments of human destiny" (B/xv), motivated by a reverence for life, governed by love, mindful of a higher power behind the humanity whose good stewards they are.

An Immolation in Perpetual Hope

> "To travel hopefully is a better thing than to arrive."
> —R. L. Stevenson

We should not be surprised by the wonderful resolution to a life such as Casher's; we are to have faith and hope. Just as we can make our own projection of *"God is Love and all Life; we know Love and Life; God, Life and Love is us,"* so we should accept the stories' idea that it is in each of us, through knowing love, to be able to work miracles.

There is always the suggestion of this miraculous, transforming dimension. Talatashar makes a significant remark to the recuperating Veesey:

> "You saved us all.... You tuned in help. You let Sh'san work. It all came through you. If you hadn't been honest and kind and friendly, if you hadn't been terribly intelligent, no cube could have worked. That wasn't any dead mouse working miracles on us. It was your mind and your own goodness that saved us."
> (I/118)

In other words, despite a scientific and empirical basis, it is goodness and faith that summoned up the mystical wardens (all of whom are strong archetypes). Love and a kind heart can work miracles, whether it be from Veesey, Go-Captain Taliano, or Casher O'Neill; in C'mell or in Mercer down on Shayol. Such prospects always lie behind mankind's somewhat wearying progress.

Perhaps our best and truest comfort is contained in the "fringe" story, "Nancy," when Gordon Greene returns from space reflecting how:

> The effect of Nancy was an immolation in perpetual hope, the promise of something that could never be lost, and a promise of something that cannot be lost is often better than a reality which can be lost. (I/200)

An "immolation in perpetual hope" is what Smith's stories provide. When we cannot be sure of arriving at our destination, nor be certain of the shape our destiny will take; when the journey is all we know; then all we can seek to do is travel hopefully, with faith. And as the technician tells Veesey:

> "The hard part is when you don't quite succeed and you have to keep on fighting. When you must keep going on and on and on in the face of really hopeless odds, of real temptations to despair." (B/56)

These "real temptations to despair" are the perils of the way. It is no coincidence that conflicts we have discussed recall those besetting Christian in Bunyan's *The Pilgrim's Progress*, for his, too, are struggles against self-doubt, fear and loneliness, evil and despair, and the hardships of the way.[46] And just as faith, hope, and love are Christian's weapons for obtaining victory, so are they the prime weapons for personal victory in the Instrumentality canon.

When in *Man and his Symbols* Carl Jung notes how mankind is "courting" disaster in the present century, he is speaking of a condition of carelessness and neglect very much like that unwit-

---

46. Without wishing to make more of Linebarger's High Anglican upbringing than is possibly relevant, there can be no doubt that Bunyan's work was a formative text. There is much of Mr. Worldly-Wiseman in the inhabitants of Jwindz Jo and Kermesse Dorgueil, and many correlatives for the Slough of Despond and the Giant Despair.

tingly permitted by the Instrumentality. When he also writes that change for the better can only begin "with an individual; it might be any one of us," we have a localization of responsibility onto individual commitment which closely agrees with Linebarger's beliefs. By his written work and by his own example, this is a responsibility he would urge us to accept: to be civilized and human and to each become a "lever of life" upon the times in which we live.

When, too, Laurens van der Post advances Jung's claim that the task of man is "to illuminate the ancient truths, the ancient intimations of the unconscious, the ancient intimations of the soul" so that balance is restored and healing can begin, he also reminds the individual who would do this that instead of trying to fathom these truths in their ancient manifestations, he should try to make them "immediate and contemporary, to give them a meaning in the here and now."[47]

This is what Linebarger has done in his Instrumentality canon. When we witness the hope and humanity that sustains the underpeople, that motivates Jestocost, Sto Odin and E'telekeli, that brings Casher through his moment of despair, that stands with so many of his characters in the face of the "dark forever"—we take these things together with those acts of charity and kindness and honor that marked his professional life as Paul Linebarger, the political scientist and military adviser, we see to what extent this "Cordwainer Smith" became an effective "lever of life" himself, and a true "immolation in perpetual hope" for us all.

Appendix

The collection titled *The Best of Cordwainer Smith* provides a sampling of stories which reveal Smith's major thematic emphases. (However, one wishes this collection included the

---

47. Laurens van der Post citing Jung, *The Story of Carl Gustav Jung.*

neglected "Think Blue, Count Two," which is a key thematic and stylistic work in the canon.)

SCANNERS LIVE IN VAIN

Martel and Adam Stone win freedom for the scanners and habermans and a future for humanity in space. Martel wins a normal life with Luci. "And if he won, he won Luci. If he lost, he lost nothing—an unconsidered and expendable haberman. It happened to be himself. But in contrast to the immense reward, to mankind, to the Confraternity, to Luci, what did that matter?" (B/30).

THE LADY WHO SAILED THE SOUL

Helen America wins the love of Mr. Gray-no-more, and through self-sacrifice and perseverance, she strives to keep it. "The hard part is when you don't quite succeed and you have to keep on fighting. When you must keep going on and on and on in the face of really hopeless odds, of real temptations to despair" (B/56).

THE GAME OF RAT AND DRAGON

One episode in the life of Underhill, his fellow pinlighters and their cat partners as they win new worlds for mankind. An insight into the conquest of space and the price paid to keep it.

THE BURNING OF THE BRAIN

The classic Smith adventure: tightly written, containing all the heroism, passion, honor, and formality of Smith's best stories. A classic example, too, of the importance of the theme of winning in Smith's canon. In making a routine planoform jump from the planet Sherman, the great Go-Captain Magno Taliano, master of the Wu-Feinstein, discovers that a locksheet is missing and that his ship is doomed to be stranded in transit, "lost as no ship had ever been lost before" (B/89). Taliano loses his sanity, burning out his brain to bring his lost ship home. Through this final act as Go-Captain he wins innocence and peace in love; Dolores Oh obtains her ultimate reassurance; and Dita wins all his skills and aptitudes in a wonderful "rebirth" through telepathic transference.

THE CRIME AND THE GLORY
OF COMMANDER SUZDAL

Commander Suzdal discovers the "civilization" of the once-human klopts of Arachosia—creatures who have renounced their humanity—and so threatens to lose the security of mankind. By creating a race of sentient Cats, he wins back this security. Choice is celebrated as a major factor determining the attainment or loss of our humanity.

GOLDEN THE SHIP WAS—OH! OH! OH!

Lord Admiral Tedesco and Prince Lovaduck defeat Raumsog. The decadent, effete Tedesco wins for himself a moment of pure joy in service: "Earth won and the others lost because the leaders of Earth never put other considerations ahead of survival" (B/114).

THE DEAD LADY OF CLOWN TOWN

By losing herself among the renegade underpeople of Clown Town on Fomalhaut III, the already-lost witch-girl Elaine joins D'joan, Hunter, and the Lady Panc Ashash, and is able to help "bring mankind back to humanity" (B/141) by giving the Instrumentality a valuable insight into its own decadence and nearsightedness. D'joan loses her own life to win "real life" (B/150) for all who seek a way through love. Elaine wins nobility and understanding, and "the world's great age begins anew" (B/137).

UNDER OLD EARTH

Lord Sto Odin goes down into the Gebiet to win "a cure for the weary happiness of mankind" (B/215). He does this by destroying Sun-boy and discovering Santuna, who is to become the Lady Alice More. She will become an important champion of life in the Rediscovery of Man.

MOTHER HITTON'S LITTUL KITTONS

An insight into the price of peace: eternal vigilance. With so much to lose, Norstrilia must win at any cost.

ALPHA RALPHA BOULEVARD

The discovery of self, free will, and true freedom (to choose, to suffer, to die) under the Rediscovery. Paul and Virginia, despite their impending loss, "are freer than people have been for a hundred centuries" (B/304).

THE BALLAD OF LOST C'MELL

Jestocost, C'mell, and E'telekeli work to buy time (and so a future) for the underpeople; time in which to draw misguided humankind back onto the path of love and kindness—"the best part there is to being people" (B/330). Jestocost, who had so little love in his life, wins in death a vision and understanding of C'mell's love for him. Of the plot, involving C'mell:

> She was a girly girl and they were true men, the lords of creation, but she pitted her wits against them and she won. It had never happened before, and it is sure never to happen again, but she did win. (B/315)

A PLANET NAMED SHAYOL

On the hell planet, Shayol, Mercer and the Lady Da must struggle to remain human. It is Mercer who fights "to keep the honor he knew before he came to Shayol" (B/367) and who, when "the drugs were deepest and the pain was greatest... was the one who always tried to think" (B/377). By not losing his conscious mind, by his example of humanity to others, he not only wins his humanity back, but is also instrumental in defeating the cruel Empire that has sent him there.

THINK BLUE, COUNT TWO

Veesey, Talatashar, and Trece win their way to Wereld Schemering through the ordeal of space. Good in man wins over evil; man's humanity defeats his darker side. Talatashar wins Veesey and self-realization.

Work Discussed

The page references cited in this study are to the following editions, coded in the text as indicated:

B = J.J. Pierce, ed., *The Best of Cordwainer Smith* (Ballantine, 1975)
I = Cordwainer Smith, *The Instrumentality of Mankind* (Ballantine, 1979)
N = Cordwainer Smith, *Norstrilia* (Ballantine, 1975)
Q = Cordwainer Smith, *Quest of the Three Worlds* (Ace, 1966).

Other source material includes:

Andrew Porter, ed., *Exploring Cordwainer Smith* (*Algol*, 1975)
Cordwainer Smith, *Preface to Space Lords* (Pyramid, 1965).

Dedication
From Mottile to Ambaloxi
Through Space Three and back again,
For Sheridan—a lever.

A COLLOQUIUM WITH DARKO SUVIN

QUESTIONS BY RUSSELL BLACKFORD, SYLVIA KELSO, AND VAN IKIN

[2001]

Dr. Darko Suvin F.R.S.C. was a full Professor of English at McGill University, Montreal until his retirement in 1999. His distinguished career—as academic, sf critic, writer, and poet—includes co-editing the journal *Science-Fiction Studies* from its inception until 1980 (after which time he was a contributing editor) and producing three books which the Clute/Nicholls *Encyclopedia of Science Fiction* describes as "one of the most formidable and sustained theoretical attempts to define sf as a genre": *Metamorphoses of Science Fiction: On the Poetics and History of a Literary Genre* (1979), *Victorian Science Fiction in the UK: The Discourses of Knowledge and of Power* (1983), *Positions and Presuppositions in Science Fiction* (1988). Suvin played a major role in fostering academic interest in science fiction in the USA, and is credited with introducing the concept of "cognition" to modern sf criticism. He was awarded the coveted Pilgrim Award (for services to sf scholarship) in 1979.

The following "colloquium" arose when Darko Suvin kindly agreed to be interviewed for *Science Fiction*. Russell Blackford and Sylvia Kelso joined the editor in submitting a series of questions by email, and Professor Suvin responded as set out below, sometimes answering related questions together.

Ikin: *Let us begin by getting to know something about Darko Suvin as person. In your first email, which sparked this interview, you happened to say "my 1st violin is theatre." Is all your expertise in sf and literary theory a destiny chosen for you, rather than by you? What started Darko Suvin on the path toward the pinnacle of international twentieth-century sf criticism?*

Well, I think the civic persona of Darko Suvin is only interesting because certain historical shapings happen to have crossed and possibly fused in his flesh (including the brain). As best I can make sense of those shapings, they were first of all my family ambience. My father was an MD specializing in dental prosthetics, who had the good fortune to have lived thru a socialist (well, semi-socialist maybe, but that was an awful lot then and there) revolution during and after the Yugoslav (and world) anti-fascist Second World War 1941-45. He had studied in Vienna (for Zagreb, our native city, to the childhood in which I still think back fondly, was in his youth a part of the rotting Austro-Hungarian empire), trying for the very newfangled Freudian psychiatry, only to be told by an assistant of Freud that he had no talent for discovering the proper symptoms and complexes—so I have a family inheritance (I guess) of suspicion toward individualist psychology and its facile circles and wedges. Though very small and gracile, he managed to survive 2 years as a Partizan doctor and eventually was a main founder of the Stomatological Faculty at the University of Zagreb, dying revered by his pupils, then deans and professors—happier than we are in foul PoMo times where having master-teachers is considered irksome (so much the worse for all of us and our craft). I might have from him my scholarly side, for he published oodles of articles and books on prosthetic dentistry. But as usual for sons (and Hitler's rise to power saw to it that I remained an only child), the most important shaping came from my mother, a strong and worldwise personality, who from a young bourgeois lady before WW2 evolved into somebody saving her nuclear family during the war under three Fascist states (Croatia, Germany and Italy) and a chief secretary of a research institute—one of those really running the place—in socialist Yugoslavia. Those interested in my feelings at her death can find it in my book of verse *The Long March: Notes on the Way 1981-1984* (Willowdale ON: Hounslow, 1987), in the poem "Be Still in Peace" and the shorter "The Watch Given to the Verse-Smith by Trude": for I've been writing poetry on and off from 1951 (and short prose even longer), first in Croato-Serbian and then (after I began dreaming in English in the '70s, so Freud had some good insights) in English.

I was a translator and interpreter (English-Italian) already as a very young boy who had fled with his mother in a fishing boat from a Dalmatian island across the mine-infested and German bomber-infested Adriatic Sea to the newly liberated southern Italy in October 1943. 1 remember spurning the offer to learn the piano at the age of 7 or so (my father played Vienna waltzes on it, very rarely) and choosing to learn languages instead, which resulted in an intense and lifelong but totally consumerist love of music, Bach to Bartok and the Beatles and not much further I'm afraid (one's sensibility does close down at 40 or so, which is how I explain Lukács's misunderstanding of Brecht).

I was enrolled in the daringly progressive Zagreb Montessori kindergarten (English and French) at the age of four, I think—and yes, I come from the bourgeois intelligentsia (my two grandfathers were respectively a small "colonial goods" merchant and a bank chief bookkeeper) whose nose was in the Fascist times rubbed into the betrayals our class shamefully wreaked on its own whilom ideals, Milton to Mill to Mazzini, so that they found abode with Marx. So I believe the (temporally) second main influence on me is the profound plebeian antifascist liberation movement I saw and felt viscerally indeed both in Dalmatia and indirectly in liberated Italy.

Marxism as a theory came upon its heels; it has its own huge intellectual delights but it was never (I hope) for me a bloodless dance of concepts, Parisian style; which is why I don't feel a need to jettison its still crucial insights when the historical movement—for a time—collapsed (though I've been working a lot on just what needs to be modified in it, such as 19th-Century scientism). I read the *Communist Manifesto* back in Zagreb in my early teens at the end of 1945, a wartime printing by a Partizan brigade agitprop section I got from my father; and I still remember the passage about the proletariat not being able to liberate itself without upending the whole structure of bourgeois life as vividly as I do my first love (at age 10) and my first sex experience (much later): "yes," I said to myself excitedly, "that's it"! I didn't quite know—not having yet studied the Roman kings—what the proletariat was, but I knew they were the poor, oppressed, and persecuted, so surely I belonged with them (for the Fascists had dispossessed us of everything but life and the pursuit of happiness) just as much as the peasants in Yugoslav Army uniforms. I joined the still mysterious and hush-hush Young Communist League at the end of the same year, in high school, and in 1948, during Tito's break with Stalin, I was as it were drafted—protesting my unworthiness—into a Communist Party preparing a mass basis for that tough struggle (which also meant that if the Russians occupied Yugoslavia, as was quite possible, I would have been a good candidate for one of the grapes on the city lamp-posts). I did get, as I discovered later, both into the KGB and the CIA files at the time. Well, you sheltered and cosseted people from the upper "Western" 10% of the globe can maybe see this is a quite normal—or indeed an extraordinarily lucky—East (or better Southeast) European biography: a German bomb fell 50 meters from me, and if their technoscience had been up to the Vietnam War standards (never mind today), I wouldn't have gone on to "the pinnacle of international 20th-Century criticism" as Van Ikin flatteringly puts it, or anyplace else but a small rocky grave for my pre-teen fragments. Living on borrowed time your whole life—and seeing that other children like me in Korea or Vietnam or Angola or indeed the black ghettoes of the US of A may not be so lucky—wonderfully clears the mind.

And how did I get to sf? Not by way of Sumatran jungles like Brian Aldiss or the skyscraper bureaucracies of New York like Fred Pohl or the campus oases into which a dying Native wanders like Ursula Le Guin (to mention only three people I know well enough to speculate biographically about), but by way of having lived in say six years (1940-46) in five regimes: a monarchist despotism, several Fascist militarized states, the "Western" allies in Italy 1943-45 with some insight in the corrupt business of profiting from feeding hungry Italy, the peasant communist revolution in postwar Zagreb.... And I have no words, even after a lifetime, to describe the outrageous sense of annihilating psychophysical anxiety and heart-constricting persecution a small boy in fear for his existence can feel when subjected to the monstrous threats from which the Revolution was the only salvation. Thence I guess my assiduous reading of utopias from More on (eventually sf from Lucian on) to Wells, of course preceded at age eleven or so by every European child's hefty dose of Jules Verne. I wrote an extrapolative mini-utopia of a united classless world for a high-school homework in I think 1948 (just an anatomy, I fear, though I think it did have a point-of-view narrator zooming around daringly in an airplane) which may still exist among the school papers my wife Nena retrieved last year from a friend in Zagreb. But of course I studied "high lit," there was nothing else (except sciences, in which I first did a six-year degree): English and French literature—German was still too painful, though reading Hegel, Karl Marx and Karl May, as well as a pretty young redhead from Munich on the Adriatic, eventually cured me of that. I specialized (if that's the word—I've always been easily bored and going on to new fields) in Drama, having studied that also at Bristol UK, the Sorbonne in Paris, and eventually Yale for one semester or year in each place, as an indigent foreigner imitating the vie de bohème.

I suppose Van Ikin's formulation, that sf (and, I'd add, cultural theory) was "a destiny chosen for me, rather than by me" has a good share of truth: we are given only a few choices by History (my name for destiny), and if wise we choose the one we were having elective affinities toward anyway, before conscious choice. Theatre was for me utopian oases of storytelling in the fleshly present: but I've always had a commonsense, I guess bourgeois intellectual, distrust of crassly intrusive collectivities, having gone through my share of them (I remember with some horror visiting Chip Delany around 1970 in a commune where he was living and which he has recently so beautifully described), and I've never ventured into the whipwielding-cum-cajoling role of a theatre or maybe movie director, so that the nearest I came was dramaturge (art director?) of a student theatre: and of course critic, historian, theoretician first of drama and then even of performance. But this faded after moving from Europe, my great and untranscended shows of the 1950s-60s Golden Age in Stratford, London, Paris, Milano, Berlin....

sf (always considered as between the utopian and anti-utopian horizon, as—I decided later—a sort of parable for us) was then what we weren't but could perhaps be, or at least could explore analogues of us as being. You'll understand that there's a certain importance and urgency about such a business, not simply competing (as Poul Anderson put it), for the idiot multitude's beer money.

Again, History intervened. I discovered that the revolutionary afflatus was fading back home, I dimly felt the Party bureaucracy had let the self-management project—in which I'd been involved—slide when it got too close to (their) power, I had a falling out with the dominant forces at my Faculty of Arts in Zagreb (the Nationalists hated me and the Party people didn't defend me), so that I decided I could be an alienated intellectual anywhere where I could fruitfully work.

The only proper job I could get was first in Amherst Mass. 1967, and then at McGill University in Canada from 1968 on (I retired in 1999). Students had been rioting there too, demanding power, French-language teaching, and more interesting courses—including sf. They didn't get the first two, but they got a "Marxist" teaching drama and—on and off—an sf course. Some who later became my friends confessed to an immense disappointment when the Marxist appeared in suit and tie, but I'm a European and dislike drugs of any sort, from tobacco and marijuana to Scotch and Disneyland (I do have a small chink for white wine and Italian brandy). What I taught in the first ten years can be partly seen in the *Metamorphoses*, which however doesn't include the oodles of contemporary sf I was teaching, Heinlein to Le Guin and Dick, better seen in *S-F Studies* at the time. So I never felt I had academic problems, sf was riding the wave of the epoch and became a recognized niche in academia—I even got Fredric Jameson to write for *S-FS* and sit on its Board with Northrop Frye and sundry academic worthies. Just luck. And I continued in tandem to write about Brecht and Beckett and John Arden.

Blackford: *As a cultural theorist you have been notable for your overt political engagement, and I'd like to ask you some large questions about how you see the relationships among science, politics and the work of theorists in areas such as language, literature and general culture. Two contrasting images that come to mind of politically engaged intellectuals in these fields are those of Chomsky and Foucault, who notoriously showed little connection with each other when they met in the 1970s. Does either image attract you in any sense?*

Blackford: *More generally, could you explain how you now see the relationships between the natural sciences, the study of language and culture, and the politically committed life?*

Blackford: *In "Novum Is As Novum Does," you state that you do not wish to lose the "central cognitive impetus" of science, but you also subject the program of reductionist science to a severe critique. Could you explain this and how (or whether) the evils you describe can be avoided without losing that cogni-*

tive impetus of "systematic and testable understanding of material realities"?

> *Salus rei publicae suprema lex*
> (The health/salvation of the commonwealth is the supreme law)
> —Old Roman maxim

Russell, my problem is that I've come to deeply disbelieve our dominant institutional carving of the domain of knowledge and commitment (belief). Its historically first step, the laicization of Descartes (I've written on this extensively in "Polity") was defensible as a politically liberating turf war between theologians and philosophers, though Descartes himself—probably with sincerity—conceded the final say to the Church and—what is even more pernicious—took over its split between body and soul (renamed mind by the new philosophers) to the ongoing detriment of the body. The next step, that of Galileo and Newton, was then to anathematize "natural philosophy," call it science, and allot to it the same dual role of Queen of Cognition and Supreme Good as was formerly held by theology. This shut out (better: pretended to shut out) the Subject in favor of the Object, emotion in favor of reason, female knowers in favor of male (see Donna Haraway on the early Royal Society in England or the encroachment of MDs on the delivery of babies).

So if we today ask, as a young man called Volodya Ulyanov did at the beginning of the unfortunate 20th century, "What Is to Be Done?", the hegemony of the last quarter of the millennium has brainwashed us to answer: Whatever it may be, it must be by means of, under the flag of, *science*. (And of course the only true sciences are the mathematizable ones, while the "social sciences," involved in messy human affairs which refuse to be totally quantified, are womanly soft as opposed to hard male reason; the contempt felt by the "hard" for the cringing "softies" can be wonderfully heard if you've been even at the margins of funding debates in a university Senate or a Government granting body!)

This is a powerful answer, seductive precisely for the intellectuals we need, yet on the whole a misleading one. Transmuted into technoscience, it intervenes with exponential force and speed into everybody's daily life.

Let us then further ask, on pain of extinction: What does science do? How does it do what it does? Is the power of intervention gained by this method worth the price we're paying for it (genocide, ecocide, hunger, wars)?

When "science" separated itself out of wisdom—whose backbone is care for health and salvation, theology's strongest trump card—on the basis of quantifying, it displaced the wrong qualities of theological knowledge, for example, Aristotelian "qualitative physics." But it also displaced the supreme law of the commonwealth's salus. It dispensed with any quality, except the quality of being quantified. It thus divorced scientific fact from value. This price seemed right for 300 years, but it became too high with the triumph of the Industrial Revolution (circa 1848, say), and has grown exorbitantly ever since. The project of human survival is consubstantial with a return of "specialized" sciences—most urgently the most powerful ones—into their matrix of cognitive wisdom. Truly democratic science—by and for (the) people—has to espouse being publicly taken to account as to each and every of its uses and consequences. This would be no more dictatorial than the strict control relentlessly exercised over it today by and for profit, debasing all that's not instantly marketable as quantified bytes of "information."

Modem natural science itself has given us hints how to do this spirally, by not abolishing Newton but subsuming him under Einstein as a specialized case. As just noted, human affairs are certainly messier than the Lorenz algebraic transformations which can quantify that particular subsumption. We shall have to declare that big chunks or aspects equivalent to Newton (or Bacon, or Descartes) are counterproductive and not usable after a given point of people's relationships with each other and with the environment, such as 1848 in the rich North.

Use-value qualities are by now an intrinsic and inalienable part of facts. For example, as a fact for us air is only air if breathable and water only water if drinkable. Chunks or aspects of science compatible with this may be—must be—subsumed. Genetic engineering is in the present profit-mad state of society much too risky: soon the filthy rich shall have chimaeras and sphinxes as pets, and the military sentient weapons. Any prudent society would ban it, just like research into Atomic-Bacteriological-Chemical and any other weapons, until we grow wiser (after the Revolution).

But I'm not ready to concede science to the Pournelles and Bovas, nor to the Tellers and Von Brauns. My answer is: not against science but for a science saturated with consciously chosen survival values (beginning with anti-military values). Not back to Aristotle but forward from Marx and Nietzsche.

Thus, I refuse the carve up of wisdom into science, religion, politics, economics, and similar. What today (meaning in the last 30 years) passes for politics I have the deepest contempt for, be it Blair-Clinton or Reagan-Thatcher or the various bloody sects rightly (but in wrong ways) reacting against capitalism without a human face triumphantly astride a wrongly united planet. The liberatory force of the only bearable politics, radical socialism or communism or anarchism, was defeated from without and within in the half century after 1917. I participated in it, as a Titoist (from 1945 to the mid-'60s), still believe in its original aims and achievements, and would participate again if I found it anywhere. In the meantime, we are all privatized and have to do the best we can. Chomsky does very well (better in politics than in linguistics, I think), Foucault did much less well, for his tergiversations and outright obfuscations hindered as much as helped, but he tried and should be honored for that. I could give other names: Trotsky, Raymond Williams, Stuart Hall....

The less crassly Philistine traditions of France and Germany kept an assistant Supreme Good, whose cognitive role was however unclear: Art or Poesy (from painting to verse: prose fiction joined this only in C18-19).

But I should end with a warning: alienated politics are clearly at odds with disalienating (that is, viable) art. Artists (poets) can best help by being idiosyncratically within but at the margins of fighting, liberatory movements (Brecht, Picasso...). For example, they can help by writing about the implications of genetic research by means of narrative cognition (stories). Perhaps you can find some further positions in my "Appendix on Science," planned as an entry into an encyclopedia of the twentieth century:

§

Who used in the twentieth century the scientific method, how, in whose interest, and with what results? It was used by intellectuals, as a rule, in the service of capitalist collectivities (States or corporations). In the guise of "technology," it has become a directly intervening and decisive force of production. The fruits thereof are contradictory: potentially liberating, today at best mixed, and at worst catastrophic—a good chance at destroying vertebrate life on this planet through profiteering and militarism.

The dynamics of developing sciences seem opposed to the sudden durable revelation of religion. But they are poles of the same globe. True, there is a real difference between them, of a piece with the difference between precapitalist social formations based on agricultural space and capitalism based on industrial time and then financial spacetime. Yet, the dogmatic pretension of science to get—in however deferred and lengthy ways—to a final capital-T Truth about the universe participates of the same long-durational, class-society delusion that history and human interests and evaluations in it can be brought to a stop: or that, in a Platonic-Christian vein, history is only a manifestation of the unchanging Truth.

There are by now few respectable thinkers who would not concede that of the two main kinds of scientific knowledge, "facts" and "theories," the theories—say of chemical valency—

are self-evidently useful fictions and the facts an unholy amalgam of sensual evidence and semantics plus theory (that is, fiction). Let me take Harré's example for a factual sentence, "A blue precipitate appeared at 28° C." (80), and note its referent would be rendered quite differently in cultures which see blue as not different from green (there are many such cultures), which would instead of degrees Celsius use a qualitative scale (say, "it blushed"), and which would instead of "precipitate appears" say "Mercury has been revealed" (the alchemists would). Is the sentence "Mercury is revealed when water blushes green" really translatable into Harré's lab language without remnants? If a sentence (as any linguist would know) includes presuppositions as well as positions, it is not. Is the untranslatable part simply magical mumbo-jumbo that can be suppressed? This would depend on what additional cognition it might contain: for example, "Mercury" may well be more specific (as to its look or curative powers) than "precipitate" and thus contain more bytes of information. And what about great cultures which instead of the subject-object syntax use mainly contiguity and richer if less univocal relationships, and say something like "East Dragon—green—sudden event—blush—liquid," as I fantasize the Chinese would? How come they invented gunpowder, printing, and the South-pointing compass needle?

In sum, "Many, indeed infinitely many, different sets of hypotheses can be found from which statements describing the known facts can be deduced..." (Harré 87). As a whole current of philosophers has maintained since Gassendi, theories are not true or false but good or bad instruments for research. Formally speaking, "atom" is the name of an agent in a story about "chemistry," just as "Mr. Pickwick" is the name of an agent in a story about "the Pickwick Club" (Harré 89), notwithstanding some different rules of storytelling in the two cases. "[Theoretical f]ictions must have some degree of plausibility, which they gain by being constructed in the likeness of real things," concludes the middle-of-the-road Harré (98). In other words, literary and scientific "realism" are consubstantial products of the same attitude, the quantifying immanentism of bourgeois society. Yet institutionally sanctified technoscience persists in claiming it can provide the truth, a socially enforced certainty, while the apparently "weaker" and certainly more modest Dickens did not. The philosophic and other systems of belief arising out of (and constituting) science remain stuck on this two-dimensional surface. As a planet's map is regulated and shaped by the grid of cartographic projection, so is any such system based on a principle (for example the Aristotelian excluded middle or the Hegelian necessarily resolved dialectical contradiction). And this principle is also a kind of (obviously circular) meta-reflection about, or methodic key of, the system that is in turn founded on and more or less necessarily deduced from it, and that exfoliates in the form of a finite series of propositions culminating in a rounded-off certainty. This form is finally not too different from the 19th-Century "well-made" illusionistic stage play; no wonder, they both flow out of the Positivist orientation. The Lady with the Camelias and the Laws of Thermodynamics are sisters under the skin: both show a beautifully necessary death.

Therefore, cognition is not only open-ended but also code-termined by the social subject and societal interests looking for it: the horizons are *multiple*. Not only is this legitimate, it is unavoidable and all-pervasive. The object of any praxis can only be "seen as" that particular kind of object (Wittgenstein) from a subject-driven—but also subject-modifying—standpoint and bearing. The way science has been practiced since Galileo is not only a cultural revolution but also a latent or patent *political* upheaval. The bourgeois civilization's main way of coping with the unknown is aberrant, said Nietzsche, because it transmutes nature into concepts with the aim of mastering it: that is, it turns nature *only* into concepts and furthermore makes a more or less closed system out of concepts. It is not that the means get out of hand but that the mastery—the wrong end—*requires* consubstantially wrong means. If you want to be Master of your Company, you got to treat profit-making concepts as raw material on the same footing as profit-making laborers and iron ore.

The problem lies not in the Sorcerer's Apprentice but in the Master Wizard. The scientific is the political.

The ready subservience of science to capitalist destruction of life—in theory, the crude but still very powerful scientific Positivism and philosophical Objectivism—must be decisively abandoned if we are to preserve the human species and most life as we know it.

Kelso: *"Novum is as Novum Does"* (Foundation 69 (1997), 26-43) *suggests a shift in the view of sf originally constructed in* Metamorphoses, *as a rationally based, cognitively organized, "intellectual" genre, implicitly superior to the less intellectually rigorous form that is now sold as fantasy. Having in mind the proviso that contemporary fantasy is almost as heterogeneous as sf, has your view of the former genre changed with your re-assessment of sf?*

Blackford: *You also state that "With Gautama the Buddha and Diderot, I'm in favor of enlightenment." The reference to Diderot suggests a wish to associate yourself with the capital-E Enlightenment, which seems a very unfashionable gesture, coming from a contemporary theorist of culture. Then again, you seem critical of current fashions in cultural theory. Can you explain what kind of enlightenment you are "in favor of" and how you see the current schools of cultural theory?*

Sylvia, there seem to be two questions you have posed here. The latter one, having to do with Fantasy or "fantastic fiction," I have dealt with in a forthcoming 20,000-word piece, so I had better respectfully refer your readers to it ("Considering"). I'll now focus on your first question, whether my 1997 *Foundation* article, "Novum Is as Novum Does," represents (in your words) "a shift in the view if sf originally constructed in Metamorphoses [of sf], as a rationally based, cognitively organized, 'intellectual' genre...."

In brief, no and yes. Centrally, my view was a blend of

description of sf possibilities and a prescription of which of those I deem the best (most sane and politically useful) horizon for it. This has *not* changed: the only sane way of survival for our (and other vertebrate) species—for the cockroaches and worms will with any luck survive the worst *Homo sapiens* will inflict on the planet—is a society without classes rooted in political economy, which is some form of communism (socialism, anarchism, or whatever better name we'll find for it in the future); this is best known to sf readers from the desert Kropotkinian variant in *The Dispossessed*, or differently variant approximations in Marge Piercy, Kim Stanley Robinson and others. (A languidly beautiful variant refusing machine rhythms is of course William Morris's *News from Nowhere*, in an echo of which the alternative title to my above article was "News from the Novum").

What has changed is the historical reality, devolving from the Welfare State to a new beast slouching toward Bethlehem: Global Capitalism without a Human Face; and therefore the short-range prospects into which this long-range view of mine was immersed have also changed, and entail much rethinking. Trying this for the last 15 years or so, I've concluded that—since we have to have terms by means of which to handle the new experiences of huge human groups, interpenetrating within and comprising in different ways all of us—the foci of this change can be stenographically analyzed as two questions: in the present to which all of us belong, "What is this present?" and "Who are we?" My working hypotheses for a first delimitation, without the ifs and buts no doubt necessary for further understanding, are: The what is *Post-Fordism*; the we is *Intellectuals*. Again, I've had to write about this extensively, both in the article you mention and in another one in *Utopian Studies*, but I cannot answer your question without these two somewhat lengthy detours; and for your Australian readers I may be allowed to recapitulate some main points.

§

Post-Fordism: more than forty million people die from hunger each year, which is equal to 300 jumbo jet crashes per day every day with total loss of lives; or (I don't know which is worse) the UN report that in 1996 "[n]early 800 million people do not get enough food, and about 500 million are chronically malnourished" (Drèze-Sen, *Hunger* 35 and *Human* 20). The starving hundreds of millions are joined by the couple of billion people eking out a living at the periphery of the world system or dossing down in the center of the affluent cities of the North, trying as best they can to survive the fallout from the civil and overt wars waged by the big corporations, and which with poetic justice migrate from their "hot" foci also into the "Third World inside the metropolis," the creeping war in all our slums so far best described in hip-hop and in the post-Dischian and post-Dickian dystopian sf of Piercy, Butler (Octavia, not Judith), Gibson, Spinrad or Cadigan. The argument to which I subscribe is that we are in a series of boom-and-bust cycles. An ascending part, that began in the 1930s, found in Fordism and Keynesianism the remedies to the dangerous 1920s bust. These strategies effected a limited but real redistribution of wealth: Fordism through higher wages rendered possible by mass production of goods but neutralized by total production alienation and consumerist PR, Keynesianism through higher taxation neutralized by bourgeois control of the State. They functioned in feedback with the rise of production and consumption 1938-73, itself inextricably enmeshed with imperial extraction of surplus-value, armament production, and the warfare State. In class terms, Soviet pseudo-Leninism and Rooseveltian Liberalism—as well as some important aspects of fascism—were compromises with and co-optations of the pressures and revolts by plebeian or laboring classes. In economic terms they meant the institution of a modest but real "security floor" to the lowen-nost classes of selected "Northern" countries as well as a great expansion of middle classes, including all those hearing or reading this, with a fairly comfortable financial status and an appreciable margin of maneuver for ideologicopolitical independence. Wallerstein somewhat optimistically numbers these "[sharers] in the surplus value" (us) as 10-15% of the world population, of course disproportionately concentrated in the richer North (*Historical* 123).

However, the shock of 1973, when we entered upon the "bust" part of the cycle that began with the 1930s-40s boom (the oil crisis, debt crisis, global domination of the corporate credit system, the computerized stockmarket speculations, the World Bank, etc.), revealed that our planet Earth, a finite system, cannot expand indefinitely to bear 6 or 10 or 20 billion people up to the immensely wasteful "Northern" standards (see for example Lummis 60-74). This real emergency was seized upon and twisted by the ruling capitalists into revoking both the Keynesian compromise with the metropolitan lower classes and the Wilsonian promise to the pheripheric "South." In a fierce class war from above, through a series of hidden or overt putsches by the Right wing (hidden in the "North," from Britain to the USSR, overt in the "South"—China being the pivot between the two), all protective barriers and mitigating bumpers are dismantled, so that what Marx called "the extraction of absolute surplus value" may be sharply increased: the security floor is abolished, the permanent Fordist class of chronically poor is now enlarged beyond one third even in the rich North, while the "middle" group of classes is squeezed back into full dependency by abolishing financial security (there is a wealth of uncoordinated data on this; see for example Lash and Urry 160-68). This leads to increased world concentration of capital now dominated by cartels of "multinationals." For example, the IMF 1998 "bailout" of South Korea meant in practice a cut in half of wages expressed in US$, huge unemployment of employees and bankruptcies of small businesses, opening the door to takeover of Korean banks by foreign finance, strong reduction in government spending on social programs, infrastructure, and credits to business, fracturing of the large domestic conglomerates—in brief, a whole thriving "high tech and manufacturing economy up for grabs" (Chossudovsky, "IMF").

Rocketing indigence and aimlessness provide the ideal breeding ground not only for petty and organized criminality—business by other means—but also for its legitimization in discrimination and ethnic hatred (for example in India or Yugoslavia). The warfare state had a little hiccup after the end of the Cold War but it has recovered nicely (the best estimate seems to show that two-thirds of US citizens' taxes go to pay for military technology and wars; see Ross, 4). The welfare-state transfer of wealth from one class to another goes on in spades but *for the rich*. The latest report to have percolated into public domain tells of the US Congress and FCC handing $70,000,000,000.000 (yes, *seventybilliondollars*) to the TV conglomerates in free space on public airwaves ("Bandwidth"). No wonder the number of US-dollar millionaires has from 1980 to 1988 risen from 574,000 to around 1,300,000 (Phillips, 9-10) and of billionaires, 1982-96, from 13 to 149, so that by now the "global billionaires' club" of 450 members has a total wealth much larger than that of a group of low income countries comprising 56% of the world population (*Forbes Magazine* ,1997, cited in Chossudovsky, "Global"). Whole generations, as well as the planetary environment for centuries into the future, are being mortgaged to an arrogant fraction of 1% on the top and a faceless world money market. The gap between the rich "North" and the poor "South" of the world system has doubled from 1960 to 1992, with the poor "transferring more than $21 billion a year into the coffers of the rich" (*The Economist*, see Chomsky, 62). Lowering "the cost of labor," the ultimate wisdom of capitalism, means impoverishing everybody who lives from her work and enriching top-level managers and the upper mercenaries (ranking politicians, cops, engineers, lawyers, administrators...). The dire poverty gap is turning all societies into "two nations," with good services for the small minority of the rich and shoddy ones or none for the dispensable poor. Compared to Dickens, we'll have more computers, more (or at least more talk about) sex, and more cynicism for the upper classes. Human groups divide into resentful islands who do not hear the bell tolling; Marx's "absolute general law of capitalist accumulation: accumulation of wealth is at the same time accumulation of misery, agony of toil, slavery, ignorance, brutality" (*Selected,* 483), has been confirmed in spades.

What then is the balance sheet of the capitalist social formation (cf. Wallerstein, *Historical,* 99-105 and 117-37)? Let me take the two most undoubted material achievements: production and length of life. As to the first, it is clear that human domination over nature has mightily increased: per unit of labor-time, the output of products is considerably greater. In other words, technological productivity under capitalism has finally created the presuppositions for rendering our globe habitable for all. But the habitability has been hijacked: is the required labor-time for production and reproduction per one person, per one lifetime or in the aggregate smaller? Certainly, in comparison to precapitalist formations, the working classes "work much harder in order to merely scrape by; they may eat less, but they surely buy more" (ibid 124): Paul Lafargue's right to creative laziness (by the way, this son-in-law of Marx wrote an early political sf story) is nowhere on the horizon. In the last thirty years, at the same time that a fake decolonization redrew political borders outside the metropolitan countries, from Ghana to the Ukraine, "the world proletariat has almost doubled... [much of it] working under conditions of gross exploitation and political oppression" (Harvey, 423). There is a serious possibility that the classical Marxist thesis of the *absolute* immiseration of the proletariat as compared to 500 or 200 years ago may after all be correct, if we look at the 85% or more of the working people in the world economy rather than only at the industrial workers of the metropolitan countries; and there is no doubt of the huge *relative* immiseration in comparison to the dominant classes and nations. Obviously, even the latter is politically quite explosive and morally unacceptable: it demoralizes and alienates all classes, if in different ways.

As to the second, infant mortality has been strongly reduced in peacetime: but have the pollutions of air, water, and food as well as the psychic stresses and unceasing compulsion and insecurity lengthened life for those who survived beyond cared-for infancy? The jury is out on this: but the quality and ease of life has surely fallen sharply within my lifetime, and it is bound to fall exponentially with structural long-term unemployment. The amount of social waste and cruelty was larger than ever before in the century beginning with the great capitalist world wars (1914). "[C]apitalism cannot deliver world peace" (Wood, 265): it must be considered quite probable we'll have further ABC wars after the Gulf Oil one. Capitalism is positively dependent on ecological devastation, condensing geological change into historical time. True, "really existing socialism" also badly failed at this (not at keeping peace); but ecological vandalism is a measure of capitalism's *success*, not failure: the more vandalism the more short-term profit (look at Amazonia). So I asked in "News": is our overheated society better than the "colder" one of (say) Tang China or the Iroquois Confederation? There are more of us but do we have more space or more trees, per person? Many of us have less back-breaking toil, but all have more mind-destroying aimlessness resulting in person-killing by drug and gun; we have WCs but also cancer and AIDS.... Most probably, even quantitatively—and with greater certainty qualitatively—the achievements of the bourgeoisie celebrated in *The Communist Manifesto* have been overbalanced by what it has suppressed.

From this point of view, one would have to defend the principle of enlightenment. True, the eighteenth-century Enlightenment had its limits, historically quite understandable. But they grew pernicious only when the two-faced bourgeoisie had forgotten its *citoyen* soul (see Marx's discussion of that in "On the Jewish Question") in 19th-Century Positivism. So, the principle of mass examination of all prejudgments and ruling pieties, what Marx called "the pitiless critique of all that exists," is my Supreme Good (I think any artist or writer does that all the time anyway). Diderot is better than Herder (the Nationalist Romantics), Gautama Shakyamuni—a true atheist—than

Jehoshua of Nazareth. (Lao Tse may be still better.) As for the present hysterical anti-Enlightenment consensus among "soft" sciences, as ("objectively") a bourgeois intellectual I find it a shameful abdication of our class's historical role. But I console myself with Kant's great dictum that even a thousand years of something being so does not make it right: and the Lyotardian consensus is already falling apart, the fish smells from the head after less than thirty years.

§

Intellectuals: If we are to take the "identity politics" seriously, surely the first identity of a true intellectual is his "professional" social class rather than nation or anything else. What then of our liberatory corporate or class interests as intellectuals?

In the twentieth century, as capital has been completing its molting from individual into corporate, Fordism was characterized by "hard" technology (crucially that associated with mass car transport), semi-automation, the rise of mass media and advertising, and State planning; and Post-Fordism—the watershed is c.1973—by "soft" technology (crucially computer technology and biotechnology), automation, mega-corporations and world market regulation, and the integration of the media with the computer, all under total domination of corporate marketing. In both cases more "software" or "human engineering" people were needed than before. One of the century's earmarks was therefore the enormous multiplication and enormous institutionalization or collectivization of the earlier independent artisan and small entrepreneur. This ensured not only higher production but also its supervision and general ideological updating: that is, it was "not all justified by the social necessities of production [but] by the political necessities of the dominant [class]" (Gramsci, 13).

These "new middle classes," who do not employ other people, include teachers, office workers, salespeople, the so-called "free" professions, etc. Their core is constituted by "intellectuals," largely university graduates (but see Mills, Noble, and the Ehrenreichs), people who "produce, distribute and preserve distinct forms of consciousness" (Mills, 142)—images and/or concepts. Hobsbawm calculates that two-thirds of the GNP in the societies of the capitalist North are now derived from their labor, though their proportion within the population is much inferior. Politically, they (we) may be roughly divided into servants of the capitalist and/or bureaucratic state, of large corporations, self-proclaimedly "apolitical" or "aesthetic" free-floaters, and radicals taking the plebeian side; the alliance of the first and fourth group with some non-"intellectual" classes determined both the original Leninism and New Deal.

Our new collectivism, while mouthing liberal slogans stripped of the State worship, needs other-directed intellectuals. Post-Fordism has had quite some success in making intellectual "services" more marketable, a simulacrum of profit-making. This has long been the case in sciences and engineering: industrial production since around the 1880s is the story of how "the capitalist, having expropriated the worker's property, gradually expropriated his technical knowledge as well" (Lasch, xi, see also Noble). In the age of World Wars and revolutions this sucks in medicine, law, and "soft-science" consulting experts. Now those who buck the market better get themselves to a nunnery. The class aggression by big corporations against the immediate producers, corporeal and intellectual, means that Jack London's dystopian division of workers under the "Iron Heel" into a minority of indispensable Mercenaries and a mass of downtrodden proletarians (updated by Marge Piercy in *He, She and It*) has a good chance of being realized. The increasingly marginalized and pauperized humanists and teachers are disproportionately constituted by women and non-"Whites," a sure index of subalternity. To the contrary, what Debray calls the reproductive or distributive intellectuals—the engineers of material and human resources, the admen and "design" professionals, the new bishops and cardinals of the media clerisy, most lawyers, as well as the teeming swarms of supervisors—are the Post-Fordist "organic" mercenaries, whom PoMo cynicism has dispensed from alibis. The funds for this whole congeries of "cadre" classes—"administrators, technicians, scientists, educators... have been drawn from the global surplus" (Wallerstein, 83-84): none of us has clean hands. The welfare-and-warfare State epoch saw the culmination of the "cut" from the global surplus we "middle" 10-15% were getting; and "the shouts of triumph of this 'middle' sector over the reduction of their gap with the upper one per cent have masked the realities of the growing gap between them and the other [85-90%]" (ibid 104-05).

Our position is thus one of a living contradiction: we are essential to the policing of workers, but we are ourselves workers—a position memorably encapsulated by Brecht's "Song of the [Tame] Eighth Elephant" helping to subdue his recalcitrant natural brethren in *The Good Person of Setzuan*. On the one hand, as Marx famously chided in *The Communist Manifesto*, "the bourgeoisie has stripped of its halo every occupation hitherto honored and looked up to with reverent awe. It has turned the physician, the lawyer, the priest, the poet, the scientist, into its paid wage-laborers." On the other hand, the constitution of intellectuals into professions is impossible without a measure of autonomy: of corporative self-government which allows control over one's work. This constitution was enabled by the fact that salaried men and women are "the assistants of authority" (Mills, 74), but no authority can abide without their assistance. "[The middle class] individuals live or attempt to live an elite life, evading through 'culture,' while their knowledge serves capitalism.... They live a double life...in a *jouissance* half real and half illusionary." (Lefebvre, 32-33) Our professionalization secured for some of us sufficient income to turn high wage into minuscule capital: but even the poorest intellectual participates in privilege through her "educational capital." Excogitating ever new ways to sell our expertise in producing and enforcing marketing images of happiness, we decisively contribute to the decline of people's self-determination and non-professionalized expertise. We are essential to the production of new knowledge and ideology, but we are totally kept out of establishing the framework into which, and mostly kept from directing the uses to which, the production and the producers are put. We cannot function without a good deal of self-government in our classes or artifacts, but we do not control the strategic decisions about universities or dissemination of artifacts. The list of such variants to Dr. Dolittle's two-headed Pushme-Pullyou beast, between self-management and wage servitude, could be extended indefinitely.

For me, the main realization dawning from the above little inventory on Post-Fordism is that the hope for an eventual bridging of the poverty gap is now over, and it is very improbable the Keynesian class compromise can be dismantled without burying under its fallout capitalism as a whole. Will this happen explosively—for example in a quite possible Third World War—or by a slow "crumbling away" which would generate massive breakdowns of civil and civilized relations, on the model of the present "cold civil war" smoldering in the US, which are (as Disch's forgotten masterpiece *334* rightly saw) only comparable to daily life in the late Roman Empire? And what kind of successor formation will then be coming about? The age of individualism and free market is over, the present is already highly collectivized: as a small example, control of the major US media had passed from fifty corporations in 1983 to twenty in 1992, so that four movie studios, five giant book publishers, and seven cable TV companies—all interlocked with major banks—produce more than half of the revenue in their field (Bagdikian, ix-xii and 20-26). The dazzling surface array of diversity hides bland uniformity: there are 11,000 magazines but two (!) magazine publishers dominate the field. The people running these 20 media monopolies and their bankers "constitute a new Private Ministry of Information and Culture" (Bagdikian, xxviii). Demographics as well as insecurity will make the future even more collectivized: the alternative lies between the models of the oligarchic (that is centrally Fascist) war camp and an open plebeian-democratic commune.

In this realistically grim perspective, a strong argument could be made that our class interests as intellectuals are twofold and interlocking. First, they consist in securing a high degree of self-management, to begin with in the workplace. But second, they also consist in working for such strategic alliances with other fractions and classes as would consent us to fight the current toward militarized browbeating. This may be most visible in "Confucian capitalism" from Japan to Malaya, for example in the concentration-camp fate of the locked-in young women in industries of Mainland China, but it is well represented in all our sweatshops and fortress neighborhoods (see the US example in Harvey). It can only be counteracted by ceaseless insisting on meaningful democratic participation in the control not only of production but also of distribution of our own work, as well as of our neighborhoods. Here the boundary between our, as it were, dissident interests within the intellectual field of production and the overall liberation of labor as their only guarantee becomes permeable. True, history has shown that alliance-building is only more painful than base organizing: any Mannheimian dream about the intelligentsia as utopian arbiter was unrealistic to begin with. But at least we know it can only be done by bringing into the marriage our honest interests and uncertainties, by eschewing like the plague the PoMo certainty and apodictic terrorizing, adapted in a bizarre mimicry of their two rivals, Admass and Stalinism, as the newest variant of the intellectuals' illusion that they do not suffer from illusions (as Bourdieu notes in *Other*).

Our immediate interests are oppositional because capitalism without a human face is obviously engaged in large scale "structural declassing" of intellectual work, of our "cultural capital" (Bourdieu, "Field"; see also Guillory, 134ff.). There is nothing more humiliating, short of physical injury, than the experience of being pushed to the periphery of social values—measured by the only yardstick capitalism knows, our financing—which all of us have undergone in the last quarter century. Our graduate students are by now predominantly denied Keynesian employment, condemned to part-time piecework without security: capitalism has now adjoined to the permanent reserve army of industrial labor that of intellectual labor. The new contract enforced on the "downsized" generation is: "Workers undertake to find new occupations where they can be exploited in the cleverest and most efficient way possible" (Lipietz, 77). Intellectuals never had power over productive relations, but now we are, bit by bit, losing our relatively large autonomy. The best we can expect from capitalism is the shrinking and proletarianized autonomy of a begging order—certainly not Rabelais's Abbey of Thélème, beset as it is by an unholy alliance of barbaric businessmen and what Gayatri C. Spivak (in Robbins, ed., 167) calls "corporate feminists" (or corporate ethnics). This is not good enough.

In this bind, we can at any rate say to the supposed realists: Look where you've landed us! There's no more realism without utopia! (Your reality itself works toward a negative utopia.) But what does this practically mean? A number of things.

First, I must be the bearer of painful news: the *professionalism* of which we were up to a point justly proud has been overwhelmingly corrupted—by outright bribery where it matters, by self-willed marginality in the humanities. The ivory of our towers has been largely ground into powder as aphrodisiac for the corporate bosses. Looking at our class position soberly, we shall have to redefine professionalism as including—rather than complementing—self-managing political citizenship; or we shall be political by selling our brains to the highest bidder. On the one hand, in our classes we shall have to redefine, with Nietzsche, philology not simply as the art of reading rightly (what is there) but the art of reading *well* (what we may get from it). And outside the class it may mean anything from picketing the University Board or the Faculty of Business Management to lying down on the railway tracks (to use an improbable '60s parallel). It certainly means striving for activist unionization, at a time when corporations are corrupting academic administrators by making them into well-paid CEOs in exchange for downsizing teachers (see Soley, 24-32 and Guillory). Like publishers vs artistic cognition, universities vs teaching cognition are now "the swine... in charge of the pearls" (Anthony). As Benjamin put it, in the permanent part of an essay which was alas written in a more hopeful situation:

> ...only by transcending the specialization in the process of production that, in the bourgeois view, constitutes its order can one make this production politically useful; and the barriers imposed by specialization must be breached jointly by the productive forces that they were set up to divide. The author as producer discovers—in discovering his solidarity with the proletariat—simultaneously his solidarity with certain other producers who earlier seemed scarcely to concern him. (230)

Only this can, in his wonderful polysemy, unfetter *die Produktion der Intelligenz*: the production of us intellectuals, but also the productivity of intelligence or reason. And if we at the moment don't find many proletarian organizations to meet us in the middle of the tunnel, we can start by doing utopian cross-pollinations of at least the cultural with the philosophic, economic, political, and other history studies. This is, for example, why I consider Attali's book on the political economy of music (the age of repetitive evacuation of meaning and big centralized apparati determining production and listening as commodified time, best foregrounded in muzak) as one of the most enlightening diagnoses of Post-Fordism; or why my latest book interlards seven essays and seven sequences of poetry. But I'm afraid we'll have to relearn the tradition of persecution ranging, say, from Cyrano and Spinoza, through Marx's and Benjamin's exile from universities and many countries, to the Pope's treatment of Liberation Theology: such ecumenic professionalism will entail less reading of papers and much more civic conflictuality.

For, on the citizenship end of the same continuous spectrum, it means beginning to fight two even more difficult long revolutions. One is to master what we might call, adapting Said, *critical worldliness*: Brecht called it the art of thinking also in other people's heads. Though we partly become intellectuals in order to get far from the madding crowd, our class and often even personal survival requires us now—without surrendering either our bearings or the clarity of our arguments' articulation!—to get out of the elite ghetto of writing, theatre, etc., into the mass media. The most important politico-cultural position today is obviously the TV station (rapidly fusing with virtual space), secondly the radio station, and thirdly the cinema and the video production. This is why they are also, in descending order, the most firmly controlled by billions and laws. Nonetheless, there may be limited chinks in the system, as proved by the stories of the computer groups, the three-kilometer-radius Japanese radio stations, or of the movie producing units at the end of "real socialism" in East Central Europe—all successfully used by small self-governing groups. Video production, and in particular computerization and the Internet offer many possibilities, so far used by the Rightwing subversives much more efficiently than by the Left. The second long struggle might be called *global solidarity*: it consists in fighting what would be a Fascist geopolitical involution, turning our privileged Northern continents into an insular Festung Amerika and Festung West-Europa. The Japanese dissident Muto Ichiyo called it perhaps more precisely "transborder participatory democracy," and Douglas Lummis argues on his tracks that it is a necessity of our time when "imperial power is incarnated in three bodies: pseudo-democracy at home, vast military organizations, and the transnational corporations...." (Lummis, 138). Its furthest utopian horizon, absolutely necessary if we wish to avoid oblivion or caste society, is the long revolution of achieving "democratic forms of 'social control' of financial markets" (Chossudovsky, "IMF").

The Modernist oases for exiles (the Left Bank, Bloomsbury, lower Manhattan, major US campuses) have gone the way of a

Tahiti polluted by nuclear fallout and venereal pandemic: some affluent or starving writers à la Pynchon or Joyce may still be possible, but not as a statistically significant option for us. Adapting Tsvetaeva's great line "All poets are Jews" (*Vse poèty zhidy*), we can say that fortunately all intellectuals are partly exiles from the post-Fordist Disneyland and/or starvation-cum-war dystopia, but we are an "inner emigration" for whom resistance was always possible and is now growing mandatory. The only resistance to Disneyland brainwashing is "the invention of the desire called Utopia in the first place, along with new rules for the fantasizing or daydreaming of such a thing—a set of narrative protocols with no precedent in our previous literary institutions..." (Jameson, *Seeds,* 90). This would be a *collective production of meanings*, whose efficacy is measured by "[how many] consumers it is able to turn into producers" Benjamin, "Author," 233, and see also Attali): that is, to begin with, critical thinkers. And the only chance to do this is "[to keep] in touch with all kinds of streams of protest and dissent so as to know what's important to say" (Ehrenreich, 177-78, and passim). And a final piece of painful news: this means "doing things we're not used to, like saying things that 'everybody' (meaning everybody in one wing of the profession) 'already knows'" (Bérubé, 171, and see also the whole section 164-78, especially 176). The gentle reader will notice I haven't quite managed to follow this prescription....

True, utopia as static goal has been dead since the nineteenth century, even if its putrefying cadaver poisoned the twentieth. Marx's critique of Cabet's project of emigrating to found a colony as desertion from class struggles (and I find it rather significant that Marx did not focus on criticizing Cabet's earlier—rather poor—utopian novel) could have taught us that "the place of utopia is not elsewhere, but here and now, as other" (Marin, 346). As Calvino's "city which cannot be founded by us but can found itself within us, can build itself bit by bit in our capacity to imagine it, to think it through" (252), utopia cannot die. But its latent rebirth—Kim Stanley Robinson's great *Mars* trilogy has understood this—depends on us.

This also means—to finally face Sylvia Kelso's initial question—that I think my project in *Metamorphoses* is being misread if it is taken simply as a plea for "cold" reason as against emotion, interests, and similar. Perhaps I ought to have spent even more space on defining my terms: and for other reasons I've in the meantime done so (in "Cognitive"). For it was quite clear in my mind that I switched from the use of "science" to "cognition" precisely in order to prevent the subservience to and disciplining of sf by institutionalized science of the militarized technology kind or of the cheerleading futurology kind—both US and Soviet. Sylvia is right in seeing within my rethinking of the 1990s an even stronger delimitation against these, for they have in the meantime grown both stronger and more obviously complicitous with our ruling wreckers. Therefore I insist today more on the distinction between the fake and the true Novum (radically diminishing, versus radically enhancing, the potentialities of life). But I hold that valid emotion is both articulated and in a feedback with categories of reason: as is proper for a cognitive faculty.

Blackford: *More recently, there appears to be a division in the sf community about the relentless philosophical materialism of Greg Egan's work, in particular, but also in stories such as Brian Stableford's "The Pipes of Pan," which seems to suggest that human nature itself will be changed quite fundamentally by a future science—and that this fact (as Stableford evidently sees it) must be accepted. Some would question whether this sort of* Homo proteus *vision of the future (to use Edward O. Wilson's term) is not deeply offensive to morality in some way. Politically and morally, what do you make of such transhuman and post-human scenarios?*

Blackford: *In the context of sf, some appear to question whether the expression of reductive materialist viewpoints about human nature and experience is simply antithetical to the purposes of art. That seems to come out in Rob Latham's review of the 15th Dozois* Year's Best *anthology (in the October 1998 issue of* New York Review of Science Fiction*). The fiction I'm referring to is very different from the magical fantasy which you have appeared to reject in the past, yet I wonder whether you might not be troubled by it. Do you have a view about this?*

Russell, many thanks for sending me the text of the Symposium on "Posthuman sf" chaired by you at Aussiecon 1999. 1 confess that before you sent it I was stumped by your question. Posthuman? It seemed *déjà vu*: Foucault at end of the 1960s? and then the interminable tomes of everybody else in Paris recycling their Nietzsche, best in the Guattari-Deleuze hundreds of pages jumping from plateau to plateau amid the playful rhizomes? Well, there's a limited number of fashions, so after recycling those of (say) the 1920s and 1930s why not advance to the *haute couture* of the 1960s—especially when you can disguise this in the shiny new material of teflonized cyberspace when walking down the catwalk and hoping to rake in millions from the *New Yorker* yuppies? So where are now the discussions about the death of sf after the Hiroshima bomb, or after landing on the Moon, or after the end of US protests from Selma to the Kent State University shootings (say 1961-73, the true Golden Age of US sf in that quarter-revolution)? But where are the snows of yesteryear? What will you discuss, Russell, when you get (as I hope you do) an equally brilliant panel in 2002? I'd lay you a little bet: not "Posthuman Nature in Sf"...

This is not to say that hidden somewhere within this ultra-violet herring there are no real, even central problems facing us; and I think your panelists ably dug many of them up. These are, of course—as everybody knows unless irremediably taken in by the fake extrapolation ballyhoo legitimating sf as bellwether for US capitalist technoscience and promoted by the Bova-Pournelle wing in sf—matters that have practically nothing to do with any far future but take the muddled white-gray-smoggy light of our everyday life through the sf cognitive system of parabolic mirrors or prisms so as to analyze it into clear, *pro analysis* component colors. I'll focus here only on the downfall of the nuclear Self and the correlative or consubstantial global political economy.

I do believe the bourgeois nuclear Self is fast receding on our horizons, and the adventures of nuclear physics from Rutherford on can be read as an exact and spitting image of that "long, melancholy withdrawing roar." (Let us pause for a moment and think why—to begin with, the same brains stamped with the same historical horizons were delving into either.) Seven years ago I wrote a long essay, whose full title might hint at my position: "Polity or Disaster: From Individualist Self toward Personal Valences and Collective Subjects." It evinced rich sympathy for arguments from the most diverse quarters (one of them is Marvin Minsky's work on AI cited in your Symposium, but some of my main arguments were drawn from the Chinese cultural sphere where there never was a Self in the individualist sense—just as there wasn't one in Antiquity and not fully in the Middle Ages) that if there ever was an unsplittable Self between Descartes and Mach, or Robinson Crusoe and Stephen Dedalus, it is now an assemblage of quarks and charms and whatever. That does *not* at all mean there are no Subjects or personalities: Chinese or Japanese or Hellenic history is full of them. It just means that the Individuum (non-divisible-essence-of personality) is a historical invention—the English historical semantics for that invention are admirably disentangled in Raymond Williams's *Keywords*—for which praise and blame ought to be given to two major forces: first, the Christian idea of a soul with interiority in direct communication to God, eschewing all Earthly City loyalties such as clan, city, State or other non-Godly collectivities. The problem is that this is tenable only in times of dire threat to life by war and starvation, when such collectivities are seen to work badly if at all (we're getting there again, thank you). But it does not cope with the need of halfway equal citizenship in a reasonably livable affluence. This need gets met, second, by the bourgeoisie of Machiavelli's, Luther's,

Bacon's, and Descartes's time, which transferred such inner loyalties to the new godhead of market competition, flatteringly usurping the ancient nickname of "freedom." True, the invisible hand of market competition often got into inexplicable trouble and needed to be rescued by State protection (the Left Hand of Darkness indeed), so a collateral invention came to be the Nation.

We're now, in my diagnosis, already more than halfway to new collectivities, the top-down ones; the "senator from Boeing" from Bester's *Tiger, Tiger* has been with us almost forever (Clinton seems to have been the president from the abominable broiler-chicken industry). The Cartesian delusion, culminating in Kant or Mill, is over. The only question is: will this be a bottom-up, democratic collectivism—such as envisaged by Jefferson, Marx or Kropotkin—or a top-down, oligarchic one? Commune and coop, or dictatorial war camp? Alas, I wouldn't bet any big part of my pension funds on the former: as More said at the end of his *Utopia*, I rather hope than believe it. In other words, will our "psychic" charms and quarks be able to recombine according to our bodily interests, as in Piercy's Mattapolsett or Robinson's Mars, or will they be straitjacketed into the terrorism of Bill Gates, Wall Street, and the World Bank, mortifying our flesh in the new corporate and feudal capitalisms? You can find this too in Gibson, Piercy, Gwyneth Jones, and many others in sf, probably the best X-ray instrument we have within fiction. So the dislike of the body, rampant from cyberpunk to Ken Macleod, seems to me a very bad sign. To split mind from body, sensorium from senses, is Cartesianism gone crazy. And Maureen Kincaid Speller rightly made the crucial parallel between the traditionally (in Christianity) "lower" body and the lower classes:

> ...all these portrayals of a transhuman or posthuman existence... show privileged societies, peopled by an elite who can afford to cut loose from their flesh containers and play throughout the Universe.... Who maintains

this existence for them?...who tends the machine or grows the new body? One is left to posit a mysterious invisible underclass,...rather like the servants running a Victorian country house, or the Hispanic gardeners and maids in Los Angeles. The emphasis is on choice, but choice is governed by material wealth, and that is surely no choice at all.

The lower classes traditionally (magically) include women, the lowest creatures on any religious scale. Since we don't have sf critics from global periphery or from working classes (bar one or two maybe), the female and feminist critics are as a rule most attuned to this. Not only Speller but also Helen Merrick rightly notes how "women, people of color, and gay people" are accustomed to thinking of their bodies as constructed, usually by others. Speller's Hispanic maids serve here an admirable triple purpose: they identify ethnicity, class, and gender of the oppressed and exploited, the immigrants from the colonized periphery of the global capitalist system into its core, who bring with them (in a fine show of poetic Justice) the overt violence exported by the empires into their countries and classes one or two centuries ago. But of course, the economy and daily life of the rich would collapse without the working and consuming poor: so their immigration, legal or not, is tacitly or openly encouraged, while taking good care they do not get the economico-political rights of the unionized workers they're helping to displace and vanquish.

Finally, what does this do to the techniques of writing and reading sf? Not much, I'd think. Whatever Greg Egan's or anybody else's scientific and futuristic ideas, they still inevitably write for today's readers. The problem of "rounded characters" à la E.M. Forster, taken from 19th-Century Realism and propagated (but not practiced) in sf by Le Guin, seems to me no problem: sf does not have them, nor should it, nor can it: for it is a parabolic or emblematic and not a mimetic or naturalistic genre. Kingsley Amis had it right long ago, in his *New Maps of Hell*: Gulliver cannot be a mariner out of Joseph Conrad—that is, an individual seen simultaneously from without and within, which gives the stereometric effect. All the interesting, indeed most ingenious variations involving non-human entities—for example, the "demons" of Walter Jon Williams—are simply metaphors or emblems for existing facets (charms and quarks) of the Subjects or personalities today. Personality has, as pointed out by your panelists, always been fabricated: there is no original Rousseauist Noble Savage whom we have lost through capitalist technology. True, the pace of change enforced by computerized stockmarkets seems unprecedented in duration and in global scope—the direst stresses of Auschwitz or Vorkuta or the Ithaca jail were more limited. The fragmentation thrown up by the Subjects in answer to such stress will surely present some new recombinations, not necessarily pleasant. While it is only fair to try to get the best out of any situation one finds oneself in, its particular potential delights, the yuppie delight in them, well noticed (say) in Gwyneth Jones's review of Neal Stephenson's *Snow Crash*, seems to me much too exaggerated, one-sided, and more than somewhat irresponsible. And the reader of 2001 or 2010 will be able to accept and understand more fragmentation than before, not so much because Prigogine or Foucault have by now percolated into the intelligentsia but because the reader's life will be increasingly such: run where the corporation wants you, when it wants, and how it wants; and the wants change with the profit winds. But a story will still have a beginning, middle, and end, simulacra of people and of landscapes in time, and so on. In the evolution of *Homo sapiens*, the 4,000 years from Homer and Gilgamesh are not such a big deal.

But we do kill and maim more efficiently.

Ikin: *Finally, looking at the field of sf criticism as it stands at present, what do you see as its most significant weakness or oversight? What are the aspects which we are most pressingly still struggling to grasp? What specifics would you like to see addressed in the next few years?*

Let us, in the interests of propaganda, compile a list of problems we do not pretend to have solved (Brecht).

Of course I won't compile a Brechtian list here either for sf criticism in general (Marc Angenot and I gave it a shot in the essay "Not Only but Also," now in my *Positions*, but this was in another country and the wench is dead) or for mine own. For one thing, it might be longer than the interview so far. For another, a single person cannot do it, only a group; and I should stress here that I deeply disbelieve in copyrights and geniuses, so that whatever strengths my criticism may have truly derives from my having—in a doubtless truncated way, dictated by our social (dis)organization—functioned as a focuser and formulator of group debate, incorporating selected hints, insights, scoldings, proposals... by, say, the co-editors (Dale Mullen, and then Marc Angenot) and almost the whole board of consultants of *Science-Fiction Studies* during my 1973-81 tenure—just as half of the contributions in that *S-FS* bear traces of my hands-on editing. I simply wish to indicate the most glaring gaps, which prey most on my mind. From what is to be done in sf criticism, I pick out one matter which seems to me a key: the *Parable as the strategic* (creative and critical) *tool* (which then logically entails a reconsideration of Fantasy).

When Patrick Parrinder (as editor) and I were discussing a possible title for a volume of essays by various hands somehow connected with my retirement (it is due out this Summer from Liverpool and Duke UP), I suggested that instead of "Cognition and Estrangement" it really ought to be "Cognition, Estrangement, the Novum, and the Parable." This was an only semi-joking proposal, for my (teleologically) final essay in the *Positions* book advances a view of sf that takes a new tack in comparison to the first three terms from *Metamorphoses*, though I trust it is not incompatible with them, as a further analogy or variant of allegory. In art rather than science, the nearest analogy may be the "moment of Cubism" (thus Picasso rather than Einstein), which John Berger dates around 1910-14 but in his sense of a horizon where all was possible I'd extend it to the 20 years after 1917, to the Left Modernism of Joyce, Chaplin, Eisenstein, and Brecht. It would not be too difficult to correlate this with the debates between the open and closed (Bloch's "warm stream vs cold stream," say Luxemburg or Gramsci vs Kautsky or Stalin) interpretations of Marx, in which the "cold" pole eschewed the scandal of dialectics in favor of the comforting Newtonian predictive element ("iron laws") inherited but also transcended by Marx.

I cannot here retraverse the theory of parable, but may only in the most abbreviated way (to be filled in by the kind reader reaching for the old essay in *Positions*) repeat that the parable has perennially been the privileged genre—and even more: the privileged *method*, which can therefore extend to stories of any length—of fruitfully marrying textual seduction (in the "vehicle") and cognitive consummation (in the "tenor"). You'll note it is a highly affective, nay erotic, way of bringing about what Brecht called "the gentle might/authority/violence of reason" (*die sanfte gewalt der vernunft*), the feedback between the universal and the singular that constitutes any cognition. This Way may be sneered at by people who cannot imagine that reason may be seductive—poor they! For they are weighed in the balance against Aristophanes, countless *mashal*-writing rabbis, Jehoshua of Nazareth, Gautama the Enlightened, Swift, Lessing, and so many others; "I had not thought death has undone so many" (T.S. Eliot).

All very well, I hear the dogmatic Post-Modernists reply, we know Bellamy wrote impressive parables and Wells stories which are narrativized parables (as "The Country of the Blind"), but what has this to do with us in the new dispensation? Well, maybe little with you—though I read much Derrida and Guattari-Deleuze as parables, and in fact the whole PoMo vulgate-text is one mega-allegory of the lovehate at the loss of Master Narrative and of the clever hysteria of Hegel's Serf without a Master—but a lot with the state of affairs we're trying to understand today. The parable is the most complex, refined, and populist form of allegory, opposed to the elitist theological combats of Virtues and Vices or Psychomachia, those black-and-white exorcisms. The overall horizons of allegory to my mind deal with the relationships of art to truth, or of narrative and metaphoric imagination to conceptualized, normative doctrine; in other words, allegory has to do with the interplay between what is in social hegemony held to be true (and thus in a way privileged and indeed sacred) and what is held to be feigned (and what has therefore, historically, oscillated uncomfortably between being unholy, just entertaining, or a second mode of privileged cognition). This has become more complex and exacerbated after the capitalist Industrial Revolution, which both installed inescapable social dynamics and yet held fast to the ruling-class traditional belief that history is at a qualitative end, and—in the new bourgeois variant—only quantitative growth remains (as in sports records or computer software: faster, higher, more).

What then is the role of new creativity, which is, as it were, generically discontinuous from the privileged body of normatively "true" texts, which is fiction or heresy rather than fact or orthodoxy? I have argued in a brief old text that all allegory, verbal or otherwise, is a (more or less admitted) relationship between a new proposition and an existing privileged set of normative and ruling propositions which the allegory re-produces (*egoria*) in a variant and other (*allos*, dare I say estranged?) way; and it might be apparent how discussions of the Novum necessarily intertwine with allegorical horizons. I noted there an inherent tension in a dynamic bourgeois society between piety and creativity, the static tradition of doctrine and the deviating pressure of experience, so that a modern parable can only be faithful after its own fashion: even the most believing creators are uncomfortable allies for priests, I concluded on the basis of my own heretical Titoist experience. Within such horizons, the *small forms* of proverb, riddle, animal (or Alien) fable, and parable will be more open to a conflict of authority than the "large forms" of mythical and religious systems, which are inexorably drawn into a confirmation of (sometimes new) authority.

The parable is, then, traditionally a way of intimately relating doctrine to fiction—and vice-versa. The traditional politico-religious point of the parable is to open the listener's ears to the irruption of (often new) understanding, Bloch's "aha-effect": "O now I see that the tiny grain of mustard seed growing into the biggest bush of them all is Christ's Word about the Kingdom of Heaven growing into my heaven-reaching faith in it!" Theoretically, one might expect the parable not to survive the death of God in the 20th-Century, the rise of competing macro-godheads and tribal godlets which entailed the slaughters of tens of millions as well as the starving of and psychic terror over—and thus evacuation of imaginative reason from—hundreds of millions, that have between them irretrievably sullied the alter-natives of ideology and the Id. But practice is always slyer than theory, and while Old Nobodaddy might be dead, the parable has managed to survive in two ways, identified with Kafka and Brecht (not counting nostalgic reactions back to reach-me-down Romanticism). Kafka managed to write parables—as Beckett managed to write Mystery-plays—against a backdrop of "zero doctrine," that is, the painful absence of community values and interhuman sense that was traditionally codified into a more or less religious doctrine, so that his isolated protagonist became a grotesque lone creature (my favorites are the animal fables of "The Burrow" or "Josephine the Songstress" rather than the clearer almost-sf of "The Penal Colony," but the overt thumb-nail sketch is in "The Door of the Law"). Brecht on the whole successfully navigated the whirlpools between the Scylla of nihilism (Kafka) and Charybdis of pseudo-religious Marxism as belief-into-scientific-destiny (not confined to Stalin) to approach a paradoxically experimental doctrine in which it is the method of fitting the *sight* to the *situation seen* that matters, and not any system. The allegorical Little Man Schweik meets finally the allegorical Ruler Hitler at the end of one of Brecht's most engaging parables of how to survive despotism, and Hitler fails: he is not prepared for Winter.... Neither is Joan Dark in the slaughterhouses of locked-out Chicago, an awful warning—the first "new map of hell," in fact—how the unemployed and dispossessed have to stick to each other or miserably die (*St. Joan of the Slaughterhouses*). It's a cold world, my masters, and you better be prepared—by slyness, wit, and method.

I shall try now to apply this to K. S. Robinson's *[Color] Mars* trilogy to make my point by using a brilliant unpublished essay of Fredric Jameson's, in the book edited by Parrinder. As I was arguing, after Marx and Nietzsche it's no go for parables (or any other allegories) which trust in the Transcendental Signifier, the doctrinal tenor as soul or static essence, to which is then adjusted the imaged story, the vehicle as sensual body: they cannot satisfy. If there is to be any soul or essence (I argue in "Two Cheers" that a dynamic, changeable essence is necessarily to be posited in order to speak about anything, so that I was emboldened by reading in Robinson that "Terra sees [in Mars] its own essence"), it can only be decisively co-constituted by the body—here the story with its figures and metaphors. Surely all flesh is grass and in a way perhaps the vanity of vanities, but it's the last line of defense and offense, delight and memory, left to us. In fact, if the Platonic-Idealist doctrine of two realities is thereby refused—the soul being either a changeable disposition of flesh or nothing at all—it is no longer quite true that the vehicle is concrete (plant) and the tenor abstract (belief in the Kingdom), and we might even pose the question whether this understanding of allegory is not characteristic of German Idealism and Romanticism, a late and degenerate form. Was King Pluto concrete but riches an abstract concept for Aristophanes, was Christ's Kingdom To Come really abstract for medieval believers? In this intimate interaction, the fact that the tenor is being elicited by such-and-such a Possible World (in Robinson, by all the features consubstantial to the three changing colors of Mars) cannot be simply subsumed by the tenor's concept or even image and then forgotten, otherwise we'd have to equate any such fictional text to a leading article written against the same horizon. (This is my problem with the useful "discourse theory," debated for years now with Marc Angenot.) An irreducible surplus is engendered by the humanizing features of World, Figuration, and Narration of their interactions; Jameson names it after Althusser's "overdetermination," but I suspect pluricausality is only an important synecdoche for what is happening and at stake here.

To exemplify it by contraries: the contingent grain of mustard-seed gives rise to a stout suspicion that whatever tenor is built by means of it may get into trouble once the world of the listener is sufficiently removed from Mediterranean agriculture. A post-industrial Kingdom of Heavens may have to cease being a Kingdom and in Heavens, acquire a dynamic vector, etc. In fact, it may have to become a utopian something to which the *Mars* trilogy relates as Dante's equally outrageous Mount of Purgatory does to his planetary Paradises. Post-industrial cognition can only proceed by experimental construction out of "nature"'s (the production mode's) constriction, the main constriction or resistance as well as source of strength in capitalism being the money economy (on which Balzac's realism is founded). Thus, science—as Jameson argues—is no doubt an allegory for human relationships, from which it anyway stems and which it then strongly inflects, but also the philosophical— or better, methodological—model for steering their dynamics.

While Robinson might demur from any such residual triumphalism (utopia is for him indeed the unnamable color on which Jameson zeroes in, approachable only by symbolic detail), what we can clearly see in his *exemplum* is how our bourgeois categories of institutionalizing, fragmenting, and alienating cognition into politics, religion, economics, psychology—the entire organigram of our social science Faculties, against which Marxists and Nietzscheans of all stripes have always struggled—begin to break down here. The ideal equivalent of the rainbow coalition is cognitively debated in the story's interplay of what we poorly classify as ecological, political, economical

(Martian and Corporate Terran), ethnic, and even psychological matters (only religion seems to have been displaced into ecological politics on Mars). This is of a piece with a cognitive recovery of History. Let me call it "the filling in of King Utopus's trench"; in Robinson, the most astounding image and *pars pro toto* standing for it is the space-elevator cable which "wraps itself twice around the planet like a broken necklace" (Jameson): an anti-trench which has always to be reckoned with as an unclean (but for this age's horizons unbreakable) birthcord from mega-capitalism, which may yet strangle any attempt at new birth.

Thus, it becomes clear that Stan Robinson has managed a Herculean feat which we might at first, within sf, call the reconciling of an almost Stapledonian grand sweep with a micropolitics out-Delanying Delany's individualist and sometimes whimsical details (see Broderick). But then, I'd go further, to the highest level: Robinson is giving a new twist to the Kafka-Brecht dilemma. His mega-parable is certainly not nihilist, though it shares with Kafka (or Nietzsche) the refusal of the Law as transcendental signifier. Updating the Brechtian (or Marxian) tension between the need for orderly learning and for productive anarchy, it plumps for nearness to the latter but on the same globe: we could call it the Tropic of Anarchy on the globe of cognition. Brecht's equidistant Equator, halfway to the Tropic of Order, seems out of reach today. In storytelling terms, this means no explicit "moral" of the fable or tenor of the parable is imaginable and thus tellable today, unless it be the moral of open-endedness: History does not end, and this is no small matter when all the *gleichgeschaltet*—or forcibly coordinated mass media—tell us it's ended definitely (and as we can see, badly). And conversely, the "show" of vehicle is to be much "thicker," much more validated by material(ist) details or "realistic," much more livable-in and seductively ostended, than the usually laconic and somehow reticent, wry European brevity of Brecht or indeed Kafka. Both of them knew roughly or precisely what to expect; we today—and Robinson as our story's teller—do not know: we must not believe Kafka, we cannot believe Brecht (who is politically equivalent to a warm halfway house between Lenin and Rosa Luxemburg). Indeed, from where I stand, the fact that Lenin is, as Jameson notes, conspicuously absent in Robinson even as a false alternative (which was still there in Piercy's *Dance the Eagle to Sleep*) seems a serious—dare I say American—gap not well compensated by the utopian optimism of *eppur si muove*. One hopes he will return to this gap, for no serious utopianism can fail to work through the problem of vanguard organization versus bloody defeat. Yet the most important matter remains that in any such ongoing history Kafka's and Brecht's Judgments are inescapable, and the Trial may be upon us sooner than we think.

Works Discussed

Amis, Kingsley. *New Maps of Hell*.

Anthony, Piers. Letter to Darko Suvin of 11/11/1997.

Attali, Jacques. *Bruits*. Paris: PUF, 1977.

Bagdikian, Ben. *The Media Monopoly*. 4th edn. Boston: Beacon Press, 1992.

"Bandwidth Bonanza." *Time* (Canadian edn.) Sept.1, 1997, 35.

Benjamin, Walter. "The Author as Producer" in his *Reflections*. Trans. E. Jephcott. New York: Schocken, 1986, 220-38.

Bérubé, Michael. *Public Access*. London: Verso, 1994.

Bourdieu, Pierre. "The Field of Cultural Production." *Poetics 12* (1983): 311-56.

— *In Other Words*. Trans. M. Anderson. Stanford: Stanford UP, 1990.

Broderick, Damien. *Reading by Starlight*. London and New York: Routledge, 1995.

Calvino, Italo. "Per Fourier" in his *Una pietra sopra*. Torino: Einaudi, 1980.

Chomsky, Noam. *Year 501*. Montréal and New York: Black Rose Books, 1993.

Chossudovsky, Michel. "The Global Financial Crisis." Electronic article Nov.9, 1997, from <chosso@travel-net.com>.

— "The IMF Korea Bailout." Electronic article Jan.1, 1998, from <chosso@travel-net.com>.

Debray, Régis. *Le Pouvoir intellectual en France*. Paris: Ramsay, 1979.

Drèze, Jean, and Amartya Sen. *Hunger and Public Action*. Oxford: Clarendon Press, 1989.

Ehrenreich, Barbara. "The Professional-Managerial Class Revisited," in Robbins ed. [see below], 173-85.

Ehrenreich, Barbara, and John Ehrenreich. "The Professional-Managerial Class," in P. Walker ed., *Between Labor and Capital*. Boston: South End Press, 1979.

Gramsci, Antonio. *Selections from the Prison Notebooks*. Ed. and tr. Q. Hoare and G. Nowell Smith. New York: International, 1975.

Guillory, John. "Literary Critics as Intellectuals" in W.C. Dimock and M.T. Gilmore, eds., *Rethinking Class*. New York: Columbia UP, 1994, 107-49.

Harré, R[on]. *The Philosophies of Science*. London: Oxford UP, 1972.

Harvey, David. *Justice, Nature and the Geography of Difference*. Oxford: Blackwell, 1996.

Hobsbawm, Eric. *The Age of Extremes*. New York: Pantheon, 1994.

Human Development Report 1996. Ed. UN Development Programme. New York and London: Oxford UP, 1996.

Jameson, Fredric. *The Seeds of Time*. New York: Columbia UP, 1994.

Jones, Gwyneth. *Deconstructing the Starships*. Liverpool: Liverpool UP, 1999.

Lasch, Christopher. "Foreword" to Noble (see below), xi-xiii.

Lash, Scott, and John Urry. *Economies of Signs and Space*. London: Sage, 1996.

Lefebvre, Henri. *La Survie du capitalisme*. Paris: Anthropos, 1973.

Lipietz, Alain. *Towards a New Economic Order*. Trans. M. Slater. New York: Oxford UP, 1992.

Lummis, C. Douglas. *Radical Democracy*. Ithaca: Cornell UP, 1996.

Marin, Louis. *Utopiques: jeux d'espaces*. Paris: Minuit, 1973.

Marx, Karl. *Selected Writings*. Oxford: Oxford UP, 1977.

Mills, C. Wright. *White Collar*. New York: Oxford UP, 1953.

Noble, David F. *America by Design*. New York: Knopf, 1977.

Phillips, Kevin. *The Politics of Rich and Poor*. New York: Random House, 1990.

Robbins, Bruce, ed. *Intellectuals*. Minneapolis: U of Minnesota Press, 1990.

Ross, Andrew. *Strange Weather*. London and New York: Verso, 1991.

Soley, Lawrence C. *Leasing the Ivory Tower*. Boston: South End Press, 1995.

Suvin, Darko. "On Cognitive Emotions and Topological Imagination" *Versus* no. 68-69 (1994): 165-201.

— "Considering the Sense of 'Fantasy' or 'Fantastic Fiction'" (forthcoming, *Extrapolation* 2000).

— "Polity or Disaster: From Individualist Self Toward Personal Valences and Collective Subjects." *Discours social/ Social Discourse* 6.1-2 (1994): 181-210.

— "Two Cheers for Essentialism and Totality: On Marx's Oscillation and its Limits (As Well As on the Taboos of Post-Modernism)." *Rethinking Marxism* 10.1 (1998): 66-82.

Wallerstein, Immanuel. *Geopolitics and Geoculture*. Cambridge: Cambridge UP, 1992.

— *Historical Capitalism [with] Capitalist Civilization*. London: Verso, 1996.

Williams, Raymond. *Keywords*. New York: Oxford UP, 1985.

Wood, Ellen Meiksins. *Democracy Against Capitalism*. Cambridge: Cambridge UP, 1995.

CHAPTER SOURCES IN CHRONOLOGICAL ORDER

"The Lever of Life: Cordwainer Smith as Ethical Pragmatist," by Terry Dowling: *Science Fiction: A Review of Speculative Literature* 10 (Vol.4, No.1) 1982. (Originally published as "The Lever of Life: Winning and Losing in the Fiction of Cordwainer Smith.")

"The Disquieting Terrain of the Spirit: Gerald Murnane, *The Plains*," by Yvonne Rousseau: *Science Fiction: A Review of Speculative Literature* 15 (Vol.5, No.3) 1983.

"Warriors of the Tao: David Lake's Xuma Novels," by Russell Blackford: *Science Fiction: A Review of Speculative Literature* 16 (Vol.6, No.1) 1984.

"Sexuality in Science Fiction," by Russell Blackford: *Science Fiction: A Review of Speculative Literature* 17 (Vol.6, No.2) 1984.

"Catharsis Among the Byzantines: Delany's *Driftglass*," by Terry Dowling: *Science Fiction: A Review of Speculative Literature* 17 (Vol.6, No.2) 1984.

"Sex as a Hard Problem in SF," by David Lake: *Science Fiction: A Review of Speculative Literature* 20 (Vol.7, No.2) 1985.

"The Non-Science Fiction Novels of Philip K. Dick," by Bruce Gillespie: *Science Fiction: A Review of Speculative Literature* 35 (Vol.12, No.2) 1993.

"The Golden Age of Australian Science Fiction," by Sean McMullen: *Science Fiction: A Review of Speculative Literature* 36 (Vol.12, No.3) 1995.

"*Diaspora*, by Greg Egan," by Russell Blackford: *Science Fiction: A Review of Speculative Literature* 40 (Vol.14, No.2) 1997.

"Thawing the Frost Garden: *Komarr*, by Lois McMaster Bujold," by Sylvia Kelso: *Science Fiction: A Review of Speculative Literature* 41 (Vol.15, No.1) 1998.

"'SF Worlds in Darkness and Joy': An Interview with Tess Williams," Questions from Van Ikin and Helen Merrick: *Science Fiction: A Review of Speculative Literature* 42 (Vol.15, No.2) 2000.

"Me, Hydra: Postcards from a Swamp," by Tess Williams: *Science Fiction: A Review of Speculative Literature* 42 (Vol.15, No.2) 2000.

"Agape, Eros and the Zoophilous: An Appreciation of Peter Goldsworthy's *Wish*," by Bruce Shaw: *Science Fiction: A Review of Speculative Literature* 42 (Vol.15, No.2) 2000.

"A Colloquium with Darko Suvin," Questions from Russell Blackford, Sylvia Kelso, and Van Ikin: *Science Fiction: A Review of Speculative Literature* 43 (Vol.16, No.1) 2001.

"Imagination, Fantasy, and Fiction," by George Turner: *Science Fiction: A Review of Speculative Literature* 44 (Vol.16, No.2) 2002.

"'*I Wasn't Expecting That*': The Career of Norma Hemming," by David Medlen: *Science Fiction: A Review of Speculative Literature* 45 (Vol.17, No.1) 2008.

CONTRIBUTORS

Russell Blackford is a philosopher and critic. He is known especially as an outspoken defender of secularism and individual rights. He has published three novels set in the Terminator universe, among others, co-edited *50 Voices of Disbelief: Why We are Atheists*, and holds a law degree and a pair of Ph.D.s. He and Jenny Blackford live in Newcastle, New South Wales.

Damien Broderick has only one Ph.D., but has published some 45 novels, scholarly tomes, and popular science books on the paranormal, the technological singularity, the prospect of radical life extension, and the very far future. In 2010 he was runner-up for the Theodore Sturgeon short fiction award, and received the A. Bertram Chandler Memorial Award. These days he lives in San Antonio, Texas, but remains a senior fellow in the School of Culture and Communication at the University of Melbourne.

Terry Dowling holds a Ph.D. in Creative Writing from the University of Western Australia, and has published many awarded and anthologized stories in all fantastika genres: science fiction (notably his Tom Rynosseros sequence), horror and fantasy. He has created several computer games, and his debut novel *Clowns at Midnight* appeared from PS Publishing in 2010. He was closely involved with *Science Fiction: A Review of Speculative Literature* from its inception until the mid-1990s.

Bruce Gillespie, one of Australia's most celebrated sf fan writers and editors, in 1969 founded *Science Fiction Commentary* (which has been nominated three times for a Hugo Award). His early writings on the work of Philip K. Dick drew attention to an author comparatively neglected at the time, and his publication of translations into English of Stanislaw Lem's criticism was of similar significance. He gained the 2007 A. Bertram Chandler Memorial Award, and lives in Melbourne, Victoria, surrounded by immense numbers of books, cats and CDs.

Van Ikin, winner of the inaugural A. Bertram Chandler Memorial Award in 1992, is co-author of *Strange Constellations: A History of Australian Science Fiction* (with Russell Blackford and Sean McMullen) and co-editor of *Mortal Fire: Best Australian SF* (the first-ever Australian *Best of* collection, co-edited with Terry Dowling in 1993). As a Professor in English and Cultural Studies at the University of Western Australia, he teaches creative writing and coordinates the postgraduate program for his School, leaving little time for sf-related pursuits and causing ever-longer delays for those which do still go ahead, as lamented in his Introduction.

Sylvia Kelso works at James Cook university of North Queensland, Australia. She is an editorial board member for *Femspec* and contributing editor for *Paradoxa: Studies in World Literary Genres*, recently guest-editing a special volume of *Paradoxa* on Ursula K. Le Guin. Two of her novels have been shortlisted in the Aurealis Awards for genre fiction.

David Lake was born in India in 1929. He has a PhD from the University of Queensland. From the age of ten or less he was fascinated by science fiction, and soon read Verne and Wells. But he only began writing sf about 1970, and from 1975 to 1985 published nine or ten novels and some short stories. Around 2000 he realized he wanted to say nothing more. About the future he is a black pessimist ("really, always was," he adds).

Helen Merrick holds a Ph.D. in feminist science fiction, and is Senior Lecturer in the School of Media, Culture and Creative arts at Curtin University in Western Australia. She is co-editor of *Women of Other Worlds: Excursions through Science Fiction and Feminism* (with Tess Williams, 1999) and her recent book *The Secret Feminist Cabal: A Cultural History of Science Fiction Feminisms* (2009) received the 2010 William Atheling Jr. Award for sf criticism.

Sean McMullen holds a Ph.D. in Medieval Literature, works on complicated technical things in a scientific research establishment, and lives in a bayside Melbourne suburb where he jogs across the solar system on most nights—there's a one billionth scale bronze model of it along the foreshore. In his spare time he has written seventeen books and seventy stories, mostly science fiction, along with a couple of hundred talks and articles. He is co-author of *Strange Constellations: A History of Australian Science Fiction* (with Russell Blackford and Van Ikin)

David Medlen had his earliest encounter with science fiction at age three when given a Captain Scarlett chocolate bar. Since then he has researched areas of interest within the field and published several articles. He is currently a Library Officer at the University of Western Australia and reminds us that Casanova became a librarian after being the world's greatest lover because it was a promotion.

Yvonne Rousseau graduated with Honors in English and Philosophy from the University of Melbourne. She lives in Adelaide, South Australia in the large equally book-crammed house she shared with her late husband John Foyster, reading prodigiously and writing wittily but publishing far too little. Her study *The Murders at Hanging Rock* is a brilliant *Rashomon*-like investigation of Joan Lindsay's famous novel. She was a joint editor, then convener, of *Australian Science Fiction Review (Second Series)*.

Bruce Shaw, author of *The Animal Fable in Science Fiction and Fantasy* (2010) and a number of studies such as *Our Heart is the Land: Aboriginal Reminiscences from the Western Lake Eyre Basin,* did his early professional work in anthropology, compiling oral history of aboriginal Australians before turning to English literature. A book on the life history of an Aboriginal woman is currently in press. He holds a PhD in Anthropology from the University of Western Australia and a PhD in English from Flinders University in South Australia. He lives in Perth, Western Australia where he is visited by a neighbor's cat.

Darko Suvin was Professor of English and Comparative Literature at McGill University, and is now its Professor Emeritus and Fellow of The Royal Society of Canada. He edited two scholarly journals, and published three volumes of poetry as well as many articles on Utopian and Science Fiction, Comparative Literature and Dramaturgy, Theory of Culture, and Political Epistemology. *The Encyclopedia of Science Fiction* describes three of his 15 books as "one of the most formidable and sustained theoretical attempts to define sf as a genre." He was awarded the Pilgrim Award (for services to sf scholarship) in 1979.

George Turner remains perhaps Australia's most highly regarded if contentious science fiction author and critic. He shared the 1962 Miles Franklin literary award for *The Cupboard Under the Stairs,* and received the 1994 A. Bertram Chandler Memorial Award. His sf novels include *Beloved Son*, *The Sea and Summer* (*Drowning Towers* in USA), *Brainchild* and *Genetic Soldier.* He died in 1997.

Tess Williams, self-described cyborg and Hydra, is author of the novels *Map of Power* and *Sea as Mirror* as well as several sf stories and articles on feminist sf. She is co-editor of *Women of Other Worlds: Excursions through Science Fiction and Feminism* (with Helen Merrick, 1999) and wrote her Ph.D.

on Shared Metaphors of Change in 'Post Neo-Darwinian' Evolutionary Theory and Feminist Science Fiction. These days she works in academe as Research Development Officer at the University of Western Australia and is thus finding less time for sf-related pursuits—which neatly returns us, here at the end, to the lament voiced in the Introduction....

INDEX

www.ingramcontent.com/pod-product-compliance
Lightning Source LLC
Chambersburg PA
CBHW021217090426
42740CB00006B/264